EDUCATIONAL TECHNOLOGY

EDUCATIONAL TECHNOLOGY

TARA CHAND

ANMOL PUBLICATIONS PVT. LTD.
NEW DELHI - 110 002 (INDIA)

ANMOL PUBLICATIONS PVT. LTD.

4374/4B, Ansari Road, Daryaganj
New Delhi - 110 002

FIRST EDITION 1990
Reprinted 1992
Reprint 1999

Reprint, 2002

PRINTED IN INDIA

Published by J.L. Kumar for Anmol Publications Pvt. Ltd., New Delhi - 110 002 and Printed at Mehra Offset Press, Delhi.

Preface

Since the development of the radio many educationists have advanced the argument that communications technology can provide major improvements in the delivery of education. Research on "teaching machines" in the developed countries of the west and especially in America goes back to the 1940s before the wholesale introduction of computers into the market place.

However the oldest instructional use of information technology is simply to present information. The textbook has been the traditional passive instructional system. Projection media-slides, film-strips, over head transparencies and pictures are modern forms. Educational radio and television have experienced quiet but steady growth since the late 1950s, and early 1960s in the developed countries of the west and America. Video cassettes and video disks will provide even more workable tools for presenting video based instructional material.

However, with all the new possibilities of improvement due to the modern technologies available the lack of sufficient theoretical framework for experimental study of the uses of the new media is a basic problem for researchers and practitioners alike.

James W. Brown and James W. Thornton JR of USA have very rightly said that the main avenues toward a better theoretical framework are the path ways of learning theory, communication theory and perception theory. They have argued that there is a serious gap not only between the "pure" science of human learning and the "applied" science of educational psychology, but that our knowledge of the whole field of learning is admitted to be fragmentary and often too specific to warrant wide generalisations.

In India where educational broadcasting and educational television are a very recent phenomenon, no worth while research is available on educational technology not to speak of statewise surveys and reports even.

In this book more emphasis has been laid on educational psychology and a theme has been introduced on educational technology. A separate discussion on educational technology may follow in the coming book. Like other disciplines we are still in the borrowing stage in the field of educational technology.

But it is encouraging to note that efforts have been made in some universities to use educational technology to improve teaching. This book has tried to provoke a discussion on this aspect of teaching.

Tara Chand

Contents

1

The Basic Principles of Learning and their Application to Teaching

Aims of the Chapter:

1. To develop a valid concept of the meaning of new learning and its implication.
2. To develop an understanding of the basic learning principles which are important in teaching.
3. To develop a proper insight of the role of the teacher in directing and guiding learning.

General Agreements Concerning Learning Prcoess

Although opinions differ regarding the many aspects of learning—how it takes place, what the best means of promoting it are, and many other matters pertaining to it, it is an accepted fact that learning does take place. That learning does take place is universally and unanimously agreed. Learning occurs in and out of school in all working hours, and is continuous from the birth until the death of any normal individual. Psychologists have come to agree that trial-success learning, conditioning, and insight are valuable as phases of the learning process if and when they are used appropriately. It is certain that all learning has to do with change going on within the organism. How these changes are facilitated depends in great measure upon the goal or, the purpose of the learner and the differentiation and integration of the factors of learning situation that make possible the attainment of the desired goal. The achievement of worthy outcomes, whether these be the forming of connections or habits, changing behavior, or the developing of insight or understanding, is not dependent upon the realization of any one point of view of learning but upon the application of the principles that fit a specific learning situation.

Although each of the different theories gives somewhat different explanations of the learning process, they have all certain elements in common. From the different studies and theories formulated were developed general principles governing. learning which are fundamental to teachers and teaching. No one theory accounts for all the problems and facts of learning. A student of education should be critical of the extreme claims of any one school, remembering that each probably has some valid contribution to make to learning and to the attainment of knowledge, in general. However, if the different theories are properly analyzed they will give us a good account of learning as essentially identifiable with the process of growth. In other words, the different theories of learning point to one important goal—that is, growth of the child in terms of integrated knowledge or behavior, understanding, skills, and attitudes. They are essentials and tools to the child's growth and development.

Basic Principles of Learning

The concept of new learning may be better understood if explained in terms of learning principles rather than in a set of laws or fixed methods and procedures. From the different studies and theories formulated were developed general principles governing learning which are fundamental to teachers and teaching. Some of the guiding principles of learning which are fully well established and quite important in teching are the following:

1. *Learning is an active or dynamic process*. Learning takes place only through self-activity. This statement is based on the

theory of self-activity by Froebel[1]—that one learns only through his own self-activity. A child learns to do a thing by actual doing, not by memorizing the rules or by watching others. In other words, we do not learn singing, oratory, or painting, by standing as passive witnesses. The individual learns exactly the reactions he practices, or he learns what he experience. It can be stated, therefore, that the learning process is essentially experiencing, reacting doing, and understanding. The recognition of the principle of self-activity shifts the focus of thought from external factors to the learner himself. The principle does not demand activity alone, but all-sided activity of the whole self. The principle of self-activity is the great and fundamental principle in all education. Self-activity is a requirement of all learning and of all mental physical, emotional, and social growth and development. The, speed is in direct proportion to the amount of activity that is aroused during the process; hence, it can be established that action promotes learning. This principle requires that pupils should participate in planning, executing, and evaluating tasks. It is on this fact that activity programs in schools are based.

To be effective, learning must be an active process regardless of the philosophy of the school, whether progressive or traditional. Directing pupil-learning experiences is the teacher's major responsibility. The creative teacher will never be so naive as to assume total responsibility for formulating, explaining, and illustrating the so-called learning experiences. As a general principle, it can be said that learning is best when it utilizes the theory of self-activity. Learning is an active, dynamic, and adjustive process.

2. *Learning is a process of integration.* Learning is best when integration occurs in the learning process. Integration is a process which operates in the unifying of separate items into a perceptual whole. Through integration, related ex-

---

1. Froebel "Education Through Self-Activity" See T. Brameld, *Patterns of Educational Philosophy* (New York: Work Book Company, 1950), p. 134.

periences are organized or tied together into bonds of greater meaningfulness. It includes the ability to perceive similarities and to organize dynamic system into a unified whole. Some learning products are themsevles an integration of similar elements. However, it can be said that integration alone is not the whole of learning. Analysis, as well as synthesis, is essential in learning.

Integration take place concurrently with differentiation. Integration and differentiation are not independent processes that operate separately without regard to the other process. Differentiation is one part of learning—a kind of preparatory process during which the learner is engaging in the process of integration. The function of differentiation is to distinguish meaning from parts or situations in order to promote understanding. Discovering relationships between the situations is an important aspect of the integrating process. The more effective the integration, the more functional will the learning be. The teacher must select appropriate learning experiences of the pupils to associate learning into a larger and larger whole. Learning tends to unify individual experiences because the learner acts as a unit in his learning. Past experiences help by furnishing organized materials, concepts, meaning, and relations through the process of integration.

3. *Learning is a process of growth and not apart from development.* This principle is based on the philosophy of John Dewey[2] "that education is growth" and on Gestalt's[3] theory "that learning is a process of development." Learning is one kind of growth which involves progressive improvement in behavior and which results from experience and maturation. Growth is a product of the interaction of the organism with its environment. The child grows as a whole, as a unified organism, as an individual in a world of things, people, and ideas. Education and learning are aspects of growth. The task of the teacher is

2. John Dewey, *Education Today* (New York: G.P. Putnam's Sons, (1940), pp. ix-x.
3. R.H. Wheeler and F.T. Perkins, Principles of Mental Development (New York: Thomas Y. Crowell, 1932). p 16.

to stimulate and to direct growth in physique, mentality, emotional control, and social personality.

Modern psychology holds that the growth of the child from birth to adulthood is a continuous and gradual process that cannot be divided into separate stages. Development therefore is not a uniform process that is general in character but rather the composite of the whole series of specific growth processes. Thorndike[4] stated that the capacity to modify response is a general characteristic of a whole life process and that the capacity is continuous throughout adult life with only a slight lessening in degree.

4. *Learning is goal-seeking or purposeful.* Purpose or goal is essential to all effective learning. Goal-seeking is one of the dynamic factors in learning. Real learning takes place only when the learning situation fills a need to satisfy a purpose of the learner and goals that constantly give direction and destination to the learning activity. When the learner has a knowledge and understanding of the goals to be achieved, he will know how to direct his energies and attention to realize them. Goals which are clearly stated and defined improve both efficiency and motivation. Learning, to be effective, must be related to needs, wants, interests, and desires. Each normal child is capable of learning anything which is related to the attainment of a personal goal. This goal can be the object which serves to satisfy some psychological drive, or it may be merely the attainment of some situation possessing secondary value. Both the teacher and the pupils should have knowledge of the goals to be achieved in any learning situation. It is, therefore, necessary for the teacher to do her utmost to make the goal evident whenever possible. The goal, in order to be most advantageous, should be purposeful. Goal-seeking is a legitimate aspect of learning.

Purposeful learning is more rapid and effective. Learning becomes more rapid and the resulting attitude becomes stronger

4. E. L. Thorndike, *Educational Psychology* (New York: Columbia University Press, 1920), Vol. I, p. 197.

when the purpose of the learnar is more intense. This is a recognized principle of learning. Unless learning is purposeful, it will be of little value to the learner. To be in keeping with the fundamental fact that learning is goal-seeking in nature, the purpose should be clearly defined and stated precisely. Kilpatrick[5] regards purposeful-activity as the essential basis of intellectual life and as the foundation of intelligent learning. Likewise, Mursell[6] insists that the purpose for which anything is learned must always become apparent in the learning. Pupils learn most effectively when they are engaged in purposful tasks that will lead desirable satisfactions after the goals shall have been attained. Half-hearted learning, learning without push and thrust, can never yield authentic results.

5. *Learning is creative.* Creativeness is defined as the ability to express oneself through writing, the arts and crafts, music, or other media of expression. Under this concept all children are endowed with creative ability to some degree, and this potential is capable of development through learning experiences favorable to creative expression as a desirable aim of education, and strives to guide children into learning situations which will stimulate creative thinking and doing. Learning is affective when the child is free to create his own responses to the situation he faces. This creativeness is a characteristic of all human learning regardless of the inherited capacity of the individual facing a life situation is the primary unit in the learning process. When the individual is free to make his own originality, then and only then will creativeness be possible.

6. *Learning is a process of discovery and exploration.* Learning achieves effective results by a process of exploration and discovery. It starts with the desire to reach a solution. It proceeds by an experimental, intelligible, varied attack in the endeavor to achieve the wish for solution. It must be remembered that learning is not caused by brute repetition. It has been shown experimentally that the degree of learning

5. William H. Kilpatrick's article in the *Journal of the National Education Association*, Vol. 24, No. 9, December 1935.

6. J.L. Mursell, *Educational Psychology* (New York: W.W. Norton and Co. 1939). pp. 170-171.

achieved has surprisingly little relationship to the number of repetitions. Learning then is an affair of discovering and seeing
the point that one wishes to know. The best learning anyone
ever does is accomplished by exploration and discovery under
the urge of strong desire. It is unsound educational practice to
organize learning simply for the sake of bringing about more
repetition, such as trying to make children put in more time
going over and over their assignments.

7. *Learning is understanding.* Purposeful and functional
learning is well aided by meaning and understanding derived
from experience. The meaning attached to any situation comes
from experience related to it. This principle calls for the use
of the pupil's past experience or background in learning. All
learning should go on in meaningful situations and should
point toward results in terms of understanding and clarification of meaning. Whenever learning goes on effectively, its
outcome is control brought about by an understanding of
intelligent response. The teacher should always try to help the
learner to achieve the best possible understanding. Likewise,
learning should be organized so that the outcome will be
understanding. History is best taught when everything is pointed
toward helping the child to some real understanding, however,
limited of the interplay, sequence, and significance of past
events. Similarly, mathematics is best taught when everything is
pointed toward an understanding of spatial and numerical
relations. Often, it is discovered that the teachers are asking
pupils to study materials for which the latter lack essential
experimental background to make understanding possible. In
the absence of direct experiences, the teacher may provide
indirect experience to make the learning situation meaningful.

8. *Learning is a social process, integrating self with environment.* Learning is best when it is made a social process, integrating self with environment. In varying degrees each person
influences others, and vice-versa. This basic principle is based
on the philosophy of Spencer[7]—"that education is a social
process and should therefore aim toward individual develop-

---

7. H. Spencer: in R.A. Tsanoff, *The Great Philosophers* (New York:
Harpers and Brothers Publishers, 1953), p. 571.

ment and social efficiency." The true principle of learning can be evolved from an analysis of the meaningful relation of the learner and the materials of learning to the situations in which learning usually occurs.

Effective learning requires a rich environment, replete with experiences. The child needs play, constructive manual activities, aesthetic activities and social activities, including the study of social life in all its aspects. Effective education furnishes the controlled environment for favorable growth and development. Environment influences the extent to which potential is realized.

9. *Learning is transferable.* Good learning transfers. This privilege states that the teaching effectiveness is improved by selecting learning experiences similar to life situations in which learning takes place. The rules of transferability apply to making learning functional in life as well as making it functional in the out-of-school life. The nearer school life is to real life, the more surely will the good reaction transfer to life. Transfer is always the hope and invention of learning. Indeed, there is no sharp distinction between transfer and application. If one cannot play, use, or transfer what is supposed to have been learned, then surely that learning is a failure. Conversely, if one can transfer, use, or apply what one has learned, this is the best proof that learning has taken place. The failure of transfer means the failure of learning.

Transfer depands on identical elements that are comprehended; that is, upon meaning. The deeper and more comprehensive the meaning is, greater also is the transfer of learning. Rich meaningful learning transfers by its own momentum. Teaching for transfer must be concerned with the kind of responses desired and the areas of living in which their use is anticipated. The teacher is the motivating force in effecting transfer of learning to pupils. Likewise, the teacher has the responsibility of selecting learning materials and methods of teaching that will bear some resemblance to later use. If transfer is to be accomplished, then both the teacher and the learner must meet some responsibilities.

10. *Learning depends on context.* The effectiveness of learning depends largely on its context. A good context for learning must be one with which the larner dynamically and strongly interacts. It must engage his interest, his will, and his active purpose. The acquisition of a concept requires a context of actual concrete experience. The real point of concrete experience is when it given the learner something to work and experiment with, something that can command his will and energy, and still keep his processes under control.

Modern teaching makes a great deal of the principle of context, and one of its greatest contributions is the discovery of the ways and means of applying the principle in the best possible way. Such teaching is often considered different in kind from the routine of the textbook assignments and recitations which are the staple organization of the conventional school.

Self-Activity the Basis of All Learning

The preceding study of learning activities emphasized the importance of self-activity on the part of the learner. There is a great need for activity in effective learning. However, too much emphasis cannot be placed on the importance of activity in the learning process on the fact that learning is promoted by action alone, for the speed and the precision of learning becomes most effective only in direct proportion to the amount of activity that is aroused during the process. In other words, speed, precision, and permanence of learning will be enhanced in proportion to the amount of activity aroused in the process. This implies that the learner must be active and must participate in as many ways as possible in the learning activity. The learning task assigned must challenge his interest and elicit the learner's cooperation. Mere seeing, hearing, and reading are not sufficient but they are all helpful forms of action. The learner must think and express himself as often as possible.

Distributed effort, overlearning, memorization, active recall and the making of applications stress the importance of activity. There are varying degrees of activity. Listening to a lecture is an activity, but experiencing, reciting, and discussing involve more activity. Activity does not necessarily involve muscular movement. One can be mentally active as well.

When we say that the pupil should be active in the learning process, we mean that there should be a large degree of involvement of the child's total personality. Greater pupil activity may be accomplished by pupil participation in planning the curriculum or the unit to be learned. Discussion and conversational methods are means of implementing pupil activity. The experience unit is increasingly being used to add meaningfulness and activity to learning. Whether the teacher adopts the unit-approach or subjectmatter approach, he can expand pupil activity through field trips, excursions, and visit to courts or business and industries. Projects which involve construction have been formed to make pupils more active.

Learning at its best is the process of discovering by one's self. It is an active end a continuous process. Learning proceeds rapidly in direct proportion to active participation. The teacher plays an important part in the educative process by furnishing the conditions that stimulate the desired physical, mental, social, and emotional experiences. His problem is to determine the different activities essential to the attainment of the goals or objectives of the classroom experiences and then to supply the conditions best adapted to bringing about the desired self-activity on the part of the pupils. It is important that such learning situations should provide for individual differences and the teacher should also take into consideration the associate and concommitant outcomes likely to result also from the classroom activities.

Methods of Self-Activity

The ideas underlying activity teaching are not new. At the present time activity teaching is practised by people with varying points of view and varying degrees of understanding. Regardless of different interpretations, it is a revolt against the mere passive learning from books which has characterized so much of our school work in the past. Activity teaching places less emphasis upon memorizing and . . .less on merely accumulating facts and more on understanding facts collected, less learning through coercion and more through genuine interest. It emphasizes the importance of needs and interest, not only in the work at hand, but interest in improvement, and the acceptance of the work as significant to the pupil's needs.

Self-activity, in the sense of ability to educate oneself, should be an objective of all teaching. Self-activity must be made a definite objective, and the pupil, under proper guidance, must be given experience in using the means that make self-education possible. In order to develop independent ability to learn, self-activity must be exercised. It is necessary also to develop those intellectual interests which make further enrichment of intellectual life a dynamic want. Extreme coercion is antagonistic to the development of interest as well as independent ability. Independent ability is only realized when it is made a special objective, when pupils are gradually thrown upon their own responsibility and guided in their efforts to utilize fruitful technique. In every method, then, provision should be made for giving as full play to the pupil's eshevity as his ability and attitude will justify. Self-activity particular method and it should be a definite objective of all teaching methods.

Importance of Self-Activity in Thinking

The principle of self-activity is of particular importance in teaching pupils to reason. Pupils will only learn to think reflectively by going through experiences of reasoning. Too much of our school work is mere repetition of what has been read or heard, and involves little real thinking on the part of the pupils. Reflective thinking results in the solution of a problem or from dealing with a situation in which pupils must use . . . or facts as found in the problems or situations. The activities in which pupils must engage in order to think through the solution of a problem or situation must be of a kind to give meaning to the factors which must deal with an understanding of the relationships involved. Training in reasoning involves more than just the activities necessary to solve certain kinds of problems or situations. It should also include a critical evaluation of the mental processes used by the pupil to the end that he may critically plan the steps of his thinking process. Thus, through experiences and reflective thinking, the pupil learns the significance of the steps of the inductive and deductive reasoning process.

In addition, the classroom teacher should make his thinking situations in school approximate as nearly as possible the situations of everyday life. Class experiences furnish thinking situations insofar as they provide opportunities for getting meanings, evaluating, comparing, estimating, generalizing, and organizing materials and relationships, etc. Every subject in the curriculum should contribute its share to the training in reflective thinking, thus accomplishing the instructional function.

Importance of Self-Activity in Acquiring Specific Motor Abilities

In acquiring specific motor abilities, it is necessary that the pupil experiences each of the sets of muscular movements essential to the development of the ability. Verbal directions, demonstrations, or various kinds of illustration may held in guiding the trial-and-error of the learning process, but actual doing and repetition are essential to the mastery of the ability. For example, in learning how to write, or how to type, the learner must experience the feeling of correct movement, and through repetition, learn to recognize and to make the desired movements. This requires concentration on the part of the learner while he goes through the trial-and-error process. Generally, in learning a motor activity, attention must be placed upon the movement as a whole or on the results obtained.

The principle of self-activity also emphasizes the need of having the learning situations approximate as nearly as possible the situations on which the motor is used. In learning to write, for example, experimentation shows that any attempt to teach the whole arm movement to the exclusion of the finger movement, overlooks the fact that some finger movement is used by all writers. Such instruction ignores the practical application of writing in every life.

Importance of Self-Activity in Acquiring General Adaptive Abilities

The principle of self-activity also applies to the acquisition of all adaptive abilities. The importance of the principle is obvious in learning to express one's ideas and feelings. For example, no high school student will expect to become a good public speaker or debater without considerable experience in appearing before an audience. Fluency in the choice and use of works, whether in speaking or in writing, comes only with correct practice in doing the necessary things—in this case, selecting the appropriate words to express the ideas and feelings to be conveyed.

The principle of self-activity applies also even where one chooses to express his ideas and feelings through artistic channel such as painting, drawing, music, etc. Pupil activity is a term of particular significance because it implies the necessity of physical, sensory, and mental reactions in understanding and acquiring abilities, new meanings, idea, relationships, attitudes, interest, ideals, etc., and in expressing and conveying meanings, feelings, and ideas to others. Class exercises then must furnish the physical, sensory, and mental experiences essential to the attainment of the above-mentioned results. They should be real activity periods instead of period of mere "lesson-learning" or recitation of learned materials.

Importance of Self-Activity in Giving Mental Association (Memorization)

Closely related to the process of acquiring mental ability is the process of memorizing associations. Under this type of learning maybe included the memorization of dates, the mastery of addition and multiplication tables, the learning of vocabularies, etc. Here, the best school procedure requires primarily an understanding of the meaning and importance of the associations to be learned. Neaning facilities memorization, and meaning is acquired only through self-activity appropriate to the particular association to be learned. Thus, in learning the meaning of multiplication, it is not enough for the child to say $2 \times 3 = 6$, nor to be able to say 6 when he sees 2×3. He should go through the experience to understand that 2×3 means taking 3 things 2 times before he memorizes the association. Experience with concrete things will help the child through the mental experience which is essentially a part of self-activity. To be effective, the learning situation should approximate as nearly as possible the situations in which the associations are to be used in life.

Importance of Self-Activity in Acquiring Emotionalized Learning Products

In learning to enjoy, the responses of enjoyment are just as essential as in any other types of self-activity. Whether it be literature, music, declamation, oratory, sports, the elements which bring about the enjoyment of these activities must be experienced before the learner discovers the possibilities of enjoyment in these experiences. While it it true that the factor enjoyment comes as a result of these leisure-time pursuits; nevertheless, other elements furnished through understanding situations may add materially to the enjoyment. For example, in reading literature, a number of elements may add singly or in combination, make the reading enjoyable. Thus—rhythm, choice of words, action, plot, character, setting, etc., are elements which the pupil needs to experience in order to find out what there is to enjoy. Without these experiences necessary to discover the possibilities of enjoyment, little progress can be made in the acquisition of emotionalized learning activities. While the foregoing point of view may be acceptable theoritically, we must be sure that the pupils are actually enjoying these experiences in actual practice.

The Importance of the Whole-Method in Learning

Most learning situations consist of an organized pattern of objects or events. Such units ought to call for an organized pattern of response. These facts had led us to ask whether it is more fruitful to handle a learning situation as though it were a single unit or whether the whole situation ought to be divided into parts. The experiments conducted by Seagoe[8] in the field of whole versus part method has added to the general conclusion that the first method is more economical than the second under a great many conditions. This result holds true both from the standpoint of time consumed during the learning period and of the degree of retention at fixed intervals after the learning period has ended. Further studies made by Cronbach[9] have shown that the whole method is superior to the part method only with respect to certain subjects. The literature suggests (a) that the more meaningful the material, the more efficient the whole method, (b) that the more efficient the learner, the more efficient the whole method, and (c) that learning of any sort is dependent to some extent on the magnitude of the unit to be comprehended.

One experimenter found that the whole method was superior to the part method except when nonsense syllables and vocabularies were used as learning materials. Still another was able to show that the whole method was superior when the material to be learned was easy, rhythmical, and well unified. When the material was difficult and the time for learning was fairly limited, the part method was superior. It ought to follow that learning becomes more efficient in direct proportion to the meaningfulness of the material. Meaningfulness often depends on the extent to which the learner can discover come sort of form or pattern that will unite many single items into a significant whole.

Learning by whole as compared to learning by the part method appears to depend upon differences in intelligence. According to Crow and Crow,[10] "the part method appears to be best for learners who have a low I.Q." It is also best for

---

8. May V. Seagoe, "Qualitative Wholes: Classroom Experiments," *Journal of Educational Psychology*, 27: 612-20, 1936.
9. Lee J. Cronbach, *Educational Psychology* (New York: Harcourt, Brace and Company, 1954), pp. 306-309.
10. L.D. Crow and A.C. Crow. *Educational Psychology* (New York: American Book Company, 1948). p. 303.

materials which are so difficult that the learner cannot grasp its general significance or get a general perspective over it. It follows that learners should not be asked to meet learning situations which stand too far beyond their ability to organize or unify. The teacher should devise learning situations commensurate with the learner's level of maturation and comprehension.

If it is true that the value of whole method lies in the extent to which meaning, order, or unity can be found in a situation, then learning tasks which are too long ought to be broken up into parts. There are several studies which show clearly that, as a piece of poetry is increased in length beyond the power of the learner to grasp it as a unit, the time required for learning increases rapidly. In general, it has been found that any material which requires more than twelve to fifteen minutes in a single reading can be learned more quickly if it is divided into parts.

The value of learning by whole method has been utilized in many recent changes in teaching methods. The assignment of a project, for example, has this advantage that it continually relates parts to unitary whole. More emphasis is being rightly placed on lesson assignment and even on rote-learning tasks that are complete units. Students who write summaries of chapters just studied do better than those who spend the same amount of time in mere reading. Outlining a chapter is an aid to learning because it enables the students to learn parts in relation to the whole. The whole method helps the learner to get a broad outline of meaning and to see relationships in the material he is learning.

Individual differences of ability among students and the type of material used in a class ought to determine the balance that shall be struck between the whole and the part methods of learning. Here, more than almost anywhere else, the learning task must be made suitable to the learner and the type of material to be learned. If the teacher is aware of the effectiveness of the whole method in most learning situations, he will develop his plans of teaching accordingly. It may be said that there is some evidence that whole learning has a more important place in modern education than it currently fills. With the emphasis on meaning and problem-solving in the present-day goals of education, the greater values of relationship in whole learning are to be sought in teaching.

New Learning and Its Implication

The fundamental concept of new learning is that the child is one whole organism whose various phases of behavior must receive attention if he is to emerge as a desirable social indivi-dual. In other words, not only must his mental develoment be looked after, as was true with the traditional way of teaching, but his physical activities, his social relationships, and his emotional adjustments must also be developed to make him a worthy member of a democratic society. These aspects of his behavior are not to be developed separately in simultaneous compartmentalized installments, but as parts of larger experi-ences. New learning gives the pupils what they need as the occasion demands. The learning is thus more permanent and meaningful.

New learning calls for application of facts learned to ac-tual situations to complete the teaching pattern and to make learning meaningful. This meeting of truly problematic situa-tions by the learner is one of the outstanding and decided advantages of the modern over the traditional way of teaching. Because learning problems are real, both the pupils and the teachers must think of ways to solve them. Teaching then will not be mechanically following a ready-made course of study which, although perpared by experts, may not meet the actual needs of a particular group or class. Experiences of the pupils and community resources are taken into consideration in selecting subject-matter to be taught or activities to be experienced.

Modern teaching not only aims to unify the behavioral aspects of the learner, but also invites him into the group to which he belongs. He acts upon the group, and the group acts upon him. This interaction which is most clearly seen in effective group planning, discussion, and evaluation, is one of the many excellent features that characterize modern teaching.

There is nothing more vital in the learning experience of a child than the way he gets along with the members of his group. It cannot be denied that many facts learned in the classroom are forgotten, especially when done in parrot-like manner, but the human relationship fostered by group planning, discussion, and evaluation will not fail to make its influence felt in democratic citizenship. The pupils would be learning the ways of democracy by actively living democratic lives in which they may ask questions, make suggestions, express opinions, etc., without fear of being scolded and reprimanded. Democracy carries with it a further implication. It means the enhancement of the individual child's personality by allowing him to grow at his own rate without having this growth forced upon him. Each child must be accepted as he is—which means that academic achievement will no longer be measured by only one yardstick. To the child and the teacher—the social, mental, physical, and emotional aspects of the learner's development are equally important. Because of this reassuring attitude toward each pupil, the former traditional situation which used to be dominated by fear and tension to longer exists, and the pupil acquires self-respect, dignity, and a consciousness of his worth as a contributing member of the group in an atmosphere of love, understanding, and appreciation.

New learning as a way of seeking the democratic socialization of individuals is characterized by: (1) unifying all aspects of behavior, (2) correlating school and community life, (3) group interaction, (4) emphasis on democratic living, (5) close cooperation between teacher and pupils, (6) recognition of individual differences, and (7) presence of love and understanding.

The fundamental objective of new learning is to help the pupils or students to clarify, intensify, and interpret their lifelike experiences so that they will be more intelligently self-directive when they encounter problem situations as citizens in our society. To obtain the greatest amount of good from their school experiences, boys and girls of all ages must have the opportunity to participate actively in the learning experiences.

The teacher's participate actively learning experience. The teacher's approach to the individual child and the group should be integrative rather than dominative. A dominative approach is defined as an attempt to one's own wishes by force, orders, attack or status.

The Role of the Teacher in Directing and Guiding Learning

This brief review of the concept of learning which is taking shape from recent research gives us a somewhat different conception of the several roles of the teacher. Since learning is an active process on the part of the learner, it is not possible for the teacher to learn for the student. In a very real sense, the teacher cannot make the student learn, but the former can have a tremendous influence on learning.

In the first place, the teacher can help stimulate or motivate the learner by bringing the latter to see the connection between the learning problem and some important need or interest of the student. In the second place, the teacher can help the learner make those reactions which are to be learned. In some cases, the teacher can help the learner's reaction by demonstrating the desired behavior, as might be done in teaching a physical skill, like writing. In other cases, the teacher may help the learner acquire the appropriate reaction by guiding his thinking through questions that focus attention on particular aspects of the problem which might otherwise be overlooked. Likewise, the teacher may guide the learner to react almost blindly to a given situation, but at the same time help the latter to eliminate the unsatisfactory reactions.

Furthermore, in the guidance of learning, the teacher may have a great influence by helping the learner get satisfaction from the right sort of reactions. As the desired behavior is repeated over and over, adequate practice can be provided and progress made toward a high level of learning.

This conception of the teacher's role in guiding learning implies that the teacher has clear objectives—that he understands what learning he is trying to help the students develop. Because of the many good things that could be learned and the small amount of time that can be devoted to schooling, not everything that might be desirable can be learned in school. Some selection must be made if the learning objectives are to be attainable. If the teacher is given effective guidance to learning, he needs to have a small number of clearly understood objectives toward which he works with students.

This conception of learning also makes it apparent that the teacher cannot be effectively guided by a series of specific rules. Since each learner must himself be involved in learning, and since the meaning of the situations has for him determines what he learns, it is clear that the specific steps that might help guide one student would not necessarily be appropriate with another. Hence, it is necessary for the teacher to utilize general concepts and principles of learning, rather then follow some collection of specific teaching methods. Recent research on learning has shown that teaching can be made more effectively by approaching it as a task of intelligence, rather than of imitation. Knowledge of learning process can help us in selecting attainable objectives and in providing basic principles to guide our teaching. Results of research are opening up for our possibilities for greatly enhanced learning.

In directing and guiding learning, the following suggestions should be taken into consideration :

1. *The teacher can direct and guide learning by determining the kind of experiences which pupils are to have.* What experiences teachers should provide for pupils cannot be determined without considering the pupil's needs and the end-product, the nature of the pupil at the time as will as the educational objectives to be attained. But the only control the teacher has over product is through experience. The teacher can never impose the product directly. It is the pupil, not the teacher, who is the active learner.

2. *The teacher can direct and guide learning, and consequently improve it by encouraging pupils to develop a method of attack in learning situations and to develop skills and attitudes that are often first steps in the attainment of certain end-pro-*

ducts. The arithmetic teacher leads the pupils in a process of discovering number relations which become tools in new learning. The science teacher must lead his pupils to develop the ability to reach science materials. The shop teacher stresses skill in reading blueprints. All of these illustrations emphasize the point that the teacher should anticipate the learning of one kind of product at a later date by providing earlier, an appropriate process.

3. *The teacher can direct and guide learning by providing opportunity for self-activity.* It is generally accepted that learning takes place only through self-activity. In other words, a child learns to do a thing by doing that thing, or he learns what he experiences. A child cannot learn to read by listening or watching others read. He has to read in order to learn. This principle demands not activity alone but an all-sided activity of the whole self. Learning activity can be made more effective if the teacher would trust the individual as an intelligent, purposing organism by insight gained through self-activity.

4. *The teacher can direct and guide learning by using motivation.* This involves both managing the initial want or need or other conditions of learning which prompt the learner to become active in manipulating the goals, incentives, and objects which he desires to attain in order to satisfy the initial want or need. A student is motivated to learn if he is satisfying a need through the learning process or if he sees a connection between his needs and the learning task. Since learning is an active process, it needs to be motivated and guided toward desirable ends. Learning must be directed by goals since the development of goals is one of the important aspects of the direction of learning. It is important for the teacher to get the learner into a state of readiness, for it increases vigor and wholeheartedness of learning. Theoretically, it is quite clear the learning will not occur in the absence of a motive or purpose.

5. *The teacher can direct and guide learning by being skillful in creating classroom experiences which provide optimum opportunity for practice.* The pupils should be provided with

abundant opportunity to use skills, habits, and abilities they have developed. Much that is learned is soon forgotten if it is not practised or used. Many learning outcomes are achieved as a result of practice, drills, review, or re-experiencing. Through correct and intelligent repetition, associations become habitual, new insights are gained, or different meanings emerge.

6. *The teacher can direct and guide learning by managing the amount, kind, and distribution of practice.* Practice is an essential condition of effective learning. However, practice alone does not produce learning, but pupils do not learn without practice. Our present knowledge of how pupils learn tells us to use practice as a method of fixing and making precise or efficient those things which other learning procedures have led us to understand. For example, there is a place for drill in arithmetic and in reading, but it follows and should not precede the development of understanding of the processes to be learned. The teacher can control learning by presenting practice materials which are important in developing the skills, habits, abilities which pupils should be learning. The practice material should be distributed so that those skills, habits, and abilities are maintained.

7. *The teacher can direct and guide learning by providing for continuity in learning.* Experience is continuous in nature. The individual meets and interprets new situations in terms of previous learning. It has already been noted that learning with meaning depends in great measure on the continuity between novel learning situations which are provided and the previous experiences of the learner. Because continuity lies in the experience of the learner rather than in the content, any highly organized curriculum procedures, such as that based in taxtbook sequence, is questioned. The type of procedure which seems to be indicated is that of planning for continuity, the previous educational history of the group and of individuals within the group must be taken into consideration. Most important however, is the kind of experiences which have been provided for the child in previous years, the kinds

of undertaking in which he has been involved, and the units of study which have been developed. These things differ from different groups and individuals from one year to the next. These things must be taken into account if even a semblance of continuity is to be provided, for the new experiences which are planned must be prepared in terms of experience which the child has already had.

8. *The teacher can direct and guide learning by providing suitable educational environment.* Learning experience has been defined as the process of interaction of the learner with an environment. To any environment, whether in the school or without, the learner brings not only a store of learning acquired previous to his school years, but also certain inherited traits and attitudes. The kind of learning experiences the learner will have depends on his previous learning, on his abilities, and on the kind of environment which the school provides for him. If that environment is narrowly restrictive in its influence on him, if the range of potential learning experience is narrow and formal, if the materials with which he is to work are few in number and poor in quality, the kind of learning he will gain will be meager and restricted. If, on the other hand, the school is able to provide a rich environment with many and varied materials, with facilities which may be adapted to many kinds of experiences, and with ample opportunities to engage in a wide range of activities, the learning experiences of the pupil will be richer, more varied and more satisfying. The pupil reacts to the complex environment which the school provides, and in the course of his experience in that environment, he not only learns subject-matter, but also a great complex of social habits, attitudes, and disposition. A good school from the standpoint of mental hygiene should provide a wholesome environment for the development and growth of the pupils. In other words, the teacher should provide the environment which will best help the pupils achieve their minimum potentials.

9. *The teacher can direct and guide learning by finding what lies back of the learner's difficulty so that he can help the*

child into a better psychological climate for learning. The teacher of the children in their formative years of schooling has a most strategic position with regard to the subsequent attitudes of boy and girl toward school and all that goes with it. Whether a child of any age likes or hates school, either attitude has much to do with his success in learning all along the line. True, a skillful teacher in the upper grades may succeed in undoing the negative attitudes a child has developed, but it would be much better for all concerned if such undoing were not necessary. Teachers in the lower grades will do will to remember that the attitudes toward school activities which are being built everyday in each boy and girl have much to do with the type of psychological content that the learner will carry with him in his subsequent learning task. It should be pointed out here that the past and present experience of children are an inescapable part of the learning situation.

10.   *The teacher can direct and guide learning by developing wholesome relationship between himself and pupils.* An unfriendly teacher has no place in the classroom because he lacks sunshine in soul and genuine human kindness. Good teaching and learning are only possible if the teacher is friendly and approachable. A good teacher is one who acts as counselor, guide, partner, and friend to the learner. Modern pedagogy recognizes more clearly then ever that in the learning situation the personal influence of the teacher is much more significant than the subject-matter achievement alone. Good relationship between the teacher and the pupils will promote a happy state of mind. Learning comes best when the teacher and learner are both in a happy, satisfied state of mind. The mental distress and apprehension aroused by a severe examination is not conducive to the recollection of facts acquired in the course under happier conditions. The state of mind of the individual should be taken into consideration in teaching and learning.

11.   *The teacher can direct and guide learning by providing opportunity for transfer of learning.* To teach for transfer, the teacher must identify and explain the factors which are com-

mon to different learning situations. Transfer will be facilitated if the subjects are studied concurrently with one another. Maximum transfer will be achieved when learning and teaching efforts are directed and devoted to transfer. To be able to promote transfer, meanings, relationships, and recurrent factors should be emphasized in teaching and learning. It is clear therefore that teaching for transfer must be concerned with the kind of responses desired by the teacher who is the motivating force in affecting transfer. Transfer of facts learned to actual life situations completes the teaching pattern.

12. *The teacher can direct and guide learning by making the teaching in the classroom psychological rather than logical.* Teaching, to be effective, must be psychological. This is based on the accepted educational concept that the learner, rather than the subject-matter, must be made the center of educative process. This means that only knowledge, skills, habits, abilities, and attitudes that are useful and very valuable to the learner must be taught and developed. Things should be taught in the manner they are to be used or applied in life. Likewise, the educational programs and other activities must be based on the interests, needs, and abilities of the pupils who are to be directed and guided by the teacher.

13. *The teacher can direct and guide learning by using whole, rather than part-method in memorizing.* Learning by whole method derives its great efficiency over part method through the learner's insight of essential interrelationship of parts. In memorizing by whole method, there must be a relating of less important facts to more important, a clustering of important points of reference to any other facts which are equally related. It is the logical association of ideas which counts in the possibility of recall. Reading the material over as a whole gives a view of the entire selection and will serve to give meaning and correlation of the parts in the whole. It will also help organize the ideas as a whole. When whole method is used, the retention is more permanent. However, if the selection to be memorized is very long, perhaps the most effective manner of employing

the whole method is to learn the material in relatively large sections instead of as a complete whole.

14. *The teacher can direct and guide learning by recognizing individual differences with respect to social characteristics of the pupils.* Any class or grade is a social group, and each individual must be treated as a personality. The teacher should bear in mind the fact that the pupils come from homes which vary widely in environmental influence. Prejudices of political, social, and neighborhood varieties affect the dealings of the teacher and the pupils. A thorough understanding of these social peculiarities of the individual members of the class not only enables the teacher to avoid unpleasant class discussion but also enables him to sound out the social ability of each pupil by properly directing and guiding class discussion and other activities. The non-social pupils must be made social. This can be accomplished by setting up the bigger aims of the daily lessons in terms of the pupil's present status and his future needs as an intelligent and efficient member of a democratic society. All that this demands is that the classroom teacher should know the social characteristics of each pupil in his class.

15. *The teacher can direct and guide learning by recognizing the problem of individual differences with respect to native ability in general.* It is an accepted fact that pupils differ in mental ability. Educators now accept the abilities of the individual members of the class to differ according to a well known law as the "normal probability curve." All pupils are not mentally equal and should not be expected to accomplish equal amounts of work. Different individuals learn at different rates in the same category of learning. Likewise, the rate of learning of an individual may vary from one subject to another. The individual pupil is not to be lost sight of in the group.

16. *The teacher can direct and guide learning by providing the learner with some criterion for indicating specifically what progress he is making.* Many pupils are interested in evaluating their success or failure in attaining desired objectives and

are motivated by a knowledge of the degree of satisfactory progress being made. The pupil who knows to what extent he is achieving finds his study periods much more meaningful than in an instance where the extent of progress being made is obscure. Evaluation thus, should be utilized as a positive form of guidance and should be designed to motivate a given learner to add effort by the simple expediency of charting their individual progress by basing teaching procedures on the testimony of test data. Such a plan enables the teacher to direct and guide a pupil's learning activities in relation with his needs as shown by his evaluation of progress.

GUIDE TO OBSERVATION ASSIGNMENT AND REPORT

Assignment for Observation :

Aims:

1. To acquaint the students with the basic learning principles which are important in teaching.

2. To gain proper insight of the role of the teacher in applying the principles of learning in teaching.

It is generally accepted that the amount of learning acquired by the pupils is determined by the quality of teaching done by the teacher. In other words, teaching if effective when it is based on the principles of learning. Learning is best when it utilizes the theory of self-activity. The principle of self-activity is a requirement of all learning and of all mental, physical, emotional, and social growth and development Learning is an active, dynamic, and adjustive process.

Class or Grade————————Section————————Grade—————

Teacher observed——————————Observer——————————

Observe a class where instruction in content subject is being conducted. Try to note the teaching done by the teacher and the learning experienced by the pupils, and make a report on the points treated in the following questions:

1. Based on your observation, was there more teaching than learning in the classroom, or more teacher-activity than pupil-activity in the classroom?

2. What learning experiences have you observed, illustrated the principles of learning?

3. What teaching principles have you observed were based on the principle of learning?

4. Did the teacher put more emphasis on memorization or on thinking? More on facts or understanding?

5. Were the facts learned applied to actual situations to make them meaningful to the pupils?

6. What are your general comments and suggestions for improvement?

SUGGESTED EXERCISES FOR STUDY AND DISCUSSION

Indicate whether these sentences are true or false (verify):

———— 1. The psychologists have come to agree that learning is continuous from the birth untill death of any normal individual.

——— 2. All learning has to do with change going on within the organism.

——— 3. The concept of new learning can be better understood if explained in terms of fixed procedures rather than principles.

——— 4. It is generally accepted that learning is a passive process of absorption.

——— 5. The recognition of the principle of self-activity shifts the focus of thought from the learner to the external factors.

——— 6. The principle of self-activity is the great and fundamental principle of all education.

——— 7. Learning is best when integration occurs in the learning process.

——— 8. Learning, to be effective, must be related to needs, wants, interests, and desires.

——— 9. Growth of the individual is a product of the interaction of the organism with its environment.

———10. Modern psychologists believe that the growth of the child from birth to adulthood is divided into separate stages.

———11. Creativeness can be best developed in a classroom which is under rigid discipline and control.

———12. The meaning attached to any situation comes from experience related to it.

———13. Learning is a social process which is based on the educational philosophy of Spencer.

———14. In teaching, there is a great difference between transfer and application.

———15. The teacher is the motivating force in effecting transfer of learning to the pupils.

———16. Activity implies that the learner must participate in as many ways as possible in the learning activity.

———17. Learning proceeds rapidly in direct proportion to achieve participation.

———18. Activity teaching places more emphasis upon memorizing and on the accumulation of facts.

———19. Extreme coercion is favorable to the development of interest as well as independent ability.

———20. Self-activity is a method and it should be a definite objective of all teaching.

———21. The principle of self-activity is of particular importance in teaching pupils to reason.

———22. It is an accepted fact that actual doing and repetition are essential to the mastery of the motor ability.

———23. Learning, to be effective, should approximate as nearly as possible, the situations in which the associations are to be used in life.

———24. Learning by whole as compared to learning by part method appears to depend upon differences in intelligence.

———25. The whole method appears to be best for learners who have a low I.Q.

———26. Part method is best for materials which are easy that the learners can easily grasp its general meaning.

------27. New learning calls for a ready-made course of study prepared by experts.

------28. This principle of self-activity demands not activity alone but an all-sided activity of the whole self.

------29. Many learning outcomes are achieved through the use of drill, review, and re-experiencing.

------30. Practice produces learning; hence learning is possible without practice.

------31. Drill or practice, to be effective, must precede the development of an understanding of the processes to be learned.

------32. It is an accepted fact that the individual meets and interprets new situations in terms of previous learning.

------33. While instruction or teaching is a group procedure, learning is always an individual process.

------34. Transfer of facts learned to actual situations completes the teaching pattern

------35. A learner must be sufficiently matured and skilled to be ready for a new learning experience.

------36. Different individuals learn at different rates in the same category of learning.

------37. There are different marked differences in the responses of children from diffrent economic levels of our society.

------38. Many desired learning outcomes are disintegrated patterns of action or activity.

------39. Learning is more efficient in an atmosphere of security and belonging.

------40. Teaching effeotiveness is improved as the pupil relates his satisfaction in relation to his new goals.

GUIDS QUESTIONS FOR STUDY

1. What are the general agreements among psychologists concerning the learning process?

2. What are some of the basic principles of learning which are fundamental to teachers and teaching?

3. Why should "self-activity" be made the objective of all teaching?

4. What are the advantages of whole method of learning over part method?

5. What is the fundamental concept of new learning and its implication to teaching?

6. What are the outstanding characteristics of new learning?

7. Why is not possible for the teacher to learn for the pupil? What principle of learning is involved here?

8. Why is it not possible for the teacher to direct and guide the learner without a clear understanding of the learning process ?

9. What is the philosophy behind the statement that "teaching must be psychological rather than logical"?

REFERENCES FOR READING AND STUDY

Barker, R. G., "Success and Failure in the Classroom," *Progressive Education*, 19: 221-24, 1942.

Burton, W. H., *The Guidance of Learning Activities*, 2nd ed, New York: Appleton-Century Crofts, Inc., 1952. Chapter 6.

Cantor, N., *The Teaching-Learning Process*. New York: The Dryden Press, Inc., 1953. Chapter 3.

Guthrie, E. R., *The Psychology of Learning*, rev. ed. New York: Harper and Brothers, Publishers, 1952. Chapter 12.

Hilgard, E.R., *Theories of Learning*. New York: Appleton-Century Crofts, Inc., 1948.

Johnson, E., and R.E. Michael, *Principles of Teaching*. Boston: Allyn and Bacon, Inc., 1958. Chapter 6.

Kingsley, H.L., *The Nature and Conditions of Learning*. New York: Prentice-Hall, Inc., 1946. Chapter 6.

Melvin, A.G., *General Methods of Teaching*. New York: McGraw-Hill Book Company, Inc., 1952. Chapter 5.

Ojeman, R.H., "Identifying Effective Classroom Teachers, in Bases of Effective Learning," *1952 Yearbook* (Dept. of Elementary School Principal). Washington, D.C.: The N.E.A., 1952. pp. 130-138.

Skinner, C.E. and others, *Educational Psychology*. New Jersey: Prentice-Hall, Inc., 1955. Chapter 17.

————, *Essentials of Educational Psychology*. New Jersey: Prentice-Hall, Inc., 1958. Chapters 10, 11, and 12.

Smith, H.P., "Individual Differences in Ability to Learn," in *Psychology in Teaching*. New Jersey: Prentice-Hall, Inc., 1954. Chapter 10.

Stephens, J. M., *Educational Psychology*. New York: Henry Holt and Company, 1951. Chapter 3.

Voeks, V. W., "Formalization and Clarification of a Theory of Learning," *Journal of Psychology*, 1950. pp. 30, 341-362.

2

The Guiding Principles and Methods of Teaching

Aims of the Chapter:

1. To develop the ability to distinguish between traditional and progressive methods of teaching.
2. To develop the ability to distinguish between method of teaching and technique of teaching.
3. To give the students adequate knowledge of the different methods and psychological principles as these apply to teaching.
4. To acquaint the students with the most recent trends, investigations, and research in order to arouse in them the desire to keep abreast with progress in the field.

Method of Teaching Defined

The guiding principles involve methods of teaching. The method of teaching refers to the regular ways or orderly procedures employed by the teacher in guiding the pupils in order to accomplish the aims of the learning situations. By methods in general is meant the process of reaching a definite end by a series of related acts which tend to secure that end. As applied to class-room teaching, method is a series of related and progressive acts performed by the teacher and the pupils to accomplish the general and specific aims of the lesson. Method has to do with the way a teacher communicates the subject to the student. Method involves regular steps to guide the mental processes of the learner in mastering the subject-matter being presented to him. It implies arrangement. Psychological studies reveal to us that the mental processes involve sense-perception, memory, imagination, judgment, and reasoning. The processes are involved in every learning situation, but they are not employed with the same degree of intensity in learning different types of subject-matter. If thorough mastery of subject-matter is desired, there must be an opportunity for the learner to repeat the process of analysis and synthesis until the act involved becomes a habit.

Risk classifies methods of teaching into two general types, namely; the authoritative and the developmental. According to Risk,[1] "the authoritative method is a procedure by which the teacher teaches by means of some kind of exposition, either oral or written, and developmental method is a procedure by which the pupil goes through the necessary learning experiences under the leadership and guidance of the teacher." Much has been written on the types of methods but no one has proven one method superior to another in every situation. In other words, there is no one best method of teaching for all situations. It should be obvious that different forms of learning require appropriate teaching methods. Likewise, there is no way to teach a particular process effectively, but there are certain fundamental principles of learning and sound philosophies of education which cannot be violated without affecting teaching methods and procedures adversely. As long as sound principles of learning are applied in the classrooms, and as long as the real aims of education are understood and are the ends toward which pupils and teachers are working, teaching methods and techniques can differ widely, even in

1. Thomas M. Risk, *Principles and Practices of Teaching in Secondary School* (New York: American Book Company, 1947) pp. 11-12.

learning the same thing. Teaching method is good when it is based on the psychology of learning and on sound educational philosophies. Teaching method, in order to be effective, must not be over-emphasized; otherwise, too much teaching and less learning will be the result.

Method of Teaching and Technique of Teaching

The literature on the subject of teaching generally makes no distinction between method of teaching and technique of teaching. Writings on educational theory and practice have presented different classroom procedures as methods of teaching or techniques of teaching. These two terms have different meanings and values, but both are integrated in any teaching and learning situation. The method of teaching covers the psychological processes involved in learning, and the technique of teaching covers the use of devices and the application of principles in teaching in order to effect the proper development of the individual pupil. The term technique is also applied in the selection of devices and method to be used as well as to the way in which they are used, Method relates to the learning performance rather than to the teaching performance, and method of teaching involves steps to guide the mental process. In brief, we may say that method of teaching refers to the arrangement of the ways or procedures through which learning is achieved while technique of teaching refers to the skill employed by the teacher in carrying on the procedure or act of teaching. Method is the course or procedure; technique is the manner of performing the various steps of the procedure. In general, method involves teacher and pupils activity, while technique limits itself to the actual performance of the teacher. Method is the key to teaching and learning, and how to use this key is what we may call technique. Teachers gain techniques and skill in teaching through experience and training. Teaching has but one prime objective—to effect the proper development of the individual pupil. To accomplish this fundamental aim, the teacher must utilize specialized teaching procedure and apply properly the accepted principles of teaching and technique. Classroom instruction cannot be sucessfully accomplished with method alone, it requires some particular teaching technique as well. Different methods call for different techniques although both are basic factors in learning. A good teaching technique is a necessary part of effective instruction.

The Old and the New Methods of Teaching

The difference between the old and the new methods of teaching can be better understood by their characteristics—as to the nature and aims or goals. The old or traditional methods are characterized by mastery of logically organized subject-matter through drills, repetition, and memorization, fixed curriculum or activities formulated by adults, strict classroom discipline, formalized instructional patterns, and fixed standards to be achieved by all pupils. Classroom activities are governed by the processes of compulsion, rigid control, formality, fear, and tension. They are based on the concepts that education is a preparation for adult life, mental discipline, transfer of training, acquiring knowledge for its sake, seeking truth and perfection, and habit formation. The traditioaal methods are subject-centered and teacher-dominated activities because their main concern is to get the pupils to master the subject-matter presented.

The new or progressive methods are based on the philosophy of John Dewey that education is life, growth, reconstruction of human experiences, and a social process. The main goal of the new methods is personality development through proper stimulation, direction, and guidance. Guidance and counseling of the pupils go hand in hand with the regular methods and technique of teaching. The new methods place more emphasis on thinking and less upon memorizing, more on understanding and less on merely accumulating facts, and more through genuine interest and less learning through coercion. Classroom activities are governed by the democratic principles and ideals, group-planning and selected activities, freedom from rigid regulations and control of authority, and friendly attitude between teacher and pupils. The new methods are child-centered because they aim principally to the total growth and development of the child.

The major disagreement between the traditional and progressive educators regarding methods of teaching centers on matters of divergent emphasis and opposing beliefs as to relative values. Most educators agree that certain fundamental principles underlie all learning, and that responsible teaching must correspond to them. However, there are the progressive educators who object to traditional methods with fixed and formalized educational procedures and standards. They advocate informality, freedom, encouragement of creative expression, recognition of the rights of the child as a free personality, life-like situation, and the fundamental importance of the interests and needs of the learner. In contrast to the foregoing philosophy, the traditionalists condemn the progressivist's easy-going tendencies, and urge the maintenance of mastery of subject-matter and mental discipline which prepares one to meet unpleasant but inevitable duties [of life in a democracy. However, there are reasons why dictation, or coercion cannot be completely eliminated in the educative process. The pupil needs to learn that life often demands what we do not wish to give. In a democratic society like ours, the good citizen needs to learn to accept a certain amount of compulsion or coercion intelligently.

With regards to our modern school curriculum, however, the writer believes that there are subjects which can be taught effectively by using the traditional methods advocated by the old school, and there are subjects which can be taught with good effect by following the practices of the progressive school as practised in the Philippine Normal College and in the Elementary, Department of Silliman University. In the teaching of Arithmetic, a systematic and logical procedure or series of steps is better for solving problems than an undirected one, as shown in the experiment conducted by Newcomb.[2] The

2. R. S. Newcomb, "Teaching Pupils How to Solve in Arithmetic," *Elementary School Journal*, Vol. 27, pp. 219-304.

experiment conducted by Washborne and Osborne[3] on the same subject gave the same result. Wrightstone[4] concluded that in the teaching of social studies the new practices of the progressive school are not inferior to the traditional methods used for developing academic achievement and skill; that these practices induce the pupils to take a more literal, tolerant, and scientific attitude; and that they provide more opportunities for developing initiative, responsibility, curiosity, and the power of criticism. The modern schools call for the integration of the two points of view in moulding the child into an intelligent and social being. The wise and efficient teacher will not throw aside traditional methods because they are old, nor will he embrace progressive methods merely because they are new. Any method should be used where it would be most effective. We must bear in mind that methods, both traditional and progressive, are means to an end. They are tools at the disposal of both the teacher and the pupils. The traditional methods when properly motivated, directed, and evaluated by democratic teachers are perhaps more democratic than the progressive methods under autocratic teachers. There are elements in both methods which must be utilized if we are to attempt to teach the coming generation effectively. One must also know the psychological concepts, principles, and techniques underlying the practices of both traditional and progressive methods of teaching.

Whatever method is to be used, the teacher must know the conditions prevailing at a given time. The most appropriate conditions for progressive or new methods are the following: (1) availability of fund, (2) small classes, (3) bright pupils, (4) variety of equipment, (5) command of the language, (6) freedom to adjust curriculum to local conditions or needs, (7) good teachers who have mastered progressive methods and

3. C. N. Washborne and R. Osborne, "Solving Arithmetic Problems," *Elementary School Journal*, Vol. 27, pp. 219-304.
4. J. N. Wrightstone, "Achievement in Conventional and Progressive School," *Progressive Education*, Vol. 13, pp. 389-395.

techniques and (8) understanding of principles and ideals of democracy. It cannot be denied that language handicap, lack of needed equipment, textbooks and teaching aids, poor educational background, and poorly trained teachers are road-blocks to the effective uses of the progressive method. A good teaching procedure will inevitably fails if its application is misunderstood or misapplied. Democratic principles and practices, if fully understood by a classroom teacher, are applicable to both traditional and progressive methods of teaching.

Factors Which Determine the Method to Be Used

The following factors must be taken into consideration in selecting the method to be used for successful teaching.

1. *The aims of education*—The general aims and objectives of education must be considered in selecting the method to be used because they embody the democratic ideals to which the schools are committed. They are the basis of educational theories and practices. The general and specific aims give direction to the needs and purposes of the teachers and the pupils and to the educational programs and activities of the school. The effectiveness of instruction is determined largely by the presence or absence of educational aims. If the purpose of the school is conceived as growth in terms of knowledge, habits, skills, abilities, and attitudes, the method of teaching which will most effectively accomplish that purpose must be employed. Method is a fundamental thing in the educative process. Educational aims and objectives give directions to the educational programs and activities in and out of the classrooms. They are the anticipated termini of the teaching methods and techniques. The teachers must, therefore have a clear understanding of the philosophical aims of education outlined in our constitution and the psychological aims of the subjects he or she is teaching if effective teaching and productive learning are desired.

2. *The nature of the child*—In modern educational practice the child is made the center of all educational programs and

activities. The nature of the child therefore should determine the nature of teaching. The method of teaching to be used must be brought into harmony with the experiences, ability, health, interest, and needs of the pupil, and with his progress and growth. The individual pupils comprising a class vary widely in mental ability. The teacher must also bear in mind that the child's interests and needs are many and varied and they change with his changing nature. For teaching and learning to be effective, it is imperative that the teachers possess a thorough understanding of the psychological factors and principles basic to pupil growth and development. Correct method of teaching is based upon the psychological laws and principles affecting child growth and achievement—his wants, needs, and potentialities. In the selection of the right method and technique of teaching, the teacher must, therefore, have a clear understanding of the nature and needs of the learners being directed.

3. *The nature of the subject-matter*—The nature of the subject-matter or lesson must be well considered in selecting the method of teaching. The term subject matter refers to what is needed to secure the desired specific knowledge or to develop the understanding, abilities, habits, skills, and attitudes. It must include tentative selection of the principal items of content that appear to be essential and desirable for the pupil experiences in attaining the goals and objectives of the course. Different types of subject-matter or lessons call for different methods and techniques of teaching. If the aim of the teacher is to develop ability to reason, the method of teaching which will accomplish that aim should be employed, and subject-matter to be selected should meet the same purpose. The subject-matter must serve as the basis of the learning process and must be interrelated with the learner's activities if effective teaching and learning are to be achieved.

4. *School Environment*—The recent educational trends in this country calls for a new type of classrooms equipped with modern facilities. Each classroom should have sufficient desks

for the meeting of the entire class. Besides adequate classrooms, availability of instructional materials, such as references, text-books, apparatus, audio-visual aids, and supplies, must be taken into account. Absence of the necessary instructional materials affects teaching and learning. The most effective teaching and learning can take place only when the environmental condition is most advantageous. It is quite difficult to do a good job of teaching in a poor building and without adequate equipment. School environment should be made conducive to good teaching and effective learning.

5. *Training of the teacher*—Mastery of the psychological principles of learning, methods, and techniques of teaching are fundamental to effective teaching and learning. The method to be used must be well known to the teacher. He must have a clear understanding of the principles and techniques involved. The teacher must not select or use a method which he is not well acquainted. He must acquire knowledge of, and skill in, the proper methods of presenting his subject-matter to the pupils who differ widely in interest and in capacity to learn.

Principles of True Method

Any method, to be effective, must have the following characteristics:

1. *The method must utilize the theory of self-activity.* Learning is the result of the pupil's activity. It is essentially experiencing reacting, doing, and undergoing. This principle states that one learns only through reaction or through self-activity which is the foundation of all learning. Teaching must be done through first-hand learning. In other words, pupils are educated by their own mental and physical activities.

2 *The method must utlize the laws of learning.* The mental activity of learning proceeds in an orderly and efficient way according to the fundamental laws governing its operation. The primary laws of readiness, exercise, and effect, must be well considered in all types of teaching and learning. It is impor-

tant for us to know that all kinds of learning activities are influenced in some measure by readiness, use, and effect. Good teaching provides an opportunity for motivation, exercise, review, examination, and emulation.

3. *The method must aid the learner in defining his own purposes by setting the situation for the emergence of a desirable purpose.* The learner must start with the purpose through originating it or accepting it. Teaching is best when the learner accomplishes his purpose and receives satisfaction.

4. *The method must start from what is already known to the pupils.* Making use of the pupil's past experiences which have elements similar to those in the lesson to be learned would facilitate learning. This can be achieved best by association and comparison. Learning is made much easier if the teacher starts it from what the pupils already know. This is known as the theory of apperception.

5. *The method must be based on the accepted well-integrated educational theory and practice which is designed to unify the work of teaching and learning.* It can be said that theory without practise is futile, and practice without theory becomes dangerous.

6. *The method must provide for individual differences and make use of procedures that will suit individual characteristics such as needs, interest, and mental and physical maturity.*

7. *The method must stimulate the thinking and reasoning powers of the pupils.* The procedure must provide opportunity for thinking activity and thorough organizing activity. The principle of self-activity is of great importance in teaching pupils to reason.

8. *The method must be suited to the progress of the pupils in skills, abilities, habits, knowledge, ideas, and attitudes.* All these are the basis of psychological aims of the subject-matter.

9.   *The method must provide the learners with numerous and diverse learning experiences or activities.* The numerous and varied activities must be provide to guarantee the acquisition of learning outcomes and to insure understanding. The activities or experiences must be unified around a central core. Learning activities, to be meaningful to the learner, must be life-like to the learner.

10.   *The method must challenge the encourage the learner to farther activities which involve the process of differentiation and integration.* The process of unifying experiences contributes much to the formation of integrated behavior. This can be accomplished best through the use of integration method of teaching.

11.   *The method must provide opportunity for the learners to ask and to answer questions.* This will give the teacher a chance to discover defects of the pupils; hence, remedial work can be given or applied. Learning proceeds effectively under the type of teaching which stimulates, diagnoses, and directs.

1?.   *The methods to be used must be supplemented or implemented by other methods.* Question-and-answer method, demonstration method, picture-method, the use of filmstrips, field trips, discussion method, and project method can be used to supplement lecture method or problem method. It is an accepted fact that a good method is a synthesis of many methods or procedures. This is based on the principle that the best learning takes place when the greater number of senses are stimulated.

Factors Which Condition the Teaching Process

In order to be able to teach effectively, it is necessary that the teacher must be conscious of the factors which condition the teaching process. Some of the factors which affect the teaching process are the following:

1.   *Physical factors*—Teaching process is conditioned by

physical factors. Such poor physical condition of the pupil as defective hearing, poor eyesight, malnutrition, constant headaches, and sleepiness are hindrances to effective teaching because it cannot be denied that to a large extent, the pupil's ability to learn is determined by his physical condition. Similarly, the teacher's efficiency is conditioned by his health.

2. *Mental factors.* Mental factors refer to the child's intelligence and mental habits. The teacher will be able to adjust hi s teaching more effectively if he has scientific evidence concerning the mental ability of each pupil. Such evidence can be obtained by the use of intelligence or mental tests. It is difficult to carry on the teaching process in a classroom where the majority of the pupils are mentally poor.

3. *Social factors*—These factors refer to the pupil's social background or past experiences. The social background of each pupil has a tremendous effect on the teaching process. The teachers should therefore gather as much information as he can about the cultural background economic differences of each pupil if he desires to approach his teaching intelligently.

4. *Emotional factors*—Emotional factors refer to the inte-rests, desires, or attitudes of the pupil. Attitude is one of the major factors if the pupil has a genuine desire for learning, or a need for the mastery of subject-matter.

5. *Language factors*—This refer to the language or medium of communication used by the pupils. Language is the instru-ment which the pupil employs in thinking and reasoning. His deficiency of the language will greatly affect the learning process. Many recent experiments point to the fact that a child's difficulty in reasoning is often one of language. Like-wise, the difficulty of the pupil in expressing himself in English is a roadblock to understanding; hence, makes teaching process difficult.

The Integration Method of Teaching

The term "integration" is used here as a process or as a method of teaching. According to Ayer,[5] "integration is unifying process that affects almost every phase of growth, thinking, and personal and social development." As a method integration denotes unity, wholeness, harmony or adequate adjustment. In teaching, integration is the process of unifying the child's mental, physical, social, emotional, and spiritual energies through learning experiences. This method of teaching emphasizes learning as conceived in terms of total growth of the child rather than in mastery of the subject-matter. Emphasis is placed on the development of integrated personality of the child—his abilities, habits, knowledge, skills, attitudes, and needs. Pupils are provided with a wide variety of learning activities and outcomes, with plenty of opportunities for participating in group planning, group discussion or execution, and group evaluation of learning activities.

In the integration method of teaching, learning activities are organized in terms of larger units rather than on an assigned isolated task. Experiences are so organized that they may become meaningful and functional in the integration of pupil's behavior and personality. In integration, the various experimental behavior in different subjects of the curriculum are fused to effect a general pattern of behavior which must subscribe to the accomplishment of the general aims of education outlined in the Philippine Constitution. These general patterns of behavior or general objectives of education would be the foci of attention of the teachers as their lighthouses for direction and guidance.

In utilizing this method, the teacher must bear in mind the aims of education, the pupil's abilities, knowledge, habits, skills, attitudes, and modes of social behavior. Likewise, the teacher must know her pupil's likes, dislikes, tastes, and their individual

---

5. F. C. Ayer, *Fundamentals of Instructional Supervision*, (New York: Harper and Brothers Publishers, 1954), p. 229.

differences. The child's nature and experience must be made the starting points in planning and organizing school programs. Conscious of the objective of the school and the nature of the pupils, the teacher must assume full responsibility in introducing the unit through abilities, interests and needs and the resources of the community.

The integration method of teaching consists simply of the major steps that are followed psychologically in developing a unit. The three major steps to be followed, irrespective of the type of unit used, are the following:

1. *Introduction of the unit*—The aim of this steps is to motivate the learners so that they may be interested in getting the worked started. A good teacher naturally selects a unit of work that will stimulate the pupil's abilities and experiences to worth-while learning activities, and should be guided by the laws of child growth and development. The teacher plans the means of motivating and stimulating the minds of the pupils so that they may be interested in pursuing the study of the unit. The unit may be introduced by using the following devices: (1) stating the objectives of the work of the unit and helping the pupils to see their worth and importance, (2) presenting a bird's-eye-view of the entire unit and the important aspects to be developed, (3) correlating the new work with past experiences, (4) placing before the class illustrative materials such as pictures, objects, drawing, maps, globes, charts, films, and slides, (5) giving the assignment through the use of outlines, guide sheets, problems, questions, and projects to be used as guides for the study of the unit, and (6) administering pre-tests or written examinations. This step includes cooperative planning of the work by the teacher and the pupils.

The introduction or initiation of the unit differs in effectiveness with the varying levels of maturity, the background, experience, and diverse economic and social status of the homes. To achieve a stimulating approach, the teacher must be alert, must have creative imagination, and must be able to see and seize opportunities in everyday happenings to initate learning activities.

2. *Point of experiencing*—This step is devoted to the development or accomplishment of a larger goal anad is essentially an assimilative period. There is no generally accepted uniform procedure to follow in this step of unit development because of the varying needs of the pupils and the various types of units. The procedure to be used therefore depends largely upon the unit or the learning situations. The methods which may be used during this period of development or point of experiencing are the following: (1) excursions, (2) fieldtrips, (3) constructions, (4) reading references, (5) discussions or reports, (6) experimentation, (7) interviews, (8) demonstrations, (9) projects, and (10) problemsolving. This period may last a week, several weeks, a month or several months, depending on the unit, the nature of the activities, and the purpose to be served by the activities.

3. *Culmination and evaluation of the unit*—The aim of this step is to integrate and evaluate the work of the unit. This can be achieved best through the use of the following activities: (1) final test or examination, (2) demonstration, (3) program, (4) exhibit, (5) play, (6) final report, (7) puppet show, (8) debate, (9) re-teaching, and (10) outlining or summarizing the unit. During this period of culmination the teacher and the pupil must sit together and appraise the pupil's progress with the aid of checklists, rating scales, results of tests, cumulative records, anecdotal records, and objectives of the course or unit studied. The teacher, in guiding the pupil, should endeavour to develop in them the consciousness of continual self-evaluation of their experience. This step will give the pupils opportunity to do reflective thinking, summarizing or organizing ideas, training in expression, and evaluation of results; thus, developing the habits of self-criticism and self-evaluation. This step further serves to completely integrate the unit. Both the teacher and the pupils must not look upon this step as a matter of getting grades.

The following important points must be taken into consideration in using the integration method:

1. The learner must be considered as an organized whole and with a unique personality. He reacts in totality with a definite aim and purpose. The outstanding fact which must be taken into theoritical account is that the learner is at all times a totally organized system and he must be given more importance than the subject-matter. The fundamental aim of the integration method is to organize dynamic systems into unified whole.

2. Learning must be conceived in terms of total growth and development of the child rather than the mere mastery of the subject-matter. Total growth of the child refers to mental, physical, social, emotional, and spiritual development of the individual. They are to be developed in as a whole and not in isolation as they function in meaningful and problem-solving situations. Education is now conceived in terms of integrated personality and social control.

3. Learning activities or program must be planned in advance and organized in terms of long or large and unified units rather than isolated or daily assigned tasks. The plan must be revised as the work in the unit advances thus, a systematic check must be kept regularly on the progress of the class.

4. Learning activities or programs must be selected and organized around real life problems, pupils' abilities, needs, interests, and levels of maturity. They must be initiated by the real needs and purposes of the learners. Interests and needs must be taken into account and should be used as guides in developing the child. A properly aroused interest, related to the natural powers of the pupils, furnishes the sustaining drive in learning.

5. Learning activities must provide opportunities for group planning, group executing, and group evaluating. Opportunties for pupils' cooperative group work must be provided. However, the teacher who is more mature and more informed, should be the leader in a shared activity although he should let the pupils decide all matters of policy.

6. Teaching must be conceived as a process of stimulating, directing, guiding, and encouraging the learner. The teacher must guide and direct the natural activities of the learner toward the desired needs and purposes. By virtue of the teacher's wider experience and professional training, he should play the role of leader and counsellor. He must consider himself a part of the group.

7. Teaching in and out of the classroom must be governed by democratic principles. The learner must be given freedom to attain his maximum growth. There should be no harshness, compulsion, or coercion in directing and guiding the child into what he was not intended to be. Integration is best accomplished through guided action—with love and understanding.

8. Individual differences should be met, not by sectioning pupils according to ability, but through the use of varied activities, assignments, materials, and chosen goals or objectives. Pupils must be provided with a wide variety of learning activities and outcomes.

9. More emphasis should be given in helping each child develop as a unique personality rather than on minimum standards or grades. Total personality development is the fundamental aim of the integrated method of teaching.

10. Integrated personality as has been mentioned, can only be developed through love and understanding. It is an inner process achieved within each human spirit; it can only be attained in an atmosphere which permits that spirit to discover its goals. Integration of personality is the fundamental aim of modern methods.

Other Methods to Supplement the Integration Method
Field Trips or Excursions

Field trips are organized visits into the immediate or distant places taken by the pupils and the teachers to further educational purposes of the regular classroom activities. They are used to develop pupil-interest in teaching units and problems, to gather information regarding them, and as culminating activities. The chief purpose of this method is to give the pupils first-hand experience that cannot be had in the classroom. Many of the objects of investigations can be studied best on their natural setting. This method provides opportunities for pupil learning through the use of many techniques other than those of reading and speaking.

The outstanding criterion to use in considering the advisability of a field trip is the possible contribution of such a trip to the objectives of the course. To be effective, the trip must be planned in relation to the other learning activities if it is to be most valuable. When properly planned, trips will stimulate new interests and will increase the appreciation of existing ones. They will stimulate pupils to study and examine familiar scenes and organizations for underlying causes and effects. Field trips may also further the development of good public relations.

While field trips have educational values, there are serious limitations, as well as practical disadvantages. Unless such trips are well planned, the pupils and the teachers prepared for the trips, and the knowledge gained from them effectively used, there will be further educational loss.

The following are the basic steps or procedures to be taken by the classroom teacher and the pupils in planning for a field trip:

1. *Planning the field trip*—The first and most essential aspects of a field trip is careful advance planning. The teacher should state and clarify the purposes or objectives of the trip. The objectives are essential in planning, conducting, and evaluating its results. The pupils should have a clear understanding of why they are going, where, and what they may be expected to find. All arrangements essential for the success of the trip should be made. The teacher should secure a written permission from the parents of each pupil making the trip. Permissions from the parents are absolutely essential. Permission to visit

the resource center must also be secured before the trip. A telephone call, letter, or personal visit may be used. All things needed for the trip must be listed and checked.

2. *Directing the Trip*—Directions for the trip should be carefully obeserved. The teacher should be solely responsible for the observations during the trip. He should direct the observations and should make only necessary suggestions and explanations. If a guide conducts the class and explains what is observed, the teacher must be on the alert to ask questions, when important points are likely to be missed. The teacher must exercise wise guidance over the progress of the observation.

The teacher must keep the field trip strictly on schedule; timing is all-important. The teacher must never, under the circumstances, dismiss the class at the place visited, or in route. He is responsible for the safe return of each pupil to the school building. The clas roll must be checked before dismissal.

3. *Evaluating the Trip*—No well planned trip is successfully culminated until it has been carefully evaluated. The teacher should help the pupils interpret and evaluate the trip at the earliest moment, while their interest is keen and while facts are still fresh. In other words, the trip must be followed by class discussion, reports, or written examination. It is necessary in this step to relate the findings of the trip to the original problems or class unit in relation to the objectives set up by the teacher and the members of the class. A letter of thanks and appreciation to all hosts, guides, speakers, and others who made valuable contributions is necessary as a final step. It should be written in the name of the class.

Dram 'zation Method

Dramatization has for a long time been one of the regular and spontaneous activities of the school. This method of teaching appeals to pupils or students because of their tendency to imitate and to create. Dramatization is depicting, through bodily action, the characters, and activities of a story. It proceeds through the use of language accompanied by facial expression, gesture, and action. This method of teaching produces more nearly the reality of life. Dramatization makes a special appeal to children and adults. It is a concrete form of play which they enjoy and understand. The greatest value of dramatization to pupils is derived from the opportunity which it gives them to clarify thought through their attempts to produce the action and expression of a story.

In the integration method of teaching, dramatization may be used during the culmination period. Dramatization as used in the culmination period may take on many forms of activity, such as the following: (1) pantomimes, (2) pageants, (3) operettas, (4) plays, (5) exhibitions, (6) fairs, (7) contests, (8) bazaars, (9) festivals, and (10) debates.

Other kinds of activity may be added to suit the needs of the class and the nature of the subject. The teachers must only direct and guide the pupils in their activities. The best dramatizations are those planned, executed, and evaluated by the pupils. This method may be used by the teacher in arousing interest in literature, history, language, character education, and health subjects. The subject-matter and materials suitable for dramatization purposes are extensive in elementary and secondary schools. Dramatization also stimulates the imagination of children, encourages inventiveness, and appeals to the creative urge.

In using this method of teaching, the following suggestions must be taken into consideration:

1. In using the dramatization method, the teacher must stimulate, direct, and guide the participants. The teacher must not dominate the planning of the activities.

2. In creative dramatic activities, a large amount of planning, discussion, and organization is essential. Setting the stage, preparing the scenery, obtaining the costumes, organizing the details of the show, and other similar tasks must be discussed

in detail before the assignment is made. The class period must be made into the planning and working period

3. In the informal type of dramatization, less work in and out of the classroom is required. In such case no assignment is necessary.

4. Close cooperation between the teacher and the pupils is important in planning and organizing dramatic activities such as pantomimes, pageants, play, and fairs.

5. Dramatic activities should be sufficiently in harmony with the other activities of the course to produce a desirable and unified effect to the growth and development of the pupils. Only dramatic activities with a definite and worthy purpose should be approved by the teacher.

The Project Method of Teaching

Someone has said that the project is not a new thing. According to educational literature the term project was first used by Richards[6] in 1900. Project, as applied to teaching, had its origin in the activities introduced into the classroom procedure when manual training, home economics, and agriculture were added to the school curriculum. It was applied to the planning and completing of some activity which was primarily manual in nature. Kilpatrick[7] wrote in order to change the essential meaning of "project" as it was employed in educational circles. He was greatly influenced by the idea of motivation which was so prominent in Dewey's educational theories. He defined project as "any unit or purposeful experience, any instance of purposeful activity where the dominating purpose is an inner urge." Monroe recognizes the philosophical nature of Kilpatrick's definition of the term project.

6. Richards, through articles written for *Teachers College Records* in W. Burton, *The Nature and Direction of Learning* (Boston: D. Appleton-Century, 1929), p. 255.
7. W. F. Kilpatrick, An Introductory Statement," *Teachers College Records*, Vol. XXII, September 1921, p. 283.

Hosic is in general agreement with Monroe[8] when he labels Kilpatrick's definition "a point of view rather than a procedure." The project method is one name given to the method of learning through experiencing, and it emphasizes purposeful activities carried on in a life-like situation. Practically all pedagogical writers agree on four steps in the project-method procedure and agree likewise on the nomenclature of those steps, which are:

1. *Purposing*—The purpose is created in this step if the pupils have been able to select and determine the nature of the project. In purposeful activity the child feels the aim himself or the children feel the objective of the group. It is with the inherent features of purposeful activity that the teacher begins in simulating the present interest of the pupils. The importance and educational values are also considered. The teacher's role is mainly to stimulate and to guide the pupils.

2. *Planning*—In this step the pupils plan the work to be done and the procedure to be followed. The materials and other necessary expenses must also be considered in planning. The pupil or the class should carry the chief responsibility of planning the project. The planning and preparation, although in the hands of the pupils, should proceed under the guidance of a thoroughly informed teacher whose part is active, not passive; cooperation, not aggressive. The teacher must participate in planning the project.

3. *Executing*—This refers to the actual carrying out of the project according to the plan made. This execution varies with the nature of the project and the character of the subject-matter. The project must be executed in the class under the supervision of the teacher. Every phase of the activity should be directed toward the realization of the objectives that brought the project into being. In this step the teacher has an active part to play, both as a guide and as helper. He needs to observe closely the

8. W. S. Monroe, *Directed Learning in High School*, (New York: Doubleday. Doran and Co., 1927), p. 449.

progress made while the execution phase is going on. He must stimulate and encourage. He must also see to it that the plan is being followed carefully.

4. *Judging*—This refers to the evaluation of the results which may take the various forms. They maybe in the form of an exhibition of materials, a report, a floor talk given before the class, a dramatic production or a debate, or the publication of the product. The pupils should be trained to judge the products of their own efforts. Psychologically, it is a well-established fact that self-criticism will be received more graciously than good suggestios from others.

The four steps given above apply to all other kinds of projects as well, such as: the producer project, the consumer project, the problem project, and the drill project. In using the project method of teaching the following points must be taken into consideration:

1. The project must have an educational value which can be appreciated by the pupil. It should take the pupil's interests and needs into consideration. To be of interest, it must be adapted to the mental level and maturity of the pupils. The time consumed must be commensurate with the values received from the execution of the project.

2. The project method can be used effectively if one starts with a purpose or an object in view, instead of an assigned lesson. Activities which aim to attain a purpose are always satisfying. Creating a purpose or a desire to do the work, which is based on the principle that effective learning is purposeful, is an important phase of the project method.

3. The project method should be carried out in its natural setting or in given life-like situations. Rather than artificial, the approach must be practical or functional. If education is thought of as a life process, pupils should live under circumstances in school that are hot artificial.

4. The project method must be based on the principles of creativity and cooperation. Creativity denotes and encourages growth, and cooperation improves personal and social relationships essential in a democracy. The project method is a creative and cooperative enterprise in which initiative, originality, experimentation, and cooperation are encouraged.

5. The project method must be used according to the needs of the course so that an orderly development of learning may take place. This method is not adaptable to all units in the course of study; however, it can be used successfully in such subjects as English, physics, biology, and history. It is also used best in the teaching of industrial arts and vocational subjects where manipulation and construction are involved.

6. The project method should be used occasionally but not regularly. It must be used to supplement or to coordinate with other teaching processes. Individual projects may be assigned to bright pupils to supplement other methods used by the teacher.

7. The project method involving construction or experimentation must be used only when materials needed are available. The cost of the materials should also be considered in the selection of a project. Many worthwhile projects are impossible because of the scarcity and high cost of the materials needed.

8. The project method must be evaluated in terms of educational values received by the participants. The teacher must exercise judiciousness in evaluating its merits for a specific learning need.

9. A time schedule should govern the project method. The economy of time involved partly decides the effectiveness of this procedure in comparison with other methods. Whatever values are received by the learner must be commensurate with the amount of money spent and the time consumed in the project. The most economical means in achieving the desirable ends

must be applied in any project.

The Developmental Method

The developmental method may be classified as a general method of teaching. This method is considered as one general method of wide application in the educative process. This teaching procedure is adaptable. Developmental method is the teacher's application of some theory of educational experience and learning principles. What the teacher should do in this method depends upon what is required to secure the qualities of experiences he seeks. The teacher considers such qualities of experience in selecting ends and means while planning, teaching, and evaluating the activities of the learning-teaching relationship.

The developmental method refers to the procedure whereby the learner follows the steps of the learning process to attain understanding, interpretation, and generalization. This method is generally used if the aim of the teacher is to formulate rule, principle, definition, and general conclusion regarding important relationship. In this procedure, a rule, a general principle, or a generalization is arrived at through the study of many examples or particular situations. The learner goes through the different steps of the learning process in order to reach a conclusion or generalizations. This method provides a direct learning procedure wherein the pupils react under the wise stimulation, direction, and guidance of the teacher.

When used to develop thinking which involves the manipulation of idea, data, or facts, the developmental method is the best procedure. The ultimate aim of thinking is to reach a conclusion or generalization. It is a process of inquiring, of investigating, of seeking, and of looking into things. Thinking is acting with the aims and purposes in view. Teaching, to be of real value, must provide the opportunity and urge for thinking. This method is also valuable as a means of diagnosing class and pupil's needs, abilities, and difficulties. It also provides for the psychological application of the principles and laws of learning. A teaching method is good when it stimulates thinking and reasoning on the part of the pupils.

The developmental method will be effective insofar as the teacher provides the following steps:

1. *Motivation* (Prepare the learner)—The aim in this step is to prepare the learner for the work or lesson to be learned. Preparing the pupil for learning is the first step in a good teaching procedure. How the learner is to be motivated or stimulated is conditioned by the aims of the lesson, the nature of the learner, the nature of the subject-matter, and the instructional materials available. In other words, how the learner is actually motivated depends upon the circumstances of the particular learning situation. A mental set to learn is important to achieve the goal that appeals to him.

2. *Development* (Direct and guide learning)—The purpose of this step is to realize the aims of the teacher and the pupils. Actual learning takes place in this step wherein the teachers helps the pupils to compare, contrast, generalize, and evaluate the facts experienced or ideas presented. Pupils are led to formulate a generalization or general summary. Generalization gives assurance of real learning. Guidance and analysis are the teacher's most instructive functions in this step. Generalization or conclusion is the function of the pupils. Much developmental work can progress more efficiently under the direction of the teacher.

3. *Application* (Evaluate learning)—This step refers to the application of the facts learned, or principle, or rule through the cooperation of the teacher and the pupils. Application of facts learned or experiences gained to the actual situation completes the teaching pattern and makes learning more meaningful. Real learning comes only when facts or skills learned are used in real situatious. Application affords a natural means for "reviewing old knowledge," and offers the best opportunity for drill work. The application of facts learned or principle formulated is the test of the whole process.

This step is also important in determining as to whether re-teaching is necessary.

The following points must be taken inio consideration by the teacher in the use of the developmental method:

1.   This method should be used only if the teacher has a thorough mastery of the subject-matter and when the pupils have the ability and experience necessary to understanding. This method is a reasoning procedure; hence, the teacher must be a master of the learning situation.

2.   The teacher must bear in mind that effectiveness of this method depends upon the direction and guidance given by the teacher and the participation of the pupils in the learning process. This method must be employed under the careful guidance of the teacher.

3.   The materials or activities to be experienced must be planned and organized psychologically. In other words, activities or subject-matter must be organized according to the interests and needs of the pupils. The teacher should select those activities essential and desirable for the particular learning situations. Likewise, the objective of the learning situation and the generalization to be developed must be taken into consideration.

4,   The principles of apperception plays an important role in the operation of this method. First-hand experiences of the pupils must be utilized in the formulation or generalization. Conclusion or generalization must be the product of their own thinking.

5.   The principle of belongingness must be utilized in developing the lesson. Only the experiences of the pupils belonging to the new lesson must be brought out in the discussion. They must belong to the content of learning that the pupils had already experienced. Knowledges and skills learned in the classroom could be of real use to the pupils if these are

in some way related to past learning.

6. There should be judicial use of illustrative materials in developing the lesson. Illustrations facilitate understanding and are a source of interest. Illustrative materials or devices must be made regular parts of the developmental method.

7. The principle of exercise plays an important part in the last step of this method. Excrcise or use is a powerful aid to learning. Application must be planned to make maximum use of recall or exercise. Subject-matter is mastered by use, drill, and review. Practice in applying insight is the best test of real mastery of understanding.

8. The use of this method varies from one learning situation to another. There is no one best procedure in developing a lesson or organizing the activities. Both inductive and deductive procedures may be used in developing the lesson or subject-matter. Skillful questioning is essential in bringing out relationships sought.

Unit Mastery Plan or the Morrisonian Method of Teaching

In the educational field the Unit-Mastery Plan is sometimes called the Morrisonian Plan of Instruction. This method which has been briefly described in several courses of study issued by the Bureau of Public Schools is the one suggested for teaching the different units in such subjects as geography, history, government, and economics. Since this method is built around group instruction, provisions for individual differences must be made through such means as special coaching for the slower pupils and extra work for brighter or superior pupils.

The popularity of unit-teaching in the elementary and secondary schools in this country in recent years cannot be denied. Practically all our next textbooks in history and other social science subjects are organized on the basis of unit-teaching. It is this type of teaching that a teacher who is trained in subject-matter can best appreciate and use to advantage. This method has this formula to observe: pretest, teach, test the result, adapt procedure, teach and test again to the point of actual learning.[9]   The following steps are suggested:

1.   *Exploration*—The teacher explores the pupils' knowledge of the lesson to be learned by written tests, oral questions, or informal discussion.   The purpose of the test is to find out what they already know and what they do not know about the new lesson or unit.   It serves also to eliminate needless repetitions of what has been previously studied by acquainting the teacher with the pupil's background for the unit to be studied.   It also serves to tie up the experiences of the pupils with the problem or problems to be studied.   The main purpose of this step is, therefore, to enable the teacher to discover what is known and what is not known to the pupils and to stimulate the interest of the learners in the new activity or lesson.   In other words, this step is designed to ascertain the appreceptive mass, to arrive at a suitable starting point, and to eliminate repetition and waste of effort and time.

2.   *Presentation*—Here the teacher present to the class by lecture or demonstration, the essential features of the unit to be covered.   In this presentation the details of the unit are omitted.   The general idea can be presented by means of lectures, with the help of illustrative materials such as maps, pictures, outlines, etc. A presentation test is given to determine what the pupils failed to understand.   The objective in this steps is, therefore, to give the pupils a preview of the entire unit so that they may approach it intelligently and without waste of time, and at the same time stimulate and maintain the interest already aroused.   This step has no other purpose than to motivate and arouse interest and to establish goals or objectives.   The pupils are to be tested for mastery of this step.

3.   *Assimilation*—In this state the pupil's work is to assimi-

9.   H. C. Morrison, *The Practice of Teaching in Secondary School*, (Chicago: University of Chicago Press, 1931), p. 81.

late or to gather information through the use of guide sheets which give the problems and the reference books to be read. The work is individualized or socialized and the pupils make progress according to their individual abilities. Before going to the next step, the teacher must give a test to aid the pupil in determining whether he has sufficient information of the proper kind to enable him to organize and present sound conclusions relative to his work. The fundamental aim of this step is to place the whole responsibility of the learning process on the pupils. This step is but a supervised study based upon a guide sheet prepared in advance by the teacher.

4. *Organization*—In this step the information assimilated or gathered is put together in the form of an outline or conclusion. The organization may be a cooperative understanding of the class. This is the acid test of the pupil's understanding of the whole unit. In brief, this step calls for the construction of the students' outlines of the unit without resource to notes assimilated.

In the use of the Morrisonian Plan, the following points must be taken into consideration:

1. In using the Morrisonian Method of teaching, the teacher must plan his work on the basis of the unit-operative technique. A chart showing the objectives and nature of the work, a brief outline of the unit, and the activities to be undertaken by the teacher and the pupils must be planned in advance. The planning in order to be comprehensive, and the execution, in order to be effective must, by the requirement of the method, consider the primary importance and urgent necessity of available, suitable, and sufficient references within the reach of the pupils to save time and to make the educative process productive and stimulating.

2. The exploratory and the mastery tests to be given must posses the criteria of a good test. It is necessary for the teacher to know the pupil's knowledge of the content to be covered and to know what pupil's may need special help. This

can be accomplished by the use of pre-testing, discussion, or oral questioning.

3. In presenting the unit to be covered the teacher assumes the full responsibility. The teacher may present the bird's-eye-view of the unit to orient and motivate the pupils. The manner of presenting the unit may be conditioned by the nature of the subject-matter and aims to be developed. Presentation should be followed by presentation test on items which the pupils have not understood.

4. To make assimilation period effective, guide sheets and a list]of references must be mimeographed and given out to the pupils. If workbooks are to be used, these may be given out with proper instruction.

5. The effectiveness of this method must be evaluated in terms of pupil's mastery of the subject-matter. It is important, therefore that the unit test must be comprehensive. To cover all phases of the unit, objective tests should be used.

The Problem Method

This method is usable in associational or integrated learning. The procedure in this method is similar to the unit-mastery plan of Morrison. The primary purpose of the problem-solving procedure in the classroom is to develop the thinking and reasoning power of the pupils. The importance of reflective thinking as an educational goal is the essence of this method. Dewey[10] points out that reflective thinking is characterized by a process of careful, conscious consideration of facts, beliefs, or other items of mental experience for the purpose of arriving at rational conclusions about some problems or perplexity in the light of data bearing upon such problem or perplexity. In the light of Dewey's point of view, problem-solving method is therefore a process of raising a problem in the minds of the

10. John Dewey, *How We Think* (Boston: D. C. Heath and Company, 1933), p. 12.

pupils with the aim to stimulate reflective thinking in arriving at a rational solution of the problem.

The Problem-Method uses two well-known general teaching procedures, the inductive and the deductive. If the problem calls for a general law, formula, principle, definition, or generalization, the procedure is deductive. These two procedure of problem-solving are adaptable to a variety of learning situations.

The steps in Problem-Method involving inductive procedure are the following:

1. *Stating and defining the problem*—It is the duty of the teacher in this step to help the pupils formulate and define the problem. The pupils must keep the problem in mind and must know the objective of the problem or problems.

2. *Formulating the hypothesis*—This refers to the tentative formulation of possible suggestion or generalization. This is mainly a responsibility of the pupils who have analyzed the situation and may recall certain general principles related to the problems.

3. *Collecting, tabulating, and organizing the materials*—In this step the pupils seek and examine data, ready to modify or discard the hypothesis in the light of more complete data.

4. *Drawing a tentative conclusion*—This refers to the tentative formulation of a general conclusion based upon the data collected, tabulated, and organized.

5. *Verification*—This refers to the final check-up of the conclusion to test its validity and reliability.

The steps in the Problem-Method involving deductive procedure are the following:

1. *Realizing the presence of the principle, rule, law, or generalization*—In this step the pupils are required to keep the

general rule or principle in mind.

2. *Inspection*—This refers to the breaking up of the rule or principle into parts for examination analysis.

3. *Inference*—The pupils deduce the hypothesis or formulate the conclusion in this step.

4. *Verification*—In this step the conclusion is applied to different situations to test its validity.

In the use of this method the following points must be taken into consideration:

1. In using the Problem-Method, the subject-matter must be organized on a problem basis. The teacher must always be conscious of the practical value of this procedure. The materials, such as references necessary for the solution of the problem, must be placed at the disposal of the pupils. The teacher must bear in mind that only problems which stimulate thinking and reasoning are educative. The steps in problem-solving should be followed consistently.

2. The problem should be set up and formulated by the pupils. The teacher should be alert to select problems based only on the interests that are legitimate, fairly permanent, and of efficient group appeal. They should be within the experiences and understanding of the pupils and those which they fell are important. They should be of permanent value to the pupils in life.

3. The problems should not be too broad in their scope. Many such problems make the pupils lose interest long before a solution is reached. In such circumstances, the big problems should be divided into smaller related problems, and each smaller problem should be solved independently of the larger problem. Later, all the minor problems should be reviewed as the basis for the solution of the larger problem.

4. The principle of cause and effect should be emphasized in the use of this procedure. The development of reflective thinking is the fundamental aim of this method. The problem should involve both thinking and reasoning. Facts should be learned as part of a reasoning situation and should not be for mere memory work.

5. The teacher must help the pupils define the problem clearly and to keep it in mind. The teacher must endeavor to make the members of the class conscious of the purpose and value of the problem at hand.

6. The teacher must assist the pupils to recall as may related facts or ideas as possible and to formulate hypothesis or to recall general rule or principles that may be applied. The teacher must be alert in guiding the discussion into worthwhile channels. In addition to this direction and guidance of the pupil's activities, the teacher must be ready, through the mastery of the subject-matter, to supply additional information bearing on the problem.

7. The teacher must guide or train the pupils to evaluate carefully each suggested conclusions and being systematic in the consideration of the evaluation. After the mass of material is collected, it must be organized so that the entire class may profit from group efforts. The pupils may resort to the teacher for verification.

8. The teacher must keep in mind that problem-method involves a complex act, or a series of acts, that varies with the nature and scope of the problem. This means that no teacher can assume that careful direction in one or two problem-solving situations is adequate for all problem-solving needs. The problem-solving activities must be directed and guided in a variety of situations.

GUIDE TO OBSERVATION ASSIGNMENT
AND REPORT

Assignment for Observation

Aims:

1. To observe the teaching of the lesson and the learning of the pupils with a view to developing an understanding of the method or procedure used in teaching and in learning.

2. To develop an appreciative understanding of the procedure used.

The method of teaching is the process employed by the teacher and the pupils to accomplish the general and specific aims of the lesson. It must be remembered that different types of learning call for different methods or procedures. Method of teaching must not be confused with technique of teaching for they have different meanings and values. Method is to learning technique is to teaching; both, however, are basic factors in learning.

Class or Grade————Section———Date—————

Teacher observed——————Observer————————

Go to the classroom where teaching is being conducted in related subjects. Observe the activities of the teacher and the pupils and note the method used, and be able to answer the following questions in your report:

1. What method of teaching was used by the teacher? Was it a traditional or progressive type?

2. Was the method used in conformity with the principles of true method given in Chapter VIII of the text?

3. What factors given in the text did you notice were utilized by the teacher in the selection of his method? List the factors.

4. In the execution of the method, did the teacher make any provision for individual differences in the ability to comprehend?

5. Do you consider the method used by the teacher and the pupils the best for the accomplishment of their aims or objectives?

6. What are your general comments and suggestions for improvement?

SUGGESTED EXERCISES FOR STUDY AND DISCUSSION

I. Indicate whether these sentences are true or false verify):

———— 1. It is an accepted principle that method is to learning and technique is to teaching.

———— 2. Teaching method is good when it is based on the psychology of learning and on sound educational philosophies.

———— 3. The traditional methods are characterized by mastery of the subject-matter through drills, repetition, formalized instructional patterns, and fixed standards.

———— 4. The progressive methods are subject-matter-centered while traditional methods are child-centered.

———— 5. The traditional methods are based on the concept that education is life, growth, and a social process.

———— 6. The educational aim of the teacher will largely determine the teaching method that is used.

———— 7. A true method is one which utilizes the theory of self-activity and the laws of learning.

———— 8. The most effective learning can take place only when the environmental condition is most advantageous.

———— 9. Any method, traditional or progressive, should be used where it would be most effective.

————10. In modern educational practice, the subject-matter

is made the center of all educational programs and activities.

——11.   In the integration method of teaching, learning activities are organized in terms of assigned isolated tasks.

——12.   The fundamental aim of the integration method is personality development through stimulation, direction, and guidance.

——13.   As a method of teaching, integration denotes unity, wholeness harmony, or adequate adjustment.

——14.   The Project Method is used only in teaching subjects which aim to develop skill.

——15.   The dominating purpose of the pupils in a construction project is to solve the problem for enjoyment.

——16.   Kilpatrick considers a project as any purposeful activity carried on in a life-like situation.

——17.   The project method can be used effectively if one starts with an assigned lesson given by the teacher.

——18.   Execution is the second step in the Project Method of instruction.

——19.   Drill and review methods are good examples of the developmental method of teaching.

——20.   It is generally accepted that there is but one best procedure in developing a lesson.

——21.   Assimilation in the Unit Mastery Plan of Morrison refers to the supervised study period.

——22.   Presentation in the Unit Mastery Plan may be either by narration or by exposition.

——23.   In the Project Method of teaching, the teacher should carry the chief responsibility of planning.

——24.   The Morrisonian Plan of Instruction is built around individual, rather than group instruction.

——25.   The last step in the inductive method of teaching is in reality deductive.

————26.   The problem method is related to the abstraction and manipulation of symbols.

————27.   It is generally accepted that the Unit Mastery Plan is a synthesis of many methods.

————28.   Inspection as used in the deductive method refers to the application of the general conclusion formulated.

————29.   The primary purpose of the problem method is to develop the power of memory.

————30.   Like the Project Method, the Unit Mastery Plan stresses the unit assignment.

————31.   If the problem calls for the application of a general law, rule, or principle, the procedure is inductive.

————32.   The organization period in the Unit Mastery Plan is the acid test of the pupil's understanding.

————33.   The last step in the developmental method affords a means of reviewing old knowledge and offers the best opportunity for drill work.

————34.   Problem-solving develops the ability to criticize suggestions in an open-minded and unbiased manner.

————35.   In teaching, all problems must be expressed in the form of questions.

————36.   Good teaching proceeds on the basis of dictation, tension, and coercion.

————37.   The last step in the integration method is essentially an assimilative period.

————38.   Social traits can be best developed in the individualized type of instruction.

————39.   The process by which a problem is solved is called reflective thinking.

————40.   In using the problem method of teaching, the subject-matter must be organized on a problem basis.

————41. The problem-solving activities, to be effective, must be directed and guided in a variety of situations.

———— - 42. Real learning comes only when facts or skills learned are used in real situations.

————43. Preparing the pupil for learning is the first step in a good teaching procedure.

————44. Project method is adaptable to all units of learning in any course of study.

————45. Based on the concept of integration method, individual differences should be met by sectioning students according to ability.

GUIDE QUESTIONS FOR STUDY

1. How do you differentiate method of teaching from teachnique of teaching?

2. What are some outstanding characteristics of the progressive method or procedure?

3. What are come of the important factors the teacher should consider in selecting a method or methods to be used?

4. Give and explain the criteria of a good method of teaching.

5. How does the Integration Method differ from the Unit Mastery Plan of Morrison?

6. In what subjects can we best use the Project Method of teaching to accomplish good results?

7. How does the Problem Method contribute to the development of mental skills, concepts, and attitudes?

8. What are some of the outstanding principles of learning found in all the methods discussed in this chapter?

References

Bossing, N. L., *Teaching in Secondary School*, 3rd ed. Boston: Houghton Mifflin Co., 1952. Chapters II, 12, 13.

Cantor, N., *The Teaching-Learning Process*. New York: The Dryden Press, Inc., 1953. Chapter 3.

Douglas, H. R., and H. H. Mills, *Teaching in High School*. New York: The Ronald Press Co., 1948. Chapter 11.

Garrison, N. L., *Improvement of Teaching*. New York: The Dryden Press, Inc., 1955. Chapter 5.

Grambs, J. D., and W. Iverson, *Modern Methods in Secondary Education*. New York: William Sloane Associates, 1952. Chapter 4.

Hansen, K. H, *High School Teaching*. New Jersey: Prentice Hall, Inc., 1957. Chapter 7.

Morrison, H. C., *The Practice of Teaching in the Secondary School*. Chicago: University of Chicago Press, 1931 (revised). Chapters 14-17.

Wiles, K., *Teaching for Better School*. New York: Prentice Hall, Inc., 1952. Chapter 6.

3

Principles Underlying Drill and Review Methods

Aims of the Chapter:

1. To provide the students with adequate understanding of the meaning and importance of drill and review methods in teaching and in learning.
2. To acquaint the students with the various principles involved in conducting drill and review methods.

The Nature of the Drill Method

The term drill, as used in this chapter, is applied to the process of repetition to authomatize a certain response or mental association for ready use. Drill is one of the most frequently and widely used procedures in teaching. Likewise, drill or practice is the usual method adopted by all classes of people for habit-formation. Drill has for its purpose the strengthening of connections to make them stronger and more automatic. It has also for its purpose the perfection of skill. Drill and practice have the same meaning and purpose. There are numerous experiments which show that practice is a funda- mental procedure in habit-formation. Otto[1] brought out the

1. H. J. Otto, *Principles of Elementary Education*. New York: Rinehart and Company, Inc., 1949, p. 347.

fact that appropriate practice engaged in at an opportune time is valuable and essential in education. Improvement due to correct practise serves to illustrate the operation and effect of the law of use, exercise, or repetition. Repeated correct practise results in mastery permanency.

Drill is one of the oldest types of teaching. The teachers of yesterday were largely drill teachers. They drilled their pupils in all types of subject-matter. Most of the early text-books were written for the drill type of teaching. Probably there is little need today to argue against the conception of teaching which makes teaching simply and solely a matter of drill. The teacher should only drill the subject-matter that requires a response to a stimulus to be automatic, instantaneous, and accurate or correct. There should be drill only after the significance of each is understood. Drill must follow understanding.

Drill is important in education when the right material is drilled. The teacher must be careful not to drill those things that should be taught about and appreciated. Drill must be confined to tools that are used for specific purposes.

Drill is a method of habit-formation. In teaching there must be drill, and drill must be well conducted if certain facts are to be learned as permanent possessions and if certain reactions are to be made automatic. If permanency in learning is desired ordinarily, intelligent practice is required. Different studies and the practical experience of teachers have revealed to us that in learning such things as tables in arithmetic, dates in history, skill in writing and in drawing, facts in biology, rules in English, and vocabulary in reading, drill or practice is necessary. All experiments point also to the economy of learning which results when sound processes of drill method are employed. Besides the available scientific evidence proving the need for drill, there are experiences of everyday life involving the varied activities of many persons which indicate the need for essential drill as a natural learning activity.

In evaluating drill as a teaching procedure, it is well to remember that it is not mere repetition of the condition of learning that is effective. Drill can be effective if properly conducted, or it can be ineffective if not properly distributed. The teacher must remember that the pupils do not necessarily learn just because they engage in drill work. Drill must be recognized and appraised for what it is worth. Progress in drill work has developed new principles governing its use by the teachers and supervisors.

Features of the Drill Exercise

To be most effective, drill exercise should possess the following characteristics:

1. *The drill should be conducted under definitely controlled or standardized conditions so that results obtained in one period may be compared with those obtained in others.* Drill exercise provides the conditions which develop the higher level of performance.

2. *The purpose of drill should be made clear to the pupils.* The fundamental purpose of drill is to increase speed accuracy, facility, or quality of the performance. It has also for its purpose the strengthening of connections, mastery of facts, and perfection of skill. Be sure that all the pupils realize the function of drill procedure.

3. *The results of each period of drill should be measured scientifically and objectively.* The objective type of tests may be used for this purpose. Testing must be made a regular part of drill work.

4. *The results of each period of drill work should be noted and their relations to appropriate and inappropriate techniques discovered.* The results of drill work should be recorded by the teacher in order to have instructional value.

5. *The results of successive drill periods should be displayed*

in such a way as to reveal the improvement made by the pupils. This will give the pupils opportunity to know of their improvement. Knowledge of results defines success and failures. A pupil should know his degree of success in reaching a goal immediately after practice.

6. *Appropriate lengths of drill periods, of intervals between periods, and other mechanical aids to learning should be adopted.* In other words, space drill periods in line with research findings or spaced practice. These findings indicate that shorter periods of drill, spaced over a period of time, are more effective than longer drill periods, with longer intervals of time between them.

7. *Drill materials should be so prepared that the pupil can himself manage the whole learning process.* Such materials increase interests and enable pupils to develop initiative in educating themselves. The materials covered should be clearly related to the other aspects of the course in well-integrated fashion.

Uses of Drill Method

The drill method should find some use in every subject, but it should not be used exclusively in any subject. Its function is limited; but when used properly to appropriate data, its use is most productive. In situations where exact knowledge, abilities, habits, skills, and attitudes are desired, specific drill must be conducted. The amount of such drill is dependent on a variety of factors, such as the nature of the process, the past experiences, the manner of presentation, and the interest and need of the learner. Drill is nothing more than the application of the principle of practice or the law of exercise. The teacher must be concerned, not only with the fixing of habits, but also with the task of keeping them permanently fixed. The only infallible rule to prevent loss of knowledge, habits, skills, abilities, and attitudes, is use or practice. Drill must be confined to tools that are used for a specific purpose. Its use is highly productive where a high degree of proficiency, speed, accuracy, facility, or precision in certain reactions, especially those which constitute tool skills, is needed.

Drill work is essential in developing habits and skills. Recent trends in Psychology strongly emphasize the fact that one of the types of outcomes to be realized in learning is habit or skill. Habit may be defined as ways of actions or the tendency to action in a particular situation. Habit is the tendency to repeat activities of all kinds. Habit adds the element of mechanicalness or fixedness to the making of any reaction, regardless of the degree of perfection. A person may acquire skill in performing an act, but he may not carry it to the point of habit where the responses are fixed and automatic. Automatism means saving of time, the freeing of consciousness for other tasks. It may also denote a high degree of efficiency. Habits are of great importance in teaching and learning. Habits save power and lessen fatigue. Habits also strengthen power. Exercise is the fundamental law of growth of any kind. Habit widens the circle of the pupil's knowledge and increases his capacities. Education consists in the formation of habits.

Skill may be defined as any refined pattern of performance. The development of skills has long been recognized as an important aim of education, especially in the lower grades. Much of the attention of teachers and parents has been centered upon this aspect of child development. These divergent opinions arise from conflicting conceptions of values or aims in the education of children and in the process of learning. The degree of skill which an individual possesses at a given time is the degree of refinement in his pattern of performance. Higher levels of activities are equally, if not even more, dependent on skills. All types of experiences derive their qualitative characteristics in important respects from the skills which the individual is able to bring into play for the attainment of his objectives. In all types of activities, skills play an important part, and they should receive consideration in the educative process.

Skills are a necessary aspect of one's ability to meet new

situations as they arise. The subtractive actions of all kinds employed to meet emerging situations are composed of skills that have been previously mastered and that might be integrated into a new pattern of behavior. These are a host of skills which are of great importance in the education of an individual. Motor skills, which are often neglected after early childhood, may be developed to higher levels of competence and be of significance to individuals at all ages. Skill in using tools may provide an important bases for constructive experiences. Skills associated with collecting information, evaluating ideas, and using references are also of great importance.

Because of the close relation between skill and habits, some writers use the single term skill to include any habituation that may be necessary in teaching and in learning. Habit, of course, always includes the skill required when the activity is made automatic. All skills involve a certain amount of habit in the minor reactions and most of them are habituated to a certain extent. There is no dividing line between skill and habit for any activity. The value of habit and skill is universally recognized by educators, although assertions are sometimes made that certain groups of educators deny such value. Any attempt to ignore habit and skill formation in the curriculum would be impossible since both the teacher and the pupils develop them in the course of their assertion.

Principles to Be Observed in Drill Work

Perhaps we can dispel part of the confusion about drill work by considering some of the guiding principles.

To make drill work more effective, the following principles are suggested:

1. *Drill work, with knowledge of results, is an important factor in learning.* This is true as indicated by experiments.

on practice with or without knowledge of the result. Stroud[2] showed that when the learner is aware of the results of practice, the work is much more interesting and effective. The results of studies show that practice without knowledge of the result does not produce learning; that the amount of practice is not so important as accurate knowledge of the approach to the goal; and that the amount of improvement tends to increase with the accuracy of the knowledge of results. Drill work must have a goal and the teacher must devise practices that will lead to the goal. A clear idea of the result to be accomplished is very important in fixing facts and forming habits. When a learner knows the goal in mind as he practices, better result can be expected by the teacher. It is advisable, therefore, to have with drill a record system which will show the pupil his progress from day to day and from unit to unit.

2. *Drill work must be intense.* The desire of the individual to form the correct habit must be present. It should put forth a maximum of interest, effort, and attention during practice. He must himself be aware that he lacks a certain skill or efficiency, and must wish to achieve it. The learner must have a conscious desire and need for drill. In order to secure repetition while the response is being made habitual, clear attention is necessary and this in turn demands lively and sustained interest. The pupil must attend to what he is doing; he must compare each effort with the model, or with his own previous efforts, to see what gains are yet to be made and by what means they can be achieved. Attention to the process of learning shortens the time for making acts automatic; and it is absolutely necessary to bring about improvement in ways of doing things to increase skill. Practice alone does not make perfect, but practice with attention will advance the learner toward that end because it keeps him conscious of what he yet has to accomplish and makes him alert as to the possibilities of improvement in his method of working. Practice with intent

2.   J. B. Stroud, "The Role of Practice in Learning," *National Society for the Study of Education*, 41 (Part II), 1942, 353-376.

to improve is more effective than that done for temporary use. Practice with good attention is the first condition of good habit-formation, or effective retention.

3. *Drill work must be short and well distributed.* It is easy enough to prolong drill beyond the point at which returns justify the effort involved. Drill work is more effective when it is short and properly distributed. A part of the class period may be devoted to drill activity, which should cease before the point at which the returns begin to diminish is reached. If the lesson consists entirely of drill materials, the period should be shortened accordingly to avoid fatigue and failing attention. The incidence of fatigue greatly hinders and probably stops learning. Psychological research has furnished reliable data relative to the most economical and effective distribution of such practice. Ten minutes spent in different types of drill work produce better results than fifty minutes marked by interruption, fatigue elements, and the like. Rarely should a drill exercise on a particular subject for children in the elementary grades exceed fifteen minutes. Scientific evidence upon this point has established this limit to a high degree of reliability. This was also proved by the experiments conducted by Cook[3] and Erickson[4]. It can be said that the length of the drill period depends upon the age of the pupils, the stage of learning that the pupils have reached, and the difficulty of the task that is to be learned. On the other hand, drill period should not be so short as to break up the task into meaningless units.

4. *Drill work should be distributed according to the difficulty of the task, and so as to provide the right amount of practice for each habit to be developed.* Begin drill work with easy exercises, gradually increasing their difficulty after general improvement

3. T. W. Cook, "Massed and Distributed Practice in Puzzle-Solving," *Psychological Review*, 1934, 41, 330-355.
4. S. C. Erickson, "Variability of Attack in Massed and Distributed Practice," *Journal of Experimental Psychology*, 1942, 31, 339-358.

is made by the group. The pupil's greatest effort should be centered on the most difficult parts. If the practice exercises are relatively easy during the early stages of the learning process, interest is ordinarily forthcoming. Difficult reactions should receive more practice than the easy ones. However, when a task is difficult, a short practice period will prove to be less tiring. Experiments brought out the fact that in a number of forms of skill or of memorization, the rate of improvement was markedly affected by the distribution of practice periods according to the difficulty of the task.

5. *Drill work should be applied when the point of error is made and should be stopped when the correction is perfected.* This refers to the common practice to stike while the iron is hot. Therefore, to make teaching and learning more effective, the pupil should be given a thorough examination and diagnosis in each school subject, to discover his points of error, and then to apply remedies that are best adapted to the correction of these errors. Prompt correction avoids the fixation of errors. However, repetition must be provided over a period of time with gradually lengthening intervals between drills. Only right practice makes for perfection.

6. *Drill work should be adapted to individual needs, and a practice period should be arranged whenever a need for drill arises.* Drill must be individualized in terms of individual needs and ways of learning. Opportunity for individual practice on individual needs is included in a good drill lesson. The teacher, therefore, should give more drill work to those who need practice. It is good to give a test before the drill work, after which drill should be given only to those who need it. Frequent testing is necessary and beneficial to subsequent practice. Making the pupils aware of the results of the test arouses a strong desire among them to improve. The slow or average pupils need more drill work than the bright pupils. Besides drill on the common general difficulties, pupils should practice to overcome their own particular ones.

It is the function of the teacher to help the learners to

realize the degree of efficiency that each should accomplish. The standard of achievement will vary according to an individual learner's ability to achieve. The degree of skill required should be adjusted to the mental maturity and interests of individual learners. The practice periods for the young children should be shorter than those for much older children. It must also be remembered that the time needed to reach the respective levels of skill varies with individuals.

7. *Drill work should be delayed until a correct start is assured to avoid waste of time and energy.* In forming correct habits accuracy should be established before developing speed. The teacher must see to it that a correct start is followed by correct practice. Accuracy in the beginning of a habit is essential as first impressions and associations are apt to be lasting. Practice for speed should be subordinated to practice for accuracy first, and the two will be progressively balanced. When accuracy is established, speed should be sought. But accuracy should not be sacrificed for speed. In drilling on any one part or on all parts of the sequence, accuracy of response is very essential. No exception to the correct response should be allowed.

It is, therefore, most desirable that the teacher who consciously trains pupils in habit-formation should take pains to see that the first associations or reactions are correct, and that the first acts are those which are to be fixed by exercises. The utterance of sounds in phonics drill, the position in writing and the manner of holding the pen, the forms of letters, the number combinations, and many other details which should become automatic are all matters which should be started correctly. It is always safe to begin with the correct habit and thus make sure of it.

8. *Drill work should be properly motivated.* To make the drill work more effective, a motive other than to please the teacher must be had by the pupils. There must be sufficient motive actuating the pupil and making him anxious to form the habit or to acquire the skill or other automatic response.

There should be effective motivation so as to secure proper attitude and attention conducive to maximum effort and results. Learning is more effective when we take into account the readiness of the pupil to learn. The desire for practice can be created by stating the educational value or purpose of the activity. A normal person will practise the things that he believes have value. According to Stroud,[5] "one of the prime determinatives of the efficacy of practice is motivation."

9. *Drill work should be made a part of the regular teaching procedure.* To make teaching and learning more effective, the law of exercise must be utilized. Important connections formed should be exercised to make them stronger and automatic. It has been the writer's experience that the beginning of the class period is most favorable for drill work covering the past lesson. The teacher should put forth a maximum of interest, effort, and attention during the drill period. The drill should be continued, from time to time, until the desired association or habit is fixed. Practice should extend far beyond the requirement of the immediate situation. The associations should be applied as often as possible in new tasks or situations. However, there will come a time when drill may be discontinued, but experience shows that it should be diminished by degrees and not stopped suddenly.

10. *Drill work should make use of play activity or the instinct of competition.* Play and competition will stimulate the pupils to achieve better results and satisfaction. Play, games, and competition are good motives to learning. The innate tendency to play can be best utilized in the lower grades. The desire of a pupil to do well as other members of his class, or the desire of a class to equal the record of the other classes of the same grade, will do much to keep attention fixed on the work. The personality make-up, past experiences, and individual differences of the pupils must be taken into consideration in competitive situations.

5. J. B. Stroud. *op. cit.*, p. 366.

11. *At the end of a drill period there should always be reflection, analysis, criticism, self-appraisement, and reorientation.* Drill should be used as a means to an end. It should always be purposive—an exemplification of the purposeful process of exploration, discovery, and understanding which is characteristic of all good learning. In other words, it can be said that the essential characteristic of learning is not the mechanical establishment of connections between isolated stimuli and isolated responses.

Devices Useful in Drill Work

While drill devices must be made effective, the teacher should also close those that are attractive and interesting. To create strong and genuine motivation in drill process, the following devices[6] are suggested:

1. *Competition*—Several experiments have revealed that children work better and faster and improve more rapidly when working under the spur of competition than when working alone. Competition stimulates the interest and increases the attention of the pupils. When competition is utilized in drill work, the teacher must see to it that the pupils competing against each other are of equal ability, to make the contest more interesting.

2. *Games or Play*—Play activity will also stimulate the interest of the pupils, especially in the drill work. The echo game, the guessing game, and visiting and traffic games are useful in drill work in Phonics and in Reading. Likewise, climbing games, playing store, crossing the river, and running a race can be put to effective use in drill work in Arithmetic. It has been proved by psychologists that pleasure or joy is an aid to drill work.

6. For other drill devices, see P. R. Mort and W. S. Vincent, *Modern Educational Practice.* New York: McGraw-Hill Book Company, Inc., 1950. pp. 309-324.

3. *Song and Rhythm*—In habit-formation, music is very useful. Songs are valuable in teaching writing where rhythmic movement is involved. "Singing" a poem set to music facilitates speed in memorizing. The pupils can do more and better work when they are kept in a happy frame of mind.

4. *Variety of Methods*—Different kinds of activities should be brought to play in drill work to gain the interest and to maintain the attention of the pupils. For variety, flash-card drills may be followed by blackboard drill or oral drill work. Interest and attention make the work pleasant.

5. *The Whole-Method*—Psychological studies have proved that the whole-method is much superior to the part-method in memorizing, and that the whole-method requires fewer repetitions than the part or piecemeal method. The most effective method in learning either poetry or prose is to read through the selection from beginning to end until the material is fairly well understood. In learning material of extended length and great difficulty, it is probably better to divide the material into large units which represent complete thought, to learn these units separately, and to correlate them by some means which will hold the various parts together. Crafts[7] concludes that neither method will invariably be superior but that the whole method may be expected to be especially advantageous with easier and more closely related materials. Learning to memorize by the whole method increases the formation of pertinent associations and the comprehension of isolated parts in a way that cannot be accomplished when material is learned in part. Learning by the whole-method distributes the practice equally in all parts.

6. *Flash-cards*—Speed in reading and skill in arithmetic can be best attained through flash-card drills. Flash-cards will also challenge the attention of the pupils.

7. L. W. Crafts, "Whole and Part Methods with Visual Spatial Material," *American Journal of Psychology*, 1932, 43, 526-534.

The Functions of the Teacher in Habit-Formation

The following general principles are suggested for the teacher's consideration and application in the training for habit-formation:

1. *The teacher should know what habits are to be formed or practised, or what reactions are to be habituated.* Only reactions of relative importance or of immediate use to the pupils should be formed into habits. The first concern of the teacher is to see that pupils understand why the particular result to be gained through the drill lesson is necessary. Drill should be employed whenever a high degree of skill is required.

2. *The teacher should arouse in the learner a strong desire to form a strong habit.* Stating the educational purpose of the habits to be formed is essential to increase intensity of effort. The teacher will find that the task is easier if the pupils are brought to see and understand the values of their daily routine. Other things being equal, when a pupil is convinced of the instructional values of certain habits, he will be more than willing to practise.

3. *The teacher should apply appropriate procedures and devices so that the learner will maintain a proper attitude throughout the period of repetition.* The procedures, materials, and devices to be used should be adapted to the physical and mental maturity of the pupils. This close adaptation of procedures, drill materials, and devices to the individual child's ability and needs is necessary to insure a clear and full understanding on his part of just what he is to do. The teacher must not attempt drill work on something beyond the possiblity of reasonably efficient mastery.

4. *The teacher should bear in mind that a pleasant feeling facilitates progress in learning.* The teacher should provide exercises satisfying to a required degree to the learner. The teacher who emphasizes the making of correct responses step by step builds confidence in the learner that serves as a motive to

further practice. Satisfiers and annoyers are great teachers.

5. *The teacher should recognize a variation of methods in drill work to stimulate and to maintain the intererst and attention of the pupils.* Variation in procedure reduces monotony lengthens the span of the pupil's interest, and minimizes fatigue.

6. *The teacher should not lose sight of the fact that bright pupils need less drill work than the average or slow pupils.* The teacher should not drill the few at the expense of many. Only pupils who need drill work should be drilled.

7. *The teacher should provide guidance in the selection of the correct response to be made.* This can be best accomplished by setting up a correct model before the learner or by means of demonstration. Guidance in the acquisition of motor skills is desirable. It is the work of the teacher to know what the pupil should learn and how he should learn it. The formation of habit or skill requires knowledge of what to do and how to proceed to do it.

8. *The teacher should instruct the pupils to memorize by the whole-method rather than by the part-method.* Experimental studies have shown that in memorizing a poem or a prose work, and in vocabulary-building, the whole-method is superior to the part-method. This method means going through the whole material from beginning to end until it is mastered. In using this method the difficult and important materials should be given more attention than the easy and unimportant ones. The size of the unit to be mastered should determine whether there should be whole or part learning. The whole method is more effective than the part method in memorizing a short poem or material.

9. *The teacher should bear in mind that the essential principles of learning by which habits are built and skills are acquired remain the same, whether the plan for securing practice makes use of specific drill or is merely incidental to voluntary projects.* Varying the procedure used in practice will decrease efficiency

and automaticity if not properly done.

10. *The teacher should make the pupils feel the need for practice.* Drill must fix attention of specific facts that are highly important to the pupils. Select difficult and important points and drill upon them. The value of motivation is well recognized in habit-formation. Like any other learning activities, drill work should be motivated.

11. *The teacher should make use of the scientifically assembled and organized drill materials used in American elementary and secondary schools, such as the Courtis Practice Tests in Arithmetic, which provide effective means of discovering and overcoming the pupil's weakness in the fundamental operations, and the graded lists of minimally essential spelling words like the Ayres list.*

12. *The teacher should seek the most scientific information in planning his initial and subsequent drill exercises so that over-learning and under-learning could be avoided.* Scientific investigations disclose that the aquisition of the desired amount of skill, the formation of habits, or the retention of information is best achieved by repetition which is decreased in extent over increasingly lengthened intervals. Drill must stop when optimum learning has been attained so as not to waste time and effort.

13. *The teacher should remember that the purpose of drill is to fix certain facts securely and accurately in the minds of the pupils so as to facilitate the recall of such facts whenever they are needed in the performance of any act.* To achieve this purpose it is necessary that the teacher should make use of the most effective and improved drill techniques.

14. *The teacher should bear in mind that drill is most effective when it furnishes multiple associations—visual, auditory, and motor—to the concepts that are being fixed.* The same concept or particular should be utilized in different situations because isolated drill is of little value. Using several senses,

such as sight and hearing, will help memory and recall.

15. *The teacher should bear in mind that by drill, a child learns the fundamental skills required in the operation of all tool subjects.* Habits and skills can only be developed through attentive, intense, and well-distributed d ill work. Likewise, drill work must be directed toward a goal and guided by a knowledge of the approach to it.

The Nature and Importance of Review

Much confusion still exists as to the real meaning of the term review. Further confusion exists because of the tendency to use the term review to cover the process of drill. The review exercise is assuming new meaning and importance in the school procedure of the present day. Review is a teaching procedure and not a testing device. It should not be interpreted as a testing process. It has not been many years since a review lesson was an exercise in which pupils passed a second time over subject-matter previously studied. The purpose of such exercise was to fix facts so firmly in mind that they would be remembered by the learner. We have come to ragard this lesson as drill, since its function is to make certain associations habitual. The present conception of the nature of a review differs widely from this view once prevalent.

The term "review," according to Risk[8] means a "new view." This means that the old must be presented in a new view or in a way that will bring out points of relationship, association, and meaning between the old the new facts, information or lessons. It is seeing facts in a new relationship. The term "review" applies more particularly to tool subjects which may be interpreted, summarized, and organized into a unit of thought. Wherever important facts or skills have been involved, review is thought to be necessary procedure. It has also its place as a constant educative influence. To make teaching more effec-

8. T. M. Risks, *Princ'ples and Practices of Teaching in Secondary Schools*, 2nd ed. New York: American Book Co., 1947. p. 386.

tive, review should be made a part of the teaching procedure. A lesson should be reviewed soon after it has been learned for the first time. By means of review, knowledge should be organized into points to be able to show relationships. Review is the organization and integration of facts, information, and skills in the light of new experiences. Review is necessary to insure the presence of the correct basis for the process of correlation. In any form of school exercise which involves interpretation of ideas, whether it be a process of thinking out the solution to a problem, or the application of ideas to some form of activity, review may be required. Hence, the review is a means of relating the old to the new so that growth will be natural, gradual, and efficient.

Review must be recognized as an indispensable element in the various stages of teaching and of learning. The review is a highly important classroom procedure or exercise because it measures and diagnoses the teacher's teaching and the pupil's learning. It is necessary in fixing ideas, in insuring retention, and even in complete understanding. Besides, it shows also the progress or achievement made by the individual or class, and thus gives the teacher a basis upon which to build the future lesson. Review is essential in order that the pupil may organize his subject, and get a clear view of it in its proper order. Review work distributed throughout a term is much more valuable than cramming at the end. It results not only in knowledge, but also in power to work independently and effectively.

Review and Drill Work

Further confusion among some teachers still exists because of the tendency to use the term "review" to cover the process of drill. Review and drill are not identical in character, although they may appear to be alike in functions. To think of these two terms as having the same meaning is to confuse entirely two fundamentally different educational processes. Drill and review may be considered supplementary concepts. The drill exercise is concerned with repetition, with the main purpose of strengthening the connection or connections formed to make them rapid, automatic, and accurate. Drill seeks to fix relations already established. Its purpose is to fix certain facts or items of knowledge for ready recall. A review, while serving to promote this end, has in fact, different ends and a different setting that results in a new understanding or relationship, a changed attitude, and different purposes such as the following:

1. *To strengthen or fix in mind activities or materials learned.* The concept of review is, in some measure, associated with that of drill. Review gives meaning to drill. The repetition involved in review work insures greater retention. Any repetition will tend to establish connections previously formed more firmly in mind. Review is necessary in strengthening ideas and in insuring retention. Such procedure gives pupils practice in thinking and organizing, and this should contribute to their ability to work independently.

2. *To organize the important facts and experiences into a larger unit for understanding, to bring out the relationship between the old and the new materials, to revive old knowledge and to work aud enlarge on it.* All small units should be put together or formed into a larger unit for interpretative purposes. Effective reviewing will help the pupils to reorganize the subject-matter and the activities from a new point of view, for better understanding and greater returns. Review is necessary to insure a correct basis for correlation. In any form of school exercises which involve interpretation of ideas, whether it be a process of thinking out the answer to a problem, or the application of ideas to some form of activity, review may be required.

3. *To diagnose whether the lesson is adequately presented or properly discussed.* By carefully guiding the review, the teacher will be able to determine what desired educational results have not yet been achieved. The review will offer an opportunity to reconcile any inconsistency that may appear. Sometimes an added word of explanation and an intensive marshalling of additional information by means of the lecture

method will help in clarifying a confused point in the review. The review period should not be regarded as a test period, because a well-conducted review will reveal a mistaken point of view or misconception. When viewed in this light, the review places the teacher in the eyes of the pupils as one who is a valuable guide rather than a harsh judge. Review is a teaching method, not a testing device or drill procedure.

4. *To motivate the pupils to future study.* Review is a means of directing pupil's activities into new channels of experience in which they will find a need for utilizing it. If the new lesson is related to the lesson just studied, then it becomes merged with the apperceptive function of the assignment. This use of review applies particularly to such subjects as history and mathematics.

5. *To check up on the teacher's teaching and the pupil's learning.* A good review would reveal the teacher's and the pupil's success and failure in preparation and understanding. Frequently the success or weakness of the teacher is in reality the success or weakness of the learner. At any rate, the teacher should not look upon the review merely as an index of the pupil's success or failure. The teacher should remember that the review which would test his own teaching, as any good review would, is valuable to the pupils. Review furnishes excellent proof of the kind of teaching which has been done. It often reveals the weakness and the ignorance which the teacher must overcome in later teaching.

6. *To give a finishing touch to the teacher's work.* The finishing touch is generally administered by the teacher in lecture form. This kind of review need not be given regularly by the teacher, but should be given often enough to unify the work. Some teachers make use of such brief review frequently at the close of the class period, where it serves as a means of summarizing work previously discussed and prepares for the introduction of a new lesson. This procedure will give the pupils a broader perspective of the subject-matter-field as a whole.

It is then safe to say that the main purpose of a review exercise is the organization of knowledge. It also serves to repeat points in need of additional attention, to recall old knowledge in preparation for the new, to discover whether a topic has been learned adeqately, and to test the work that the pupils have done. It is also given for the purpose of preparing for an examination and for appraising habits of study. But when the review is given for the purpose of examining the pupils, it is not so effective a learning tool as when it is given to form the basis of a new series of experiences. The best type of review, then, is that which is a natural activity growing out of a preceding natural activity.

Types of Review

There are five types of review known in educational parlance. However, there is no general rule as to what type is most effective in conducting review work. The nature of the subject-matter and the dominant purpose will have some bearing on the type of review to be had. The different types of review are:

1. *Cumulative review*—This refers to the daily review or short questioning given every day as a part of a lecture summary. It is applicable to units and daily recitations where a definite continuity of theme is present. The daily review is an important aid to pupils, particularly those who learn more slowly. This serves to recall to the whole class the setting for the day's work.

2. *Problem review*—This type is one which calls for the summary or organization of the important points. It is best adapted to the natural and social sciences. The teacher may frame the problem in the form of questions. Some questions suited to this type of review are: questions asking for comparison questions asking for cause-and-effect of things, questions asking for a summary of events, factors or results, and questions asking for analysis. These are all good examples of thought-provoking questions.

3. *Socialized review*—This type of review is generally given to prepare the pupils for the examination and to stimulate interest and activity. It emphasizes memory work rather than the organization of materials. It is most effective in courses where social problems, questions prepared by the pupils, and debate are involved.

4. *Review quiz*—This is sometimes given to check up on the mastery of the subject-matter. It is a review given in the form of a short written test. It is also given to test or to measure the individual or class achievement.

5. *Oral report*—The oral report type is essentially individualized. However, there is a tendency to organize work of this type around a small group. This type of review is effective if followed by discussion and questions from the floor. It is best adapted to social and natural sciences.

Time for Review

When to give review depends generally upon the need of the class, the aims to be accomplished, and the nature and importance of the subject-matter. A review may be given:

1. *At the end of each unit of study to find out whether the pupils are ready for the new unit.* At the conclusion of any unit of work there should always be a review. It is an important aspect of aiding pupils in retaining the materials learned.

2. *Before the weekly, monthly, quarterly, semestral or final examination.* The review may be given before the final examination to organize, summarize, select, and fix important points. To test mastery, the pupils should organize the materials from a new viewpoint. The review procedure should be related to the evaluation procedure. It is frustrating to have a review over broad concepts when the pupils know that they will be quizzed on specific details.

3. *As a part of the regular teaching procedure*. Experimental studies have revealed the good effect, as far as the mastery of the subject-matter is concerned, of giving a short review every day before taking up a new lesson. A short review every day is necessary to mastery. Daily review may be conducted in different ways. The teacher may make a brief summary of the pevious lesson or conduct questioning and discussion. The brief daily review should be oral.

4. *During the recitation*. Here the ground may be laid best for the solution of a new problem by the recall of the previous materials or experience, thus making use of the Law of Apperception.

5. *At any time*. This may be given for diagnostic purposes. Remedial instruction, based upon the result of the written or oral review, may be considered review work. Such review may provide the basis for student-teacher planning of the next steps.

A review should therefore be had daily, and should be systematic and persistent in character. Each recitation should begin with a review of previous work in order to connect the known with the unknown and what is already possessed by the pupils, to serve as an introduction to the new material that is to be presented. A review also deepens the impression of the old lessons, clarifies such points that are not fully understood, and fixes the past lessons, while the class is being prepared for the reception of the new lesson. The questions are put differently in the review; the subject is presented in a new light —different from that of the ordinary recitation; thus the pupils will obtain a firmer hold of the lesson.

But, besides the daily review in connection with each recitation, there must also be a more extended and formal review which would reach back over the work of days and weeks. Pupils forget what they have gone over, and their knowledge, in this respect, would be revived and fixed by the review. The review should aim to look over the entire field and bring all the parts into a relation, comprising symmetrical structure of imparted knowledge.

While frequent review may be given to keep the interest alive and to preserve the whole work before the class, the general and exhaustive review should be given when a unit or subject or some part of it is completed, rather than periodically, for instead of attaining the educational aims sought, the fixed or periodical method would only prove a means to defeating that end. A teacher can do much to stimulate regular reviewing by giving a few unannounced quizzes. Pupils will review regularly if the teacher gives them good reason for doing so.

Review should be both oral and written. By oral review, the pupil will be trained to express himself frequently upon a topic. Oral review gives training in the formation of accurate, connected, and logical statements, in good English. The written review accomplishes the same end in written expression. It has an advantage in that all the pupils answer each question simultaneously; therefore, the review may be complete and satisfactory. Care must be taken not to let a written review develop into a test.

Making Review Worthwhile

Review method, which is considered traditional, is necessary and productive. Review activity can be made productive or worthwhile by taking into consideration the following points:

1. *Review activity, to be worthwhile, must be appropriate to the needed learning.* For example, if a review on fundamental principles of physics can put the students into a position to understand some challenging, interesting parts of the physic textbook that lie ahead; then such review may be extremely useful. The review should be so conducted as to bring together related facts in the pupil's experiences. The teacher must bear in mind that the purpose of review is to establish new relationships of ideas by means of knowledge possessed.

2. *Review, to be worthwhile, must be understood by the pupils.* It is not enough that learning which may result from such a review is needed, the pupil must know why it is needed. He must be able to understand and be made to see clearly why review will give him needed achievements that have value for him. To have value, the review should deal with relevant material. In general, details of less importance should be omitted. In this case, the essentials will be raised to greater prominence.

3. *Review activity must not only be needed and understood by the pupil, but it must be accepted to be worthwhile.* Of course there are many levels of acceptance of the necessity for review. Some pupils may never get beyond the point of accepting it as a necessary evil, compensated by their desire to pass a course, to get a good grade. Others may accept it merely as a means of keeping their status with the teacher. But there is always a good possibility that if review is made meaningful, then a majority of the class will accept it with reasonable interest.

4. *Review, to be worthwhile, must put the results to some use.* Unless the materials reviewed by the pupils are actually used in some situations, then review itself will have no meaning for the pupils. Review without meaning does not result in learning of a very high order.

5. *Review, to be worthwhile, must be used as a teaching device.* The review can be used by the teacher for measuring the result of teaching. Similar reviews for different subjects will improve teaching because they reveal where expected results have not materialized and where, in consequence, effort must be directed. Review furnishes excellent proof of the kind of teaching done and the amount of learning achieved.

Principles to Be Observed in Review

In review, whether oral or written, the following principles are suggested:

1. *The teacher must have a clear perspective of the meaning and nature of drill and review.* Drill is for the purpose of fixing certain facts or items of knowledge for ready recall. Review is primarily for the purpose of broadening and clarifying the understanding of the relationship being discussed or studied.

2. *The teacher must make a thorough preparation for the review.* The review should be most carefully planned to fit the specific purpose desired. Care must be exercised in the selection of the type of review to be given. The success of any review exercises which is an important part of a lesson or series of lessons will depend largely upon the thoughtful preparation of the teacher and upon his foresight in creating the right attitude and spirit for it.

3. *The teacher must teach the pupils how to review the subject-matter.* The teacher must illustrate how to outline and summarize important points or materials. The nature and method of review must be known to the pupils.

4. *The teacher must see to it that new and interesting experiences are utilized from time to time.* Play, games, and contests must be provided to stimulate interest. The teacher must conduct the review lesson differently each time.

5. *The teacher must make some provision for a review of the entire unit or course before the final examination.* The assignment of some type of work that will require a synthesis of the main points, facts, and ideas which have been discussed should be given to guide the pupils. The exact nature of such a summary would, of course, depend upon the materials studied. The assignment should call for a thorough review of the entire unit or course in such a way as to make the pupils organize the details, find the important facts, or ideas, and isolate their own weaknesses.

6. *The teacher must use some kind of device to measure the effectiveness of the review work.* The results of a review are commonly measured by essay or by objective tests. The making

of an outline, a generalization, a summary, a chart, and a graph is also a good test of the effectiveness of review.

7. *The teacher must remember that the review which would test his own teaching, as any good review would, is valuable to the pupils.* A well-conducted review will determine the pupils' mastery of the past lesson and their readiness for the new lesson or activity.

Suggestions to Students Concerning Review

To be able to promote effective review, the teacher should offer suggestions to guide the pupil. The following suggestions may be of great help to the pupils even without the teacher's help:

1. *Review the past lesson as a preparation for the test.* If the test involves enumeration, important points should be memorized. If true-and-false statements are to be used, all important sentences should be analyzed.

2. *Review the points where you are weak.* Direct the review to points where understanding is lacking. Pupils should be given reviews for mastery of subject-matter. Review will make your work easier.

3. *Review should help establish coherence and continuity between different parts of the course.* Different units should be viewed as a whole instead of as so many different or separate parts.

4. *Make the review a check-up and a verification.* Test yourself by answering questions at the end of each chapter. Use sets of test questions to see if you can answer them.

5. *Read previous notes and make an outline of the important points in the course.* An outline is an appraisal of the pupil's understanding. Never memorize the outline.

6. *Review both at short and long intervals.* Frequent review conserves learning and gives a broader view of the subject. Make the review in part a process of checking and verification.

7. *Use review questions as guides; they will facilitate speed and lead to the more important points in the course.* Review for main points rather than for details.

GUIDE TO OBSERVATION ASSIGNMENT AND REPORT

Assignment for Observation:

Aims:

1. To develop a clear understanding of the nature and purposes of drill and review methods.
2. To acquaint the students with the proper technique in conducting drill and review activities.

Habits are of great importance in teaching and in learning. They are formed through the application of the law of use or exercise. The law of exercise is closely related with drill and review though they have different aims and functions. It must be remembered that exercise is the fundamental law of growth. Drill is required if permanence in learning is desired. Review is used in teaching to bring out points of relationship. Review is the organization and integration of facts, information, and skills in the light of new experiences. Drill or review is an integral part of the teaching procedure.

Class of Grade————Section————Date————

Teacher observed—————————Observer————————

Go to a class where drill or review is conducted in preparation for a test or examination. Observe the drill or review work carefully and make a report based upon the following questions:

1. Was the drill work or review work properly motivated? Was the purpose of drill work or review work explained to the pupils?

2. If drill work was observed, were the drill responses put under time pressure? Did the teacher encourage speed of response?

3. Do you think the length of the drill period was just about right, or do you think that it was rather too short, or too long?

4. If review work was observed, was the review work justified from an educational point of view? Was the aim of the review accomplished?

5. Were facts associated, organized, established, and added to the pupil's permanent store of knowledge?

6. What are your comments and suggestions?

SUGGESTED EXERCISES FOR STUDY AND DISCUSSION

Indicate whether these sentences are true or false (verify):

——— 1. Drill work is but the application of the law of exercise or use.

——— 2. The principle of habit-formation is to insure the right response in the future.

——— 3. It is an accepted fact that habits are inherited traits.

——— 4. According to the law of exercise, repetition weakens the mechanism responsible for response.

——— 5. It is an accepted psychological principle that practice makes perfect.

——— 6. Drill work is more efficient when practice is concentrated in one period.

——— 7. Practice periods should be arranged whenever a need for practice arises.

——— 8. In teaching, habit can be utilized as a motive to learning.

———— 9. Practice, to be of value, should be applied at the point of error.

————10. Mere repetition is sufficient to produce efficient learning.

————11. Practice is less efficient when the purpose of the learner is known to him.

————12. In drill work, well-distributed practice produces effective results.

————13. Habit-formation is closely related to the law of exercise.

————14. In drill, the emphasis must be on the repetition of correct work rather than on the correction of specific errors.

————15. Habits can be formed or developed without reactions of some kind.

————16. The larger the length of the practice period, the better will the result be.

————17. The law of disuse is the negative aspect of the law of exercise or use.

————18. Diagnosis should always precede and follow the drill method.

————19. The acquisition of skills in arithmetic is a matter of forming correct habits.

————20. The law of effect has a weak influence in the development or habits of skills.

————21. In memorizing short material, the part-method is superior to the whole method.

— — —2 2. The kind of practice that makes perfect depends upon the number of repetitions.

————23. The fundamental aim of a review is to bring out points of relationship between the old and the new lesson.

————24. Review work is effective when it involves a new meaning or point of view.

————25. A review can be used to check up on the teacher's teaching and the pupil's learning.

————26. Drill and review have the same aims and functions.

————27. The review is a mere repetition of the work that has been done before.

————28. Review is a valuable aid to the securing of good teaching results.

————29. A good review serves as a finishing touch to the teacher's work.

————30. The testing function of a review should be mainly incidental.

————31. Review can be utilized to motivate the pupils to future study.

————32. Review is the organization and integration of experiences to give a new view.

————33. In review work, the emphasis is on the repetition of the old and correct responses.

————34. The teacher should look upon review merely as an index of the pupil's success or failure.

————35. Review method, to be effective, must be used regularly by the teacher.

————36. Review is necessary to insure a correct basis for correlation.

————37. Subjects taught by units require the application of review technique.

————38. It is generally accepted that review is a teaching procedure and not a testing device.

————39. To make teaching more effective, review should be made a part of the teaching procedure.

————40. Review applies more particularly to tool subjects which may be interpreted, summarized, and organized.

GUIDE QUESTIONS FOR STUDY

1. What is the difference between drill method and review method with regards to aim?

2. What are some outstanding features of the drill exercise?

3. What are the uses of drill method in education?

4. What responses in school should be habituated or be made automatic?

5. Why should the slow pupils be given more drill work than the bright pupils?

6. How is review related to drill in use?

7. What are some of the many functions of review? Explain your answer.

8. Why should devices such as outline, charts, and graphs be used in reviewing?

9. How may the review be used to reorganize materials and experinces?

10. Of what value is the review as a means of diagnosing weaknesses in teaching?

References

Bossing, N. L., *Teaching in Secondary Schools*, 3rd ed. Boston: Houghton Mifflin Co , 1952. Chapter 13.

Bossing, N. L., *Progressive Methods of Teaching in Secondary Schools*. Boston: Houghton Mifflin Co., 1942. Vol. I. Chapter 9.

Butler, F. A., *Improvement of Teaching in Secondary Schools*. Rev. ed. Chicago: University of Chicago Press, 1946. Chapter 16.

Doughlas, H. R., and H. H. Mills, *Teaching in High School*. New York: The Ronald Press Co., 1948. Chapter 13.

Halley, C. F., *High School Teacher's Methods*. Illinois: The Garrard Press, 1937. Chapter 15.

Hansen, K. H., *High School Teaching*. New Jersey: Prentice Hall, Inc., 1957. pp. 200-203.

Kettlekamp, G. C., *Teaching Adolescents*. Boston: D. C. Heath and Co., 1954. Chapter 6.

Lancelot, W. H., *Permanent Learning*. New York: John Wiley and Sons, 1944.

Morgan, C. T., *Introduction to Psychology*. New York: McGraw-Hill Book Company, 1956. Chapter 5.

Mort, P. R., and Vincent, W. S., *Modern Educational Practice*. New York: McGraw-Hill Company, Inc., 1950. Section 15.

Risk, T. M., *Principles and Practices of Teaching in Secondary Schools*. New York: American Book Co., 1947. Chapters 10 and 17.

Witherington, H. C., *The Principles of Teaching*. New York: Prentice Hall, 1939. Chapter 6.

4

The Technique of Teaching

Aims of the Chapter:

1. To give the students adequate knowledge of the technique of teaching in the light of a philosophy of education which measures success in terms of the pupils' growth.
2. To acquaint the students with the recent trends in this field as shown in different teaching activities.

Technique of Teaching Defined

The history of education reveals to us that in the past, technique was stressed. Webster defines technique as "the method of performance in any art; technique skill; artistic execution." To Good,[1] "technique is a process, manipulation, or procedure required in any art, study, activity, or production." The technique of teachnig refers, therefore, to acts or the quality of the acts executed by the teacher in presenting the subject-matter to the pupils. It may also include the skill of the teacher in accomplishing the task of teaching. It is essentially a technical skill, or an artistic execution. Technique in teaching is a factor which promotes or effectuates learning through teaching with the aid of devices; hence, it may be defined as the skill of the

---

1. C. V. Good, *Dictionary of Education* (New York: McGraw-Hill Book Company, Inc., 1945), p. 413.

teacher in manipulating the devices so that the psychological processes of the learner may be stimulated to effective reactions, particularly in dealing with the subject-matter that is to be learned. Technique is the teacher's way of combining and emphasizing the elements of the classroom situation. The psychological processes of the learne˄ act as the starting point and the basis for determing the election of both the devices and the technique of teaching.

Successful classroom instruction depends upon the technique of teaching; through it, the learning activity of the pupils is guided. Pupil activity, without the organization of effort and material to achieve a definite goal, would be a waste of time and effort and would not achieve satisfactory results in content learned, or in study habits. It is the teaching technique that provides this guidance for the pupils. Therefore the instructional period should be a learning period for the pupils. The general principles of learning should have specific application in every actual teaching situation. Whenever a teacher is teaching, the pupils should be engaged in suitable learning activities, utilizing the proper study technique and developing skill in such activities. The technique of teaching should be adapted to the technique of learning, which the pupils use in their work. Since the outcomes of teaching and learning are both in pupil achievement, the technique of teaching as well as that of learning depends upon the learning outcomes being sought by the pupil at any time. This gives the teacher his opportunity to determine the method of teaching that should be used.

The technique of teaching must be used as a means to an end, and must be improved through research and experimentation. The technique to be used must be carefully selected and must be adjusted to the subject, to the pupils, and to the objectives. It should center upon the prima·y laws of learning. The technique employed by the teacher in the classroom is of prime importance to the education of children. The validity of any technique in teaching is measured by the extent to which it contributes to the realization of the specific and general objectives of education.

There is a specialized learning technique for each type of learning. From psychology and education we have the following general conclusion in this respect: (1) Knowledge is best gained through the technique called the question and answer; (2) skill and habits may be acquired through the drill and practice technique; (3) attitudes and appreciation may be best developed by effective use of the learning technique called appreciation.

Standards That Govern the Selection of Technique

It is generally accepted that technique is to teaching and method is to learning. The following standards must be observed by the teacher in the selection of his technique:

1. *The technique must be selected according to the nature of the subject-matter.* The presentation of the subject-matter requires a technique different from that which is effective in presenting formal materials in the same subject. Likewise, the technique that proves effective in dealing with history may not be suited to the presentation of language materials, and mathematics, government, physics, etc., may still require different technique to render their presentation effective. The teacher must adapt his technique to the nature and purpose of the subject-matter.

2. *The technique should be selected on the basis of its direct effect upon some essential phase of the learner's learning performance.* The technique will be as good as its good effect upon the mental processes involved in dealing with the subject-matter presented to the learner. Likewise, the effectiveness of any technique is measured by the growth experienced by the learner.

3. *The technique should be selected according to the nature and maturity of the pupils or of the class.* A certain technique may not be equally effective with all pupils in the group. The

teacher must be alert to discover the reactions of the pupils and to adapt his technique to the varying characteristics of the pupils.

4. *The technique should be selected on the basis of the ability and training of the teacher who would employ it.* The teacher should not attempt to practice any kind of technique that is foreign to him. He should study his own nature and know his own weakness and limitation. A phase is known to him and is easy for him to perform.

5. *The technique should be selected according to the time alloted to the subject.* A short period will require a different kind of practice from that which is best adapted for a long period. If the teaching period is devoted to drill, review, or the presentation of a new lesson, the technique must be different, even though the length of time is the same.

Rules Governing the Use of Techniques

The following rules should be observed in the use of technique:

1. *The technique should be used as a means to an end.* The teacher should never center his attention upon his technique to the extent that his chief concern is to show off his performance. Attention should center at all times on the learning performance of the pupils. As a rule, the more the technique of the teacher is evident the less effective it is, and vice versa.

2. *The technique should be judged by the effect it produces upon each particular situation.* However, the act that is effective at one time in one situation may not be effective at another time in another situation. The teacher should constantly adapt his technique to the securing of the desired results in each teaching situation.

3. *The technique should utilize the primary laws of learning such as readiness, exercise, and effect.* The values of these

laws are generally recognized in any method or technique of teaching.

4. *The technique should be used according to the nature and aims of the subject-matter.* The technique of the teacher is oftentimes influenced by the nature and aims of the lesson.

5. *The technique should be adjusted to the physical and mental growth of the pupils.* Their interest should be taken into consideration. The technique which appeals most to the pupils should always be utilized.

Technique in the Use of Question-and-Answer Type of Recitation

The Nature and Importance of Questioning. The question-and-answer method of teaching has been subject to as much the same criticism as the other traditional methods. Nevertheless, this method can also be very fruitful if used intelligently. It should be employed with rather stringent limitations. Nothing can be more deadly, more routine, than merely asking a series of questions of one pupil after another. To be effective, the question-and-answer method must be used with a great deal more imagination, ingenuity, and intelligence in order to yield its best results. It would be impossible to consider adequately methods of teaching without recognizing the question as an essential element in all teaching procedures. The question is the key to all educative activity above the habit-skill level.

The importance of questioning has been recognized by the great teachers of method for many generations. The question-and-answer method, otherwise known as the Socratic Method,[2] is an almost universal method of teaching, the techique of which all teachers should know. The technique is indefinitely more memorized, but upon the ability of the pupils to analyze, evaluate, and generalize in constructive fashion from the text,

2. Socratic Method in J. S. Brubacher, *A History of the Problems of Education* (New York: McGraw-Hill Book Company, Inc., 1947), p. 170.

which is expected only as a starting point for rigorous mental activity. The teacher must keep the class moving steadily and progressively in the direction of its ultimate goal and, if possible, toward the realization of its immediate objectives. A complete understanding of the nature of questioning and skill in its use are fundamental in all teaching procedures.

In the classroom the question assumes a still more important role. It is a key to all educative activity. In a large number of schools today, the period of pupil-activity in academically oriented subjects is a period devoted to question-and-answer. It is therefore imperative that the teacher has a clear understanding of all its aspects and its rule in stimulating, directing, guiding, and encouraging the learner. To meet the difficulties inherent in the case of the question under classroom conditions requires some personal equipment, on the part of the teacher, beyond a technical knowledge of the approved mechanics of questioning. It is necessary that the teacher has mastery of the subject-matter and is alert in his thinking. Unless the teacher has an intimate acquaintance with the content of the subject-matter and achieves rigorous habits of thought, successful questioning is not possible. The teacher must, likewise, have a sense of relative value if she is to handle questions and responses to the class to the best advantage. The teacher must have the ability to frame questions skillfully. Self-confidence on the part of the teacher is essential in questioning. Until self-confidence is achieved by the teacher, clarity of thought is impossible.

Functions of Questions. Questions perform a variety of functions. They are utilized largely, however, to perform the following:

1. *To measure the pupil's achievement in knowledge, habits, abilities, skills, and attitudes.* This is perhaps the most extensively involved function of questions. Likewise, question can be used to measure the pupil's understanding of the facts learned. Memorizing of facts does not insure their understanding. One of the fundamental aims of education is to develop understand-

ing or insight.

2. *To stimulate interest in the work at hand.* The question, to stimulate interest, must be adapted to the experience and ability of the pupil and should create a situation likely to involve a desire to know. Curiosity or interest is the best stimulus to learning that can be utilized by the teacher. Questioning is also effective as a means of securing a vital interest in the new or advance assignment. It is wise for the teacher to stimulate the pupil's thinking so that questions that lead to definite intellectual interests will arise. To stimulate interest, classroom questions should be predominantly thought-provoking in nature.

3. *To help pupils to correlate past experiences to the new lesson.* Most pupils have read, travelled, and had other experiences that may have an important bearing upon the understanding of a given lesson. It is a wise teacher who will use the question to draw upon this valuable reservoir to supplement and interpret data already before the class. Questions related to the past experiences of the pupils are useful in teaching developmental lessons.

4. *To challenge individual attention.* If properly used, the question is very effective in challenging attention. Stimulating questions will arouse intense interest which is the basis of attention. The attention of an unattentive pupil may be gained back through the use of questions. In like manner, in a class growing listless, a stimulating question will sometimes arouse intense interest.

5. *To develop the power of evaluation.* Evaluation is one phase of true thinking, though more prominent in some types of thought than in others. The teacher can, by the use of discriminating questions, lead the pupils to evaluate carefully the value of data in textbooks, both for correctness and relative significance. Pupils are constantly called upon to evaluate the merit of this fact over other facts, as the basis for intelligent generalization.

6. *To develop the power of organization.* The use of related questions will lead the pupils to see the relation of one fact to another. It is the work of the teacher to formulate questions that will lead the pupil to see the relation of one fact to another, and the possible effect of that relationship upon broader interpretation and conclusion.

7. *To stimulate thought.* It is generally accepted that at the heart of every question there is a problem. At certain stages in learning for some individuals, even the most simple memory questions will evoke thought. In modern education the primary function of the question is the stimulation of thought. To accomplish this function is therefore for classroom questions to be predominantly thought-provoking in nature.

8. *To develop appreciation.* A well-directed series of questions may create likes and dislikes. Subtle suggestions in the form of questions will serve this purpose. Social psychology has long recognized the potency of suggestion in the conditioning of favorable or unfavorable attitudes and the control of social behavior. It is important for the teacher to realize that the proper question technique maybe a help in fostering such attitudes.

The Characteristics of Good Questions

Questions, to be worthwhile, must have the following characteristics·

1. *They must be carefully planned*—Questions to be asked should be prepared in advance. They should be selected with care and formulated with reference to the objective set up. Carefully planned questions are prerequisites to good teaching and effective learning. They serve as the teacher's guide for effective teaching. Careful planning is a part of any learning process.

2. *They must be brief and direct*—Questions should be brief and direct to the point of clearness. They should be made simply and reasonably short, so that their meanings can be easily grasped by the pupils. There should be no doubt in the minds of the pupils as to what the teacher means, in order that there may be the desired concentration of thought upon the answer. This makes for easy understanding, and renders the question comprehensible to pupils of varying degrees of intelligence. Brief questions also avoid waste of time. It takes less time to state them and less also to interpret them.

3. *They must be adopted to the ability and experience of the pupils*—Questions should be adapted to the ability, interest, experience, and maturity of the pupils; otherwise they cannot promote profitable reflection and thinking. Only when they are so adapted can the pupils be expected to grasp the full significance of the question. They should be adapted also to the nature and aims of the lesson. Only questions involving the degree of comprehension which the individual has attained should be asked.

4. *They must be free from the wording of the textbook*—Questions, to be effective, must be free from the language of the textbook in order to stimulate initiative and the thinking and reasoning power of the pupils. Moreover, questions that are worded originally and apart from the textbook will require independence of thought and study on the part of the pupils. The questions in the textbooks, may, however, be used to aid in review, to direct the thought to all phases of the subject, or to awaken interest in further study or investigation. The questions in the textbook should not be used in conducting the recitation.

5. *They must be definite in requirement*—Definiteness in requirement is necessary to secure clearness. Questions which are definite in requirement are more objective, valid, and reliable. When a question is susceptible of two or more interpretations, its value is lost. The utmost care in the formulation of questions is necessary to insure that ideas are clearly con-

veyed from teacher to pupil.

6. *They should stimulate thinking and reasoning*—Questions should stimulate the thinking and reasoning power of the pupils. Thought-provoking questions will accomplish this objective and will further stimulate reflection and encourage favorable expression. Unless the lesson is of a drill type, it should contain a predominance of thought-provoking questions. Direct questions should generally be avoided. "Yes" and "No" answers do not evince thought. Single-word answers, as a rule, should be accepted only in drill work. Where thought has not been stimulated, the exercise must be considered a failure.

7. *They must follow certain aims*—Questions should be formulated according to the aim or purpose of the teacher. Memory questions should be formulated somewhat differently when the purpose is to elicit an opinion or to stimulate discussion. To the teacher, the observer, and the pupils, the questions should have direct relation to the objectives of the lesson or course. Without a specific aim, no matter how engaging the manner of the teacher, or how well he puts his questions, the desired end will not be accomplished. There must always be a clearly conceived purpose in every recitation and even in each of the questions that are put to the class. Questions that are purposeless soon kill the spirit of the class.

8. *They must be related to one another*—Questions should be properly related to one another to establish a relationship between facts or points. Related questions will lead to better organization of the points learned, for they can bridge the gap from point to point.

9. *They should be of varying difficulty*—Questions should be of varying difficulty or degree. Beginning questions should be easy enough to stimulate the interest of the pupils. As the recitation progresses, the more difficult questions should be given.

10. *They must allow logical order*—For checking up a

developmental lesson, the questions given should be in logical order so that the pupils may have a clear idea of the wholeness of the lesson. Otherwise there will be confusion in the pupils' minds in regard to the lesson. Besides, the pupil will fail to obtain an adequate conception of the teacher's purpose. This principle, however should not be observed in conducting drill or review lesson by means of questions.

When to Use the Question-and-Answer Technique

Questions perform a variety of functions. The teacher should keep in mind that one function of instrumental questions is to facilitate the teaching process toward the achievement of educational aims. The use of questions as a teaching device should not be considered as being limited to testing. The other important functions of the question-and-answer procedure which should be recognized are:

1. *In drill work*—Questions are often used to strengthen the connection formed in order to make it automatic. When the questioning is for the purpose of drill, limited responses and speed in reaction are desirable. In this case the practice must recognize the laws of learning underlying the drill process. Good teachers have recognized the value of frequent drills on important facts conducted through rapid questioning.

2. *In review work*—For centuries, questions have been used for review purposes. The purpose of review is to associate the old lesson with the new lesson so that the pupils may be given a view of the whole. It is the duty of the teacher to formulate questions that will lead the pupils to see the relation of one fact to another, and the possible effect of that relationship upon broader interpretation and generalization.

3. *In diagnosing the weakness of the pupils*—As a means of diagnosing, the test question is highly valuable in that it gives direction to teaching and learning. The teacher's questions help bring out the points that the pupils have overlooked.

4. *In verifying the pupil's interpretation of the lesson assigned*—The pupil's understanding of the lesson assigned can be checked up by the use of question. Questioning can reveal to the teacher the range and breadth of the pupil's knowledge. This is perhaps the most extensively involved function of the question.

5. *In directing attention to certain points*—Questions can help bring out the important points or facts in the lesson. They also can guide the pupils in their studies. The teacher can direct the attention of the class to the important points in the lesson through questions.

6. *In guiding the pupils in the recitation*—By means of questions, the teacher can guide or help the pupils in the organization, analysis, and evaluation of the lesson. The interpretation of the reading materials may be aided by careful questioning.

7. *In developing or stimulating thinking*—Reflective thinking is best stimulated by means of questions. Classroom questions should be predominantly thought-provoking in nature. The inductive or deductive development may be utilized.

8. *In furnishing incentives to careful preparation*—Most often, the teacher makes use of questions to create a strong desire in the pupils to do their work. Questioning is especially effective as a means of securing a vital interest in the advance assignment.

Classification of Questions

For the most part, questions should challenge thought and test the pupil's knowledge indirectly, rather than directly. Based on this concept, questions may be classified according to their purpose or function and according to the mental process involved. There are several ways of classifying question into types. The types of question based on purpose are drill questions, factual or memory questions, developmental questions, and pivotal questions. The purpose of drill is to make mental associations automatic. Good drill questions should be short, definite, and factual. They are purely memory questions and do not demand much thinking on the part of the pupils. Memory questions require simple recall of facts. They are used in teaching content subjects. Like drill questions, memory questions do not demand much reflection. Developmental questions are often used in teaching developmental lesson. The developmental questions are useful in getting pupils to associate one detail with another so as to see their proper meaning and significance. This type of questions is often used in the teaching of history and literature. Pivotal questions are used to direct the pupil's thinking to important points. A pivotal question is a comprehensive one which goes straight to the heart of the lesson under consideration. This type is often used to help pupils to think straight and to lead him quickly to the point of difficulty.

The other type of questions based on the mental process involved are the thought-provoking questions and the factual questions. Thought-provoking questions require reflective thinking before the answer can be given. The examples of thought-provoking questions are analytical, organization, cause and effect, explanation, comparison, and imaginative questions. Factual questions require simple recall or one-word answer, requiring less thinking on the part of the pupil. A question which can be answered by "Yes" or "No" is another example of factual or memory question.

Technique in Asking Questions

Technique in asking questions in any teaching situation concerns the skillful way and manner of questioning. There is no hard and fast rule governing the way questions are to be presented before the class, but there are practices that experience has shown to be ineffective. All the suggestions given in this book are subject to exception. But they are based upon the experiences of good teachers. No teacher of elementary and secondary subjects can succeed in his teaching who does not have a fair mastery of the art of questioning. The following principles are suggested:

1. *Questions should not be asked hurriedly*—They should not be given too fast nor too slowly. All questions should be asked in a slow manner and with apparent deliberation. The speed should be based on the purpose of the teacher. Only ᐧdrill and review questions should be put under time pressure. Drill questions should be short and drill work brief and rapid. Such a procedure will give all the members of the class an equal opportunity to formulate tentative answers in their minds. The teacher who calls upon the pupil to answer immediately after the question is asked makes reflective thinking almost, impossible. There is little incentive to thorough and accurate thinking. Psychological studies show that teachers tend to ask their questions in a manner too fast for the average pupils to grasp.

2. *Questions should be evenly distributed among the members of the class.* As much as possible all pupils must be given an opportunity to take part in the class activities. However, in a large class, it is not always desirable that every pupil should participate each day. Each pupil should be given questions according to his need and interest. The fundamental purpose in distributing questions is to make the pupils feel that they have a share in the recitation as well as a responsibility. To accomplish this purpose, it will be well for the teacher to examine his class roll from day to day to see that he is distributing his questions accordingly. Too often the bright pupils are over-questioned, especially when a supervisor is present.

3. *Questions once given should not be repeated.* The practice of giving questions only once will, no doubt, make the pupils attentive during the period of questioning. Attention is challenged by not repeating the question. To repeat the question is to invite inattention. Of course, a question may be repeated when unavoidable noise at the instance of asking the question makes the hearing difficult. If a teacher makes a

practice of repeating his questions, he will soon create a very undesirable atmosphere of inattention which fosters careless answers.   Under certain circumstances the questions may need to be repeated, but the habit of repeating questions is pedago- gically unsound.   Such a policy will do much to stimulate attention.

4.   *Questions may be asked first before calling on the pupil to answer the question.* More pupils will thereby be stimulated to think and the recitation will not become centered upon the teacher and the pupil asked.   Such a practice has the further advantage of securing general attention to class procedure and to the answer given.   If the pupils know in advance that a particular pupil is to do the answering, inattention will result. This is especially true with the traditional practice of calling on pupils by turn.   If the pupils do not know when their turn is to come they will be more alert.

5.   *Questions should be asked in a natural and modulated voice rather than in imperatively formal classroom manner.* This will give the pupils opportunity to react under favorable condi- tions and proper stimulation.   Psychologically, a quiet manner of questioning stimulates the best thinking and reveals the willingness to teach.   Questioning should be natural and inter- esting, and the conversational tone of voice is considered the best.

6.   *Questions that are quite difficult should be addressed to the bright pupils unless the slow or average pupils show a sign of readiness to answer.*   Such a practice is a true recognition of individual differences and of the law of satisfaction.   Thus the bright puplis will be given an opportunity to develop their thinking and reasoning power if the difficult questions are addressed to them.   This should not be construed to mean that the slow pupils are to relax and to wait for an easy question while the brighter pupil is answering a difficult question.   What the teacher should do is to formulate questions that will best challenge the ability of every member of the class and the answers to which are within the comprehension of all.

7.   *There should be no regular or systematic order in asking questions, such as the order of seating or the alphabetical order so that there will be proper distribution of questions, and all the pupils will be put on the alert.*   By following a systematic order in questioning, the teacher unwittingly suggests to the pupils their turn to recite;   therefore, they will be more likely to pay attention only when they are about to be called upon.   Following a regular or systematic order in asking questions will make the recitation mechanical rather than rational.   A pupil should be called upon for some good reason apparent in the situation and often to all or several members of the class.

8.   *Inattentive or mischievous pupils should be made the targets of questions.*   The main purpose is to gain their attention or to interest them in the lesson.   This method is a good means of handling disciplinary situations arising from inattention.   When pupils know that they are called because of inattention, they are apt to give respectful attention, especially if they failed to study their lessons.   Questioning should be done to arouse interest and to stimulate the pupils into activity.

9.   *Never made the pupil conscious that he or she is through with one question.*   The consciousness that his recitation is finished for that period is often the cause of inattention or poor classroom discipline.   The practice of calling on the pupils by turns, or the use of a systematic order of questioning should be done to draw every pupil into activity throughout the whole period.

10.   *The pupils should be encouraged to ask questions*—This will give them the opportunity to clear their doubts on certain points in the lesson presented or discussed.   The teacher should use every possible means to make the pupils participate in class work through questions.   It is not an uncommon experience for the writer, as a supervisor, to observe teachers being embarrassed when questioned by the pupils.   In a democratic country like the Philippines, the pupils, like the teachers, have the right to ask questions.   However, only questions related to the lesson should be entertained.   Questions asked by the pupils are not

necessarily to be answered by the teacher. It is a good practice to ask the pupils to help answer their own questions.

11. *In giving assignment the difficult questions or problems should be assigned to bright pupils and the less difficult should be given to the average of slow pupils.* The teacher must bear in mind that some pupils have greater ability than others. The teacher should avoid giving the same sort of questions to all pupils.

12. *The teacher should show adaptability in questioning.* It is impossible for the teacher to anticipate fully the classroom situation as it will be. Well-planned questions may need to be cast aside and new ones formulated as the classroom exigencies demand. The teacher should show such close rapport with the class and such mastery of the subject that questions will appear fresh blown for the moment, and perfectly at point. The teacher should never be afraid to venture an offhand question not stated in the lesson plan. Adaptability in questioning is essential in a democratic teaching process.

13. *The teacher should require courtesy in questioning.* The occasional eagerness of the pupils to ask questions leads at times to several questions being propounded to the teacher simultaneously. It is a splendid opportunity for the teacher to show the class how courtesy and self-restraint often made both for speed and for the realization of the desired objectives. Failure to insist upon one question at a time from the class inevitably leads to confusion, and later to bad disciplinary problems. It cannot be denied that some pupils are generally discourteous in their questions. Questions of this type should not be entertained by the teacher.

14. *The teacher should recognize the timeliness of the questions asked by the pupils.* Not all questions by the pupils should be entertained. Only questions related to the lesson under discussion should be welcomed by the teacher. Likewise, if they are significant to the class and have more educational value than the lesson itself, it is proper to consider them. The

more the teacher can bring pupils to ask questions, the more certain they can be that education is taking place in the classroom. A question asked by the pupils also has an important bearing on teachersuccess.

Technique in Dealing with Answers to Questions

As regards the manner of dealing with the answers given by the pupils, there is no hard and fast rule to follow. The following principles, however, are suggested:

1. *Correct answers should be followed by an encouraging remark.* This will stimulate the pupils to further study and better reactions. The nature of commendation should be judged by the nature of the response given and the ability of the individual concerned. The teacher should give appreciative consideration to all pupils' answers to make them feel that their contributions are worthwhile even though they may not be exactly what the teacher wants.

2. *Answers given by the pupils should not be repeated by the teachers or by the pupils excepts for emphasis or for correction.* The teacher should exercise discretion in repeating answers. An answers giving important facts or information may be repeated for emphasis especially if such an answer is to be the source of another question. An answer may also be repeated if the sentence construction needs correction or improvement. If the answer must be repeated, have the pupil do it.

3. *The pupils should be made to observe correct English usage in answering questions in all subjects.* The educational value of good and correct expression is beyond doubt. Modern education insists that the knowledge of correct grammatical form or correct English usage is a matter of habit formation. The teacher should require his pupils to frame their answers in good English. It is generally accepted that good English habits can only be developed through correct practice.

4. *Answering in concert should be discouraged, for such is*

oftentimes the cause of poor discipline. It should be allowed only in special or exceptional cases. not regularly. Besides, answering in chorus has little diagnostic value. This manner of answering is permissible if the teacher's purpose is either to arouse the interest of the pupils or to elicit group judgment.

5.   *Encourage liberal expression of views in answering questions.* Answers of some length should be encouraged among our pupils in grades. This will train them to express themselves with ease and intelligence. The timid pupils should be encouraged to take part in the discussion. Generally, the teacher is likely to forget the timid pupil who does not volunteer to recite. The teacher should endeavour to give such a pupil special encouragement and must refrain from commer's that would tend to belittle his contribution.

6.   *Insist on clearness on every point expressed by the pupils.* Answers which are not the result of careful thinking should not be accepted. Habits of clear thinking should be developed. This will help eliminate the necessity of repeating the pupil's answer. Many teachers make the mistake of drawing the discussion to a close too soon with an air of finality. The pupil's discussion should not be left behind in fragmentary order. With respect to the individual recitation, the pupil who has the floor should be encouraged to continue reciting until he has, if possible, made a significant contribution to the discussion.

7.   *The teacher should see to it that questions asked by the pupils are, as often as possible, anwered by the members of the class.* Such practice will give the pupils more opportunity for creative thinking. Only questions related to the lesson under discussion should be considered.

8.   *As a general rule, the pupils should never be assisted in the formulation of their answers.* Let them make their contribution unassisted. It is an accepted principle that one learns by reacting; hence, a pupil should be trained to rely on his own resources and to frame his answer without assistance from the teacher. However, slow pupils may be helped in the

formulation of their answers either by suggestions or by the use of guide questions. This practice will relieve them of the embarrassment occasioned by their slow thinking. Under ordinary circumstances, however, pupils should rely upon their own resources in answering questions.

9. *The teacher should never bluff in answering a pupil's question.* When the teacher cannot answer questions asked by the pupils, he must frankly say so. The teacher has nothing to gain by bluffing but loss of pupil-respect. Pupils are quick to detect when a teacher bluffing his way. On the other hand, a frank admission as a matter of course that the teacher is not a medium of all wisdom will be accepted with increased respect for the teacher. However, it cannot be denied that a teacher cannot afford to be too often put in a position where lack of essential knowledge must be admitted.

10. *The teacher should get the class evaluation of the partially correct response.* At times it is desirable to get class evaluation of partially correct responses made by the pupils. When the most approved question technique has been employed the class is ready for a critical constructive evalution of the answer given. Class evaluation provides good training in courteous impersonal comments on another's effort, both to the class and to the individuals whose efforts are thus subject to analysis and criticisms.

Technique in Conducting Recitation

There is no one procedure or technique that can be used for the conduct of the recitation. Rather, the plan adopted must vary with the subject and with the aims of the teacher and the pupils. The teacher must bear in mind that practically every method used in the classroom will involve elements of the lecture of the recitation. It is therefore necessary to recognize the flexible nature of the recitation and the manner of its use. There are certain suggestions on the technique of conducting the recitation with merit and consideration. A good technique in conducting the recitation involes a number of principles such as the following:

1. *The recitation should be carefully planned.* A good recitation program should be well planned if it would carry out the purpose of the teaching period. Any well-planned activity produces a good effect. The plan must be based on the modern concept of the recitation. The basic elements of planning as applied to teaching and learning must be well considered by the teacher. The plan must be centered on the growth of each individual.

2. *The recitation should be well motivated or carefully introduced to create the proper mind-set.* A carefully introduced recitation establishes a favorable attitude toward the work and provides a proper setting for the new lesson. An attitude of alert eagerness on the part of the teacher is likely to arouse a similar attitude in the class.

3. *The recitation should be so regulated as to meet individual differences.* A good recitation technique respects those differences and makes provision for a procedure that will suit individual characteristics. Attention to individual differences is an important factor in teaching.

4. *The recitation should provide for pupil activity and expression.* Class activities such as debates, dramatics, and discussion should be made a regular part of the recitation. Creative expression can come only when provision is made for a wide range of response and when differentiation of response is encouraged by the teacher.

5. *The recitation should be well organized to promote unity of thought or to show the relationship of facts presented.* A good teaching technique is one that is systematic and well organized. A well-organized recitation will give the pupils a clear picture of the wholeness of the lesson rather than its disconnectedness in units of facts.

6. *The recitation should utilize the appropriate lesson type.*

The purpose rather than the method determines the type to be used. The type should be selected with reference to the aim, subject, grade, and the maturity of the pupils.

7. *The recitation should stimulate the thinking and reasoning power of the pupils.* A good recitation technique allows for reflective thinking and provides opportunity for spontaneous expression.

8. *The recitation should be adapted to the aim and purpose of the teacher.* How the recitation should be conducted depends upon the purpose of the teacher and the aim of the lesson. Learning is effective when it is purposeful.

9. *The recitation should provide drill or review work for the pupils.* This will give the pupils an opportunity to master the subject-matter previously learned. It will also give the teacher an opportunity to diagnose the weakness of his pupils and to discover their readiness for the next lesson.

10. *The recitation should provide pupil's cooperation in the planning.* This can be done without abdication of the prerogatives of the teacher to use his mature judgement in the planning of the lesson. The degree to which the teacher may permit or encourage participation in planning depends upon the ability and experience of the pupils. It is through the pupil's participation that the most legitimate forms of cooperation may be sought.

Poor Recitation Technique

A poor recitation is often due to wrong technique such as the following:

1. *Allowing the recitation to become a dull narration of the lesson assigned.* Some teachers are contented with merely being able to hear by themselves the pupil reciting. The pupil should address the class and not the teacher.

2. *Allowing the pupils to sit lazily while reciting.* This is one of the causes of poor classroom management. Pupils should be stimulated in order that they may become active mentally and physically.

3. *Confining the recitation to a few pupils.* Most often the recitation is dominated by the bright pupils. The majority of the pupils are neglected. The questions should be properly distributed.

4. *The teacher reciting for the pupils.* The teacher should not answer his own questions nor complete the answers of the pupils. There should be more activity on the part of the pupils and less on the part of the teacher.

5. *Failure to correct errors in English during the recitation.* Errors made by the pupils should be corrected in order to develop the desired language habits. The pupils should be encouraged to correct their own errors in English; it should not always be the teacher who should do it.

6. *Interrupting pupils who are reciting.* It is bad technique to interrupt a pupil in the midst of his talk. The teacher should not stop the pupil just to criticize him.

Technique in Conducting Socialized Type of Recitation

The socialized recitation may be either formal or informal. The socialized recitation is that form of recitation in which the members of the class take turns in presiding over and in conducting the recitation. There are certain suggestions regarding the technique of conducting the formal or informal socialized types of recitation. The following principles are suggested:

1. *The teacher should repress his own tendency to mono polize the discussion.* The pupils should be given more opportunity to participate in the discussion. The theory o self-activity should be foremost in the mind of the teacher.

2. *The teacher should train the leader in the proper proce-dure.* The integrity of the group must be preserved. Fairness and courtesy must be observed by the leader and the members of the class.

3. *The teacher should encourage the members of the class to address themselves to the group.* The whole responsibility should be made to rest on the leader or group rather than on the teacher. This is one of the characteristics of a socialized class.

4. *The teacher should encourage the members of the class not to limit their discussion to the textbooks alone.* Other sources should be utilized to stimulate the interest of the class.

Techniques in the Use of Visual Devices

The alternative for pure abstraction in learning and teaching appears to be such concrete materials or illustrations as the pupils may see, feel, and manipulate. Most schools could not afford to provide a concrete basis for all educational activity, even though it were possible or desirable. In teaching and in learning, visual devices supply one form of aid to attention, understanding, imagination, and incentive to action. Visual devices are used to attract attention. The teacher who has a repertoire of good visual devices at hand usually maintains full class attention. Visual devices are also used to facilitate reasoning and understanding. The fundamental reason for the use of visual aids is to aid reasoning and understanding. Visual devices are further used to stimulate imagination and provide incentives to action. The teacher must use the power of word symbolism and concrete materials to fire the imagination, arouse the emotions, and incite to actions. Unfortunately, teachers have seriously cramped the larger possibilities of intellectual develop-ment of the pupils through the failure to adequate stimulation of the imagination and the will to intellectual activity.

To make use of visual devices most effectively, certain prerequisites must be observed. The technique in the presentation of visual aids varies somewhat with each of their type. The standard suggested does not apply with equal force in every situation. The following principles are related to the use of visual devices:

1. *The use of visual aids should be well planned by the teacher.* The teacher needs to have all visual aids properly classified and ready for instant use. When a number of materials are to be used, they should be arranged in order so that each will be used in proper turn. Where mechanisms are involved, they should be carefully checked to insure their perfect working condition before use. No detail that would detract from the effective use of the visual aids should be overlooked. Visual aids should be viewed in their relation to good teaching.

2. *The use of any type of visual aids should be for some definite teaching purpose.* The temptation to use visual devices in a vague assurance that they will be helpful too often accomplishes nothing. Visual aids should be for some definite teaching purpose or for a definite function to perform. They are not to be used just to attract attention in a general way. They should serve a specific purpose in the development of the lesson. The teacher should see clearly a real need for visual aids, and then select a concrete material that will actually assist the pupils to overcome their difficulties. The effectiveness of visual aids depends upon the way they are utilized to accomplish their purposes or aims.

3. *Visual aids should be used judiciously by the teacher.* It cannot be denied that too many devices used may confuse, rather than enlighten. One writer warns against too many devices; another insists that danger lies in the use of too few. Judged in the light of extended observation, the danger would seem to lie in under, rather than over-use. The greatest danger lies in a profuse use of concrete materials in and out of the season without due regard to actual needs. The number of devices and the extent to which they should be given must remain a matter of discretion on the part of the teacher. Real monotony develops when the same device is used day after day.

4. *Visual aids should be used to supply adequate imagery in some particular subjects.* For example, in the study of plants and industries, such visual aids as pictures, films, slides, and graphs are rich sources of imagery for the pupils. Vivid and realistic imagery should be evoked with care. Visual aids can also be used as means of correcting inaccurate imagery.

5. *Visual aids should be used only when the lesson presented does not furnish a basis for appreciation.* The approach to a new lesson or subject may be made more attractive and more interesting by the use of concrete materials. Through the use of visual aids it is possible to arouse interest in learning. The teacher can, likewise, maintain full class attention through the use of visual aids.

6. *Visual aids should be used to furnish illustrations, during the course of the lecture or development of the lesson, to permit pupils to experience the content through the avenues of sight and hearing.* The important function of illustrations is to facilitate understanding of the lesson presented or developed. Most pupils can think better if they tie their thinking to some definite concrete material observed. In addition, they insure more effective learning and more permanent retention than does lecture alone.

7. *Visual aids should be used in summarizing a given unit or phase of work.* Pictures, objects, slides, and films have given good results as teaching devices. Outlines, graphs, diagrams, and charts are also effective aids to summarization. Visual aids make it easier to concentrate on the materials learned or to see their relationship. The wholeness of the lesson learned can be illustrated through the use of visual aids.

8. *The use of visual aids by the pupils should be encouraged to give vitality to their recitations and reports.* Visual aids such as models, diagrams, pictures, and demonstrations add to the value of the recitation. They are valuable in clarifying the thinking and in perfecting the understanding of the pupils. Abstract ideas are also made concrete in the minds of the

students through the use of visual aids.

9. *The blackboard should be used by the pupil to diagram or to illustrate his ideas if such a procedure would contribute to the effectiveness of his discourses or explanation.* The blackboard is one of the most useful devices available as a visual aid in teaching and in learning. It is also used to challenge the pupil's attention.

10. *Use sparingly devices or illustrations of personal-experiences-type.* It cannot be denied that one's personal experiences is most vivid and replete in mental imagery. It is most natural that recall should bring to the free appropriate experiences to fit a given situation. The danger lies in the impression of egotism that may be left as an unwholesome after-effect. When personal experience is used for illustrative purposes, the first personal pronoun must be avoided.

11. *Varied types of visual devices should be used.* It is an accepted fact that a variety of visual aids reduces monotony to a minimum. Pupils should be encouraged to collect illustrative materials from home magazines and other publications. This can be done during an activity period. Different types of learning call for different types of visual devices.

12. *The teacher must see to it that visual aids are visible to all.* The danger in the use of visual devices is that they are not made sufficiently visible to all pupils to be of value. The teachers who use small pictures with light colors, or small models, are likely to err in this respect. To be of value to the pupils, visual aids must be big or bright enough in order to be visible to all.

Technique in Developing Appreciation

It is generally maintained that education should also aim to develop the power of appreciation and enjoyment. Appreciation may be defined as sympathetic understanding, or understanding coupled with a feeling of pleasure or satisfaction. A well-developed appreciation is exemplified in the appreciation of good books and magazines. The development of the power of appreciation constitutes a tremendous educational responsibility on all school levels. The encouragement of an appreciative attitude in learning is a recognized function of education. No less important in the educational program of any organized school system is the education of the emotions.

Appreciation belongs to the general field of feeling rather than of knowing. However, appreciation involves an intellectual state, the addition of which makes the total complex more of an emotional rather than of a cognitive nature. It may grow out of an active attitude or emotion. Appreciation always involves emotional tone, otherwise it could not be enjoyed.

If we want the rising generation to care for good pictures, music, and literature; to dislike the ugly, the unclean, the untidy, and the unfitting; and to raise the standards of living, we must definitely include training for these ends in our school plans and procedures. It may be urged that all these ends are accomplished by the lesson which impart information in regard to the various phases of knowledge, but knowledge does not always include the feeling of appreciation which affects ideals.

Types of Appreciation

Appreciation is of four different types which are of utmost importance to the teacher. They are (1) appreciation of the beautiful, (2) appreciation of human nature, (3) appreciation of the humorous, and (4) appreciation of the intellectual powers.

1. *Appreciation of beauty is usually discussed under the head of aesthetic emotions.* Most writers agree that the stimulus for aesthetic appreciation must be a sense percept or an image of some sensed objects. Nature, arts, music, literature, and the dance are chief source of aesthetic appreciation. This type of appreciation involves emotional pleasures and reactions caused by the beauty of the things. Since good taste, beauty, and other aesthetic elements are found in many forms, appreciation

has many objects upon which it may be exercised. Appreciation may be aroused in any environment, and by the work of either man or nature. Our great need is to learn to open our eyes and see the possibilities for aesthetic appreciation all about us.

2. *Appreciation of human nature denotes the appreciation of the value of human life—appreciation of great characters, and so on.* Some writers classify this type of appreciation under moral feelings. These feelings are stimulated by such studies as literature and social science subjects which deal with human life. In geography, history, and economics, we ought not to fail to cultivate it on the basis of lofty motives, hardship overcome, and suffering nobly borne. I is a valuable part of education to arouse appreciation for the spirit and labor of human beings. This appreciation has its source in the social instincts, but it must be developed and trained.

3. *Appreciation of humor has many of the characteristics of the first two types of appreciation mentioned above.* Webster defines humor as "appreciation of ludicrous or absurdly incongrous elements in ideas, situations, happenings, or acts." This type of appreciation may be exercised by reading comics in books, magazines, and newspapers which deal with human life. Humor adds to good mental health to be able to see the light side of the darkest corner.

4. *Appreciation of intellectual powers refers to the enjoyment of a piece of literature, of a debate, of an argument, or of a piece of scientific research.* Appreciation of the meaning expressed is the thing that can arouse feeling. This type of appreciation often results from the individual's desire to know and to experience the feeling of satisfaction. In brief, intellectual appreciation is an attitude or feeling toward questions of truth.

Principles in Developing Appreciation

In developing appreciation of all kinds, the following techniques or principles are suggested:

1. *The teacher must make an intensive and thorough preliminary preparation.* Everything that has to do with the subject selected must be mastered. Even the life and thoughts of the artist must be studied as intensively as possible.

2. *The teacher himself must appreciate what he is teaching.* It is quite difficult to teach an appreciation lesson if the teacher does not appreciate what he is teaching. Since emotional states are communicable and are frequently aroused in pupils through their imitation of the teacher, the teacher should keep his own emotional states alive. His enjoyment of literature, music, and art, his attitude toward historical situations, his approval of moral qualities, are quite likely to be reflected in his classes. In teaching for appreciation, therefore, the teacher must draw much upon himself in transmitting to the pupils the essence of his experience. If he expects to exert a deep and permanent influence upon the pupils his own enthusiasm must be genuinely evident.

3. *The teacher must make use of motivation in developing appreciation.* The teacher's opening remarks should develop in the pupils a mind-set, a directed interest, which will give rise to a powerful impression through the thrills and climax to follow. Giving a short sketch of the author's life illustrates the application of this principle. Motivation creates an interest in the lesson and a desire for it.

4. *The teacher must make knowledge the basis of appreciation.* Studies have revealed that knowledge increases appreciation. It is quite impposible to appreciate a thing fully without knowing something about its nature, characteristics, etc. The teacher should bear in mind that the greater the intellectual basis for understanding, the greater are the possibilities for appreciation. Without understanding, we may have no sentiment, we may have the wrong sentiment, or we may be led into unwise action. Overanalysis of the thought of the selection must be avoided. Overanalysis is fatal to emotional enjoyment.

5. *The teacher should set up a definite standard of appre-*

ciation to be followed or achieved. For this reason, appreciation lessons should be taught incidentally and should be presented through many avenues. The pupils should not be forced to give expression to the feeling stimulated. A very important fact to remember is that the aesthetic appreciation is sometimes slow in its development and it is not equally distributed. Some pupils have more of it than others, and some are more appreciative in certain directions than in others.

6. *The teacher should provide ample opportunity for developing appreciation.* There should be real situations and constant appeal to the pupil's experiences. The teacher should create situations that would stimulate the feelings and emotions of the pupils.

7. *The teacher should see to it that the appreciation lesson is adapted to the age and experience of the pupils.* I is necessary for the teacher to be on guard against attempts to develop appreciation upon an insufficient background of experience. The teacher should also take into account the varying degrees of development of the aesthetic sense or interest of the pupils. The difference in the parents' education and interests, in other words, the difference in home environment, and similar factors enter into the situation.

8. *The teacher should judge the success of his work by the interest he can arouse in the class.* The class that is truly appreciative will be alert and interested. Enthusiasm is the final test of a well-taught appreciation lesson.

9. *The teacher should direct the emotion and interest aroused into channels of purposeful activity, thus enabling the pupils to profit by the application of the law of effect.* Literary clubs, social service clubs, musical clubs, art leagues, and many other similar organizations represent the crystalization of sentiment into organized activity. The fundamental thing is to turn the sentiment into wholesome action and not to let it go to vaste.

10.   *The teacher should use both direct and indirect methods in teaching or developing appreciation.* The fundamental objective in teaching appreciation is the development of interests, attitudes, and ideals, which include the recognition of values within desirable social patterns and the emotionalizing of the acceptance of these social values by the pupil. The teacher should guide the pupils to a rational discovery of those attitudes, interest, and ideals worthy of emulation by direct teaching. Such teaching involves strong emphasis upon the intellectual elements without neglecting the emotional reactions that should accompany the development of interests, attitudes, and ideals. The direct teaching of the defects or evils of the dictatorship form of government preceding the Second World War is a case in point where both the intellectual and emotional aspects of the situation were stressed with telling effect. Some educational writers advocate only the indirect teaching of appreciation.

GUIDE TO OBSERVATION ASSIGNMENT AND REPORT

Assignment for Observation

Aims:

1.   To observe the teaching of the lesson with a view to discovering good teaching technique.
2.   To observe the teaching of the lesson with the aid of devices with a view to developing understanding of their uses in the teaching process.

Technique is important in the application of teaching principles. Successful classroom instruction depends upon the techniqne of teaching must be adapted to the technique of learning which the pupils use in their work. The validity of any technique in teaching is determined by the extent to which it accomplishes the aims of the lesson and by the type of learning involved.

Class or Grade————Section————Date————

Teacher observed——————————Observer—————

Go to the classroom assigned to you. Take necessary notes and make a written report for discussion during the conference, observing the following directions:

1. Note the technique used by the teacher in conducting the recitation in relation to the lesson taught.

2. List the number of questions asked by the teacher and the pupils during the period.

3. Note carefully the types of questions used by the teacher to stimulate the thinking and reasoning powers of the pupils.

(a) No. of thought-provoking questions

(b) No. of factual questions

(c) No. of questions asked by the pupils

4. List the principles you have learned in your textbook which you have seen violated by the teacher in asking questions and in dealing with answers to the questions asked.

5. Note whether or not the instructional devices are skillfully used by the teacher. Note the following:

(a) Material devices—pictures, maps, charts, etc.

(b) Mental devices—questions, outlines, etc.

6. Observe carefully whether the teacher appeared to appreciate that which he would have to appreciate.

7. Give your general comments and suggestions for improvement.

SUGGESTED EXERCISES FOR STUDY AND DISCUSSION

Indicate whether these sentences are true or false (verify):

———— 1. Technique of teaching may be defined as a refinement of specialized method.

———— 2. The technique of teaching should be adapted to the technique of learning to be used by the pupils.

—— 3. Each type of learning calls for specialized learning technique.

—— 4. The technique of teaching is valid when it accomplishes the general and specific aims of education.

—— 5. A recitation is good when the slow pupils are over-questioned.

—— 6. To be effective, the wording of the questions must strictly follow the language of the book.

—— 7. Answers to thought-provoking questions should be in a fragmentary manner.

—— 8. The uses and values of questioning are limited to testing.

—— 9. Answering in concert should be allowed only in special cases, not regularly.

——10. A good recitation utilizes the theory of self-activity and the primary laws of learning.

——11. Memorizing of facts is a clear index of the pupil's understanding of the lesson.

——12. Only in a review lesson should pupils be encouraged to ask questions.

——13. Reflective thinking is essential in answering memory questions.

——14. Social traits can be best developed by a socialized type of recitation.

——15. Understanding is essential in developing appreciation.

——16. A quiet, reassuring manner of questioning stimulates the best thinking of the class.

——17. It is a fast or fixed rule that all difficult questions should be addressed to the bright students.

——18. Ordinarily it is better to designate the individual who is to respond to the question before it is asked.

——19. For the purpose of distribution, the teacher must follow a systematic order in asking questions.

————20. The question-and-answer method has greater possibilities for use.

————21. A definite standard must be set before the pupils in developing appreciation.

————22. The enthusiasm of the class is a good index of a well-taught appreciation lesson.

————23. The teacher must himself appreciate the appreciation lesson he is teaching.

————24. Most of our school work ought to aim to develop the power of appreciation.

————25. The speed of questioning should be adjused to the nature and purpose of the question.

————26. A developmental lesson can be best developed by the use of factual questions.

————27. An appreciation lesson is primarily intellectual.

————28. Devices have no other purpose or function than to stimulate the learning process.

————29. The development of appreciation is limited to the teaching of music and drawing.

————30. Appreciation belongs to the general field of feeling rather than of knowing.

————31. Guide questions given by the teacher to direct the pupils in the recitation are good examples of mental devices.

————32. In a good recitation the pupils recite for the benefit of the teacher.

————33. Appreciation can be increased by the arousal of the imagination.

————34. Factual questions stimulate the thinking and reasoning power of the pupil.

————35. Questions should require general rather than specific answers.

————36. Questioning is one of the techniques of teaching which teachers will do well to study.

————37.   All answers given by the pupils must be repeated by the teacher for emphasis.

————38.   Questions should conform to the immediate objectives of the teacher.

————39.   Thought-provoking questions are good for drill work.

————40.   Questions should never be used for developing appreciation.

GUIDE QUESTIONS FOR STUDY

1. What do you understand by the terms technique of teaching and method of teaching?

2. What are the criteria that govern the selection of technique?

3. In what way will good teaching technique stimulate teaching and learning?

4. What types of questions are suitable for the development of the thinking and reasoning powers of the pupils?

5. Enumerate the characteristics of good questions.

6. What functions do questions perform in teaching?

7. What are some of the chief faults of teachers in questioning?

8. Enumerate some poor recitation techniques and the effect of each to teaching and learning.

9. In what way will the wise use of devices make learning effective and productive?

10. How might appreciation for a poem be strongly motivated in children?

11. What subjects in the curriculum are suitable for developing aesthetic appreciation? Intellectual appreciation?

12. Explain this statement—"Appreciation belongs to the general field of feeling rather than of knowledge."

References

Bossing, N. L., *Progressive Methods of Teaching in Secondary Schools*, Vol. II. Chicago: Houghton Mifflin, 1942. Chapter 12.

Bossing, N. L., *Teaching in Secondary Schools*, 3rd ed. Boston: Houghton Mifflin Co., 1952. Chapter 12.

Burton, W. H., *The Guidance of Learning Activities*. New York: D. Appleton-Century Company, 1944. Chapter 14.

Dale, E., *Audio-Visual Methods in Teaching*, rev. ed. New York: The Dryden Press, Inc., 1954.

Grim, P.R., and Michaelis, J.U., *The Student Teacher in the Secondary School*. New York: Prentice-Hall, Inc., 1954. Chapter 6.

Hansen, K.H., *High School Teaching*. New Jersey: Prentice-Hall, Inc., 1957. Chapters 7 and 8.

Johnson, E.A., and R.E. Michael, *Principles of Teaching*. Boston: Allyn and Bacon, Inc., 1958. pp. 154-157.

Kieffer, R. de and L.W. Cochran, *Manual of Audio-Visual Techniques*. New Jersey: Prentice-Hall, Inc., 1955. Unit 2.

Lancelot, W.H., *Permanent Learning*. New York: John Wiley and Sons, 1944. Chapter 17.

Risk, T.M., *Principles and Practices of Teaching*. New York: American Book Company, 1941. Chapter 23.

Wittich, W.A., and C.F. Schuller, *Audio-Visual Materials: Their Nature and use*. New York: Harper and Brothers, 1953.

5

Results of Teaching and Learning

Aims of the Chapter:

1. To develop a proper understanding of the meaning and importance of evaluation in teaching and in learning.
2. To develop a correct idea of the function and imortance of test and measurement in teaching.
3. To acquaint the students with the principle involved in measurement and in evaluation.

The Meaning of Evaluation

If education were to become a science and an art, it must develop means of determining with accuracy the degree and kind of all the changes which it brings about. Teaching becomes more productive when followed by an accurate appraisal of its results. The teacher cannot of course determine accurately how much he has contributed to the education of the pupil at the onset of his teaching. Various studies have shown that opinions on all types of educational outcomes are unreliable. The more objective and refined the measures of educational products, the greater are the possibilities of determining and putting into effect improved educative procedures.

The success or failure of the teacher in applying the principles which have been discussed in this book is evaluated by the growth and development of the children. Of course, it is also possible that the validity of the principles which we sought to establish may be called in question by the same sort of evaluation. Teaching is, after all, the adaptation of our methods to the normal growth and development of boys and girls whose growth can be evaluated in terms of knowledge, habits, skills, abilities, attitudes, reasoning, and the like.

According to the Dictionary of Education, "evaluation is the process of ascertaining or judging the value or amount of something by careful appraisal." To Wiles,[1] "evaluation is the process of making judgments that are to be used as a basis for planning. It is a procedure of improving the product, the process, and even the goals themselves." In education, the terms refers to the step taken in directed study in which the teacher and the pupils appraise the progress made in the study of a subject or unit. Likewise, the term evaluation also refers to the process of determining experimentally or subjectively the merits of a test on the basis of such characteristics as validity, objectivity, ease of administration and scoring, adequacy of norm, availability of duplicate forms, and ease of interpretation; Evaluation is closely related to educational measurement. However, it is a far more inclusive concept than measurement. "Measurement" implies the use of standardized tests, the results of which are expressed in quantitative terms. In education, therefore, measurement represents only one approach to evaluation. Both evaluation and measurement are for the adequate appraisal of the results of teaching and learning. Measurement has always a place in the evaluation technique. Monroe[2] has distinguished between measurement and evaluation by indicating that in measurement, the emphasis is upon a single aspect of subject-matter achievement or specific skills, habits, knowledge, and abilities; whereas in evaluation,

1. K. Wiles, *Supervision for Better Schools* (New York: Prentice Hall, 1950), pp. 248-282.
2. W.S. Monroe, "Educational Measurement in 1920 and 1945," *Journal of Educational Research*, Jan. 1945. pp. 339-340.

the emphasis is upon broad personality changes and major objectives of the educational program. In other words, while measurement is centered on the pupil, evaluation on the other hand, is centered on the environment and what it does to the pupil. Measurement is focused on isolated points; evaluation is focused on the whole child in his environment. Evaluation utilizes all the tools and techniques of measurement as a means for determining progress rather than as ends in themselves.

Importance of Evaluation

The effectiveness and success of any job of learning is heightened by a valid and discriminating appraisal of all its aspects. Evaluation is part and parcel of teaching. It is an integral element in the proper organization of learning. It is in no sense functionally separated from it. Testing, measuring, marking, and making reports, which are the most familiar instruments of evaluation, and also others which are less familiar but in certain respects more important, should be considered and treated as factors in the business of bringing about better learning, and not as a system separate from that of learning.

Evaluation is not just a testing program or an administrative technique. It is not something to be resorted to at the close of the school term as a culminating activity, nor should it be viewed as an end activity to be done by the district and division supervisors of the Bureaus of Public and Private Schools. In the modern school, increasing emphasis on the personal and social development of the child, as well as his academic achievement, has called for the corresponding development of a variety of techniques for appraising all phases of child growth and development, of pupil achievement, of behavior and of the teaching-learning processes. Due to the large number of factors that enter into teaching and learning including such instructional variables as objectives, methods and techniques, and subject-matter on the one hand; and such human variables as pupils, teachers, and supervisors on the other, it has been difficult to appraise the validity of the pupil's achievement. There is, therefore, a comparatively large subjective factor in the evaluation of teaching and learning that needs to be taken into account together with its objective features.

It cannot be denied that the evaluation of teaching and learning is an exceedingly complex activity. However, the efficiency of the teacher and the growth and achievement of the pupil can be evaluated through the use of such devices as check lists, rating scales, tests of different aspects of teaching ability, interview, and questionnaires. Through the use of such devices much valuable data may be gathered relative to many of the important aspects of teaching and learning.

The importance of evaluation in teaching can be summarized as follows:

1. *Evaluation is important to the classroom teachers, supervisors, and administrators in directing as well as guiding teaching and learning.* Evaluation, to be of importance to teachers and supervisors, should be diagnostic, i.e., it should reveal the specific points of strength and weakness in teaching and learning.

2. *Evaluation aids in devising more effective instructional materials and procedures of instruction.* Current educational literature is filled with enthusiastic advocacy of various cooperative research, and if worked along this line, will determine the degree of success and effectiveness of evaluation.

3. *Evaluation also helps to measure the validity and reliability of instruction.* The effectiveness and success of any phase of teaching technique can be demonstrated through the nature of the results obtained. From a purely methodical point of view, the measurement of effective teaching finds its great value in the possibilities it offers for the improvement of teaching and learning. All activities of the teacher should be evaluated in the light of their adequacy to promote the democratic way of life and on how nearly do the students realize the objectives of education.

4. *Evaluation stimulates students to study.* A questioning teacher creates incentives for students to learn more. He sets up effective and definite goals for learning. Giving oral or written examination is a good incentive for the students to study harder or to do better work. It makes the learner familiar with his own results. Likewise, he needs to understands his own high and low potential for learning, but even more, he needs help in understanding the personal problems of human relations.

5. *Evaluation helps teachers to discover the needs of the pupils.* The purpose of any program of evaluation is to discover the needs of the pupils being evaluated and then to design learning experiences that will satisfy these needs. Traditionally, the results of evaluation have been used to compare one individual with anoIher. It is an accepted fact that growth is a continuous process and that each individual grows at a rate that is unique for him. This being true, we evaluate an individual in order to discover his needs; and eventually, we reevaluate in order to determine how much progress he has made toward satisfying them.

6. *Evaluation can be used to enforce external standards upon the individual class or school.* This method should be such as to encourage a flexible curriculum which is ever responsive to the changing needs of modern life and to the variations in local conditions. Local schools should be free to select and develop instruments for evaluation which are appropriate for their curricula.

7. *Evaluation, likewise, helps to provide objective evidences for effective cooperation between parents and teachers.* The increasing complexity of our present society has emphasized the importance of the cooperation of the school, the home, and the community in making significant educational progress.

8. *Evaluation helps parents to understand pupil-growth, interests, and potentialities.* The major responsibility of the school and teacher is to help the parents understand their

children. Understanding a youth means understanding his progress in the various areas of the curriculum, his desires and motives and behavior they lead to, his potentialities for learning, as well as his achievement.

9. *Evaluation is helpful to the teacher.* It enables him to see how he can make his contribution to the accomplishment of the total goals or aims of the school system. It helps the teacher to coordinate his efforts with the efforts of others who contribute to the general educational goals. The first step in evaluating the results of instruction is to determine the general objectives of the school and the specific objectives of the different courses offered.

10. *Evaluation is helpful in securing support for the school from the government, local or national.* The people frequently complain tnat public schools in this country are inadequately supported.

Development of Educational Measurement

The movement in educational measurement started in Europe as early as 1864 with the work of Rev. George Fisher.[3] To Ebbinghouse[4] goes also the credit for devising and using what was probably the first completion test in 1885. In America the work of Dr. Rice[5] and the development of a crude Spelling Scale in 1895 marked the beginning of objective measurement in education. In 1902, Stone[6] developed the fist Standard Test in Arithmetic reasoning. This was followed by a test in

3. A.R. Lang, *Modern Methods in Written Examination* (New York: Houghton Mifflin Co., 1930), p. 11.
4. From Ebbinghouse's own account of his experiments. A contribution to *Experimental Psychology* (1885), translated in 1913 by H. Ruger and C.E. Bussenius.
5. G.M. Ruch, *The Objective or New Type Examination* (Chicago: Scott, Foresman and Co., 1929), p. 6.
6. *Ibid.*, p. 13.

Spelling by Ayres[7] in 1915. Since 1910, rapid progress have been made in the invention and development measuring devices as a means of supplementing opinions. The scientific work in education has advanced a great deal with the develoment of instruments for measurement. Every further improvement in testing and measurement makes possible further advance in education. The standardized test movement is slightly more than thirty years old. The standardized test, while generally assumed to apply to educational tests, covers a wide field. The earlier efforts at standardization were applied to tests of intelligence. At the present time, many standardized tests have been prepared to measure qualities other than intelligence or school achievement. The standardized test has made a unique contribution to the work of evaluating the results of teaching.

The non-standardized objective examination, sometimes called the new type or teacher-made objective type examination, is an outgrowth of the popularity of the standardized test movement. The development of standardized tests has brought into sharp relief the improved techniques employed in the construction of these new types of tests.

The use of tests and measurement is not new in the Philippine school system, but the use of standardized educational tests was not introduced into this country until 1924. In July, 1924[8] a section was organized in the former Academic Division in the General Office of the Bureau of Education (now the Bureau of Public Schools). The Section of Tests and Measurement became a division in 1940, and later became the Division of Research and Evaluation. From 1925 to 1941, it constructed an annual survey testing in almost all the shool subjects in the elementary and secondary curricula. At present, the Division

7. Ayres Spelling Scale, See W.S. Monroe, *An Introduction to the Theory of Educational Measurement* (New York: Houghton Mifflin Co., 1923), p. 8.
8. T. Clemente, "A Survey of the Testing Measurement," *Philippine Journal of Education*, Vol. XXXIV (February, 1956), No. 9, p. 559.

constructs standardized tests, administers them to school children, interprets their result, and conduct research studies. Standardized tests are also used in surveying the status and quality
of instruction as could be removed by remedial measures. The
Evaluation and Research Division has published some tests for
Filipino use. Among these are the Philippine Mental Test, the
Philippine Prognostic Test, the College Entrance Test, the Philippine Classification Tests, the Philippine Teacher Selection Test,
the Philippine Vocabulary Tests, and the Philippine Educational Achievement Tests in different elementary and high
school subjects adapted to Philippine needs and conditions.

Integrating Testing With Teaching

Educational tests and the information resulting from their
use in the classroom are coming to be almost universally identified with good teaching practice. If instruction consists of
teaching, training, and testing, the latter should then be made
a regular part of the teaching procedure. Testing or examination should be considered an essential part of instruction. Testing serves to guide learning and should, therefore, be an integral
part of the learning procedures. The new elements in the
situation are the extreme frequency with which some teachers
use them and their careful integration of tests with the teaching
procedures brings results. Objective tests results can be integrated in teaching, especially with review in a more immediate
way. The test-teach-test method has its values, especially in
the lower grades. It should never be used as a substitute for
all other methods or techniques. The method provides an
opportunity for the systematic remedial teaching because it
diagnoses, for both the pupils and the teachers, what has not
been mastered.

So that examinations may be educational, the teacher should
attempt to make them in such a way as to fulfill their true
functions. Testing or examination serves as a stimulus to daily
preparations. Nothing operates more surely in increasing or
in generating interest and effort than the experiencing of the
results of efforts. Testing will also enable the teacher, not only

to measure the extent and degree of learning that results from study and teaching, but also to note weaknesses and defects as revealed by the diagnosis. That diognosing is an important function of testing should be borne in mind. Results need to be cheked up constantly as a guide to teaching, and remedial teaching should follow closely upon the original presentation and study. Tests should furnish data disclosing the learning that has taken place, with respect to items of information, concepts, and appreciation. Testing should also be considered, not only as a desirable stimulus and a necessity for diagnosis, but also for the purpose cf school records. The classification and promotion of pupils are based upon the grades or marks assigned by the teacher. Classification and promotion are among the educational functions of testing.

Types of Tests Useful in Teaching

Modern tests are so numerous that it is extremely difficult to classify them closely. Tests can be classified on the basis of their forms, their functions, and their content. The types given by the writer are classified as: function, educational, intelligence, and personality tests.

1. *Educational Tests*—Educational tests have as their primary function the measurement of the results or effects of instruction and learning. They are intended to test primarily classroom learning. Educational test may be either standardized or non-standardized. A non-standardized test has no fixed norm and it is free from prescribed rules. The teacher-made test is a good example of the non-standardized test. Examples of educational tests are the following:

(a) Standard Survey Test, which aims to measure the attainment, progress or status of the pupils or the schools. It refers also to a test which measures the general achievement of the pupils in a certain subject or field.

(b) Informal or Teacher-made Test, which aims to measure the achievement, progress, weakness or defects of the individual pupils or class, or the effectiveness of the method used by the teacher. This may be either an essay or an informal objective test.

(c) Standard Achievement Test, which aims to measure the pupil's accomplishment as a result of instruction in a given subject or subjects.

(d) Standard Diagnostic Test, which aims to locate the weaknesses, and if possible, the cause of disability in performance.

(e) Inventory Test, which aims to measure the degree of mastery existing before the teaching or the learning of the subject or subjects.

(f) Aptitude Test, which aims to measure the specific intelligence as it operates in a certain field or area of performance. It may be used for prognostic purposes.

2. *Intelligence Tests*—The intelligence tests have as their purpose the measurement of the pupil's intelligence or mental ability in a large degree without reference to what the pupil learned in or out of school. The two types of Intelligence Tests are:

(a) Individual Intelligence Test—This type of intelligence test can be administered only to one pupil at a time, like the Binet and Simon Intelligence Test (1904).

(b) Group Intelligence Test—This type of Intelligence test can be administered to a number of pupils at the same time, like the Alpha and Beta Intelligence Tests, or the Philippine Mental Tests.

Values of the Educational Test

Some values of the educational test worth considering are as follows:

1. *The educational test measures the accomplishment and progress of the pupils.* Any attempt to measure the achievement of the children would result in the discovery of the progress being made from week to week, or from month to month,

or from year to year. It would be advantageous to note the progress and deficiency at all periods if comparison is to be made with the work three weeks or a month later. Some tests are designed to serve this end. This results of achievement tests are widely used for classification and promotion.

2.   *An educational test diagnoses the strength and weakness of the pupils in a subject or a subjects.* The test will serve both as a guide to teaching and as an enlightenment to the learner. When a pupil makes an error, the teacher needs to apply a diagnostic test to discover why the pupil made the error and to determine how the thinking of the pupil may be directed in order to build up a correct reaction in place of the incorrect one. Asking questions, the use of drill material, and the review are all forms of diagnostic tests. It is, therefore, a sound educatic   practice to use both oral and written tests for diagnosing what goes on in the pupil's mind.

It is important that the teacher should be able to measure the extent and the degree of learning that results from study and teaching, to note weaknesses and defects, as measured by the desired level of mastery, and to adjust remedial procedures to the deficiencies revealed by the diagnosis. That diagnosis is an important function of testing should be borne in mind. The use of evaluation procedures to disclose instructional weakness has proved to be a most valuable way of improving teaching and learning. It can be said that many so-called weaknesses of pupils are the result of poor teaching.

3.   *The educational test measures the validity and reliability of instruction.* The effectiveness and success of any phase of teaching technique can be demonstrated through the character of the results obtained. The teacher should know how to measure the results of his work in order to adapt his procedure to the needs of the varying situations. From a purely methodical point of view the measurement of teaching effectiveness finds its greatest value in the possibilities it offers for the improvement of teaching. As a matter of fact, it is only since the educational tests were developed that any significant evaluation

of teaching methods has been practicable. The teacher must keep in mind that the greater function of teaching is not evaluation but instruction.

4. *The educational test stimulates the pupils to study.* Testing serves as a stimulus to daily preparation. The teacher, by giving an unannounced or announced test of some sort will, no doubt, stimulate the pupils to study the lesson assigned or the work covered. Giving a written examination is a good incentive for the pupils to study harder or to do better work. It makes the learner familiar with his own results. The final examination given in the high school and in college at the end of the course or term funishes a very powerful stimulus to review. This function should be recognized but not stressed.

5. *The educational test opens the way to remedial work.* Test results afford a basis for diagnosing the pupil's needs. Difficulties are prevented by the early discovery of the strength and weakness of the pupil. Knowing the defect of the individual or the general weakness of the class, the teacher will be able to select the right course or procedure to follow.

6. *The educational test sets up standards of performance for the pupils.* It increases the effectiveness of education by setting up standards of achievement in terms of varying capacities. A standard test can be used in comparing the merits of different schools, different classroom methods, different organiations cf materials, and the different lengths and methods of assignment.

The use of standards has been associated with standardized test of one form or another. The norms for achievement tests in different subjects have been most useful as a basis for interpretation and comparison. Standards are, of course, not feasible in examinations formulated by the classroom teacher, and, therefore, should not be looked upon as of great importance.

7. *The educational test can be used for educational and*

vocational guidance. Test results afford a basis for the guidance of pupils. The test first came into use in a general way. It can be used to guide the pupil in school in the selection of courses or of the vocation for which he is best qualified. It can be used to discover the unusual aptitude of pupils. The guidance function of education assumes a prominent place in the modern concepts of the aims of education. It is generally accepted that intelligence tests are necessary to supplement indices of achievement as a basis for guidance. The use of intelligence tests for guidance purposes has become so thoroughly accepted that no guidance can be considered effective which does not involve the use of these means.

8. *The educational test measures the efficiency of the teacher, and the teacher's efficiency can be best measused by the results of the test given in the difficult subjects that he is teaching.* The success of teaching, as well as the efficiency of the teacher, can be best judged by its results as shown by the growth of the pupils in knowledge, skills, habits, abilities, and attitudes.

9. *Educational tests can be used in the classification and sectioning of pupils.* It has been proved that pupils learn most effectively when they are placed with other pupils having approximately the same abilities. This means that pupils of approximately the same intelligence and achievement levels should be grouped together for instructional purposes. For the accomplishment of this purpose intelligence and achievement tests can be utilized. The use of mental-age and achievement-age scores is recommended for the classification of pupils.

10. *The educational test can also be utilized to solve some disciplinary problems in the classroom.* Some educational writers have pointed out that a large proportion of misbehavior in the classroom is oftentimes due to the failure of the teacher to realize the actual ability of the pupil and to utilize it adequately. Through the proper use of well selected educational tests the teacher will improve, not only his understanding of the pupils, but also his ability to stimulate the individual pupils to

accomplish more at their own effective levels.

11. *The educational test can be used by supervisors to direct and guide the teachers.* The supervisor who appreciates the value and limitations of tests can use the data to suggest changes and improvement in teaching procedures. However, tests should not be used as the sole criterion for evaluating teacher-effectiveness. The training of the teacher, the ability of the class, the materials and resources available to the teacher, are other factors that should be taken into consideration. The test data should be used as supplementary evidence.

12. *Educational test results are a valuable part of the pupil's records.* The meaning of the test data is widely understood, and when they are entered in the pupil's permanent record they can help other teachers understand him better. The test data should be used only as background information, not as a measure of present status.

Requisites of Good Tests

The following are the requisites of a good standard or non-standard test or examination:

1. *Validity*—A test is valid when it measures what is supposed or intended to be measured. The validity of the test depends upon the purpose of the test. The term may also refer to the general worthwhileness of an examination. The other synonyms for validity are goodness and general merit. A diagnostic test, to be valid, should measure the weakness or defects of the pupils in a given subject. A test unit should accomplish the particular purpose which the user has in mind. A test ceases to have validity when applied to the measurement of abilities for which it was not intended.

2. *Reliability*—A test is reliable when the scores are constant or when it possesses a fair degree of accuracy. The reliability of a test may be determined by using the same test twice

with the same group of pupils under the same conditions. If the test is reliable, each pupil should make approximately the same score each time. Lack of agreement indicates roughly the degree of unreliability. Reliability is an aspect or phase of validity. It refers to the degree of accuracy or phases of validity. It refers to the degree of accuracy of measurement. Long tests are more valid than short ones. Reliability is most frequently expressed by the use of the coefficient of correlation.

3.   *Objectivity*—A test is objective when personal opinion is eliminated from the scoring. A question given in an objective test has but one possible answer, and the total score is determined solely by the number of correct answers given. The true-and-false or multiple-choice types of examination are highly objective. The objectivity of a test, like validity and reliability, may be expressed by the use of the coefficient of correlation.

4.   *Ease of administration and scoring*—This refers to the case in giving and taking the examination, as well as in correcting and scoring the examination papers. The direction should be understandable and easily followed by the examinee. Inability to comprehend the directions may prevent a subject from doing a task which he has the ability to do. A poorly administered test gives the pupils much opportunity to cheat. When the essay-type of test is used, however, cheating is greatly minimized. A good plan of administering and scoring tests can eliminate cheating. Efficiency requires that an examination should be administered as expeditiously as possible. This responsibility can be given to or shared by the bright pupils.

5.   *Utility*—A test possesses utility to the extent that it satisfactorily serves a definite need in the situation in which it is used. Unless tests are selected and constructed for definitely conceived purposes and their results are used in an intelligent attempt to reach the desired results of teaching, they are of little value. The teacher must make use of the results of the test to improve the pupils' ability.

6.   *Establishing a fixed norm*—This refers to the establish-

ment of a standard by which the results achieved may be interpreted. The use of the norm has been associated with the standard test of one form or another. The norm is not feasible in an examination formulated by the teacher, and, therefore, should not be considered as of much significance. However, local norms may be derived with the accumulation of records The norm is useful as a basis for interpretation and comparison.

7. *Economical*—Economy involves both time and money, and therefore, simple equipment, carefully selected items that obtain wide sampling without an excessive number of items, and ease of scoring are essential to save time. A test must be valid and reliable or the cost tag will have little meaning. It is recommended that in selecting a test, the teacher must seek the advice of experts, study published reviews of tests, and examine the test manuals.

8. *Comparability*—A test possesses comparability when it makes possible a comparison between a pupil's score in one testing and his second or third scores on the same subject. It makes it possible also to translate a pupil's score in terms of grade norm or in terms of members of other groups similar to those of which he is a member. Comparability as a criterion i useful in evaluating changes in pupil behaviour.

Objective Types of Examination

One of the outstanding features of our educational practices today is the extensive use of the objective test. Men like Micheels,[9] Wrightstone, Justman, and Robbins,[10] are convinced of the superiority of the objective test over the essay examination. The main objective of this type of examination is to

---

9. W.J. Micheels and M.R. Karnes, *Measuring Educational Achievement* (New York: McGraw-Hill Book Company, Inc., 1950), p. 115.

10. J.W. Wrightstone, J. Justman, and I. Robbins, *Evaluation in Modern Education* (New York: American Book Co., 1956), p. 103.

avoid the element of subjective judgment and to increase the objectivity and accuracy of measuring the results of education. Like the traditional examination, it may be either oral or written. There are many types of objective classroom tests and the most common are following:

1. *True-and-false test*—One means of recognizing previously learned facts is the true-and-false, or plus-minus, or right-wrong test. True-and-false tests are made up of a number of statements, some of which are true and others, false. Pupils taking this test designate which statements are true by answering T, Yes, or True; the false ones are designated by F, N, or False. In such a test, if a statement is partly true and partly false, the student is directed to judge it as false.

2. *Completion-type test*—The completion is a test of recall. Ebbinghouse, in 1885, devised the first completion test in a study of memory. This type of test consists of statements from which one or several words are missing. The pupil is directed to write the correct word or words missing to complete the sentence. In this type of test the teacher must see to it that there will be sufficient blank space in which to write the correct answer. The length of the blanks should be uniform in order to avoid giving a clue to the correct answer.

3. *Multiple-choice test*—This is another type of recognition test. The multiple-choice test commonly consists of an incomplete statement followed by three to five suggested responses which will complete the statement with varying degrees of accuracy. The pupil is instructed to choose and to place a check on the response which correctly completes the statement. The multiple-choice test is one of the best types of objective tests because of its high reliability and objectivity.

4. *Matching-type test*—The matching-type test is a more difficult form of the multiple-choice types of test, and the number of scoring points is ordinarily determined by the number of responses required of the pupil. This test consists of two lists of related facts which are to be matched by means symbols.

with numbers of letters to indicate their proper relationships. To minimize guessing there should be an excess number 'n one set or list, preferable two or three. This consists of a sentence or paragraph with significant words or expressions omitted and replaced by blanks to be filled in by the examinees. This type of test is difficult to correct objectively.

Weakness of the Teacher-made Test or Non-standardized Tests

A test tests the teachers as well as the students. The teacher may waste the efforts of his good instruction for the marking period by judging his students by a test that does not measure the course covered. To be valid, a test must measure the thing that was purported to be measured; that is, the content of a test must cover the content of the course or that portion of it on which the student is being judged. Because of this, there is the possibility of achieving in the teacher-made tests, a higher validity than in the standardized tests, provided that the teacher is skillful enough in constructing his testing instrument.

A good teacher is aware of the common weakness of the testing procedures. Perhaps the most common is to cover only a limited portion of the instruction for the period, thus injecting the chance factor to the extent that the results are not valid. For instance, an essay test of five questions in history course may cover only five of the twenty equally important phases of the course. Maybe greater validity or reliability might have been achieved by using an objective-type-test. A teacher needs to know first exactly what he is attempting to measure and to make out his test accordingly. If it is reasoning he wants to measure, he will choose an aspect of the course commonly taught to all and use perhaps an essay approach. If it is recall he is interested in, then the true-and-false or completion test invites his consideration. There are a number of common approaches for simple recall.

School teachers need to guard against the weaknesses that arise with the so-called objective tests, such as the true-and-false, the completion, the multiple-choice, and the matching type.

They may be handled with too little consideration of their shortcomings because they are easy to construct. The teachers have a general knowledge of the common errors made in test construction and the relative values of teacher-made tests in various teaching and learning situations.

Limitations of Standardized Educational Tests

Evaluative concept recognizes the fact that no one measuring device can be used to evaluate all phases of the student's growth and development. Since human nature is complex, it is difficult to devise accurate and adequate techniques of measurement. Educational tests are only means to an end. A classroom teacher or supervisor should take into consideration the following limitations of educational tests:

1. Standardized educational tests do not measure all contents in learning. The power to reason and other traits cannot be measured at all. Most educational tests are centered on factual knowledge, habits, skills and abilities.

2. They are not adapted to all conditions. The teacher's training and experience, as well as his school environment, differ.

3. Standardized educational tests tend to produce mediocrity in teaching. The norm is the goal of the majority of teachers and supervisors in the field.

4. The fixed norm penalizes the dull or slow pupils. Individual differences are oftentimes not considered in the construction of educational tests.

5. Standardized tests are not valid owing to differences in materials taught and methods and devices used. Teachers in the field do not use the same amount of teaching materials, methods of instruction, and teaching devices.

6. Standardized tests do not prove helpful in many experi-

mental situations. They seldom are satisfactory in measuring achievement in any but the most conventional subject fields. For example, there are no tests devised to measure creative power or research ability, nor are there any measuring instruments available to evaluate adequately the aesthetic or the abstract qualities of the products of creative or research skills, even at the level of the upper elementary grades.

In spite of the limitations mentioned above, measurement is a necessary tool of education; hence, it is essential that the classroom teacher and supervisors acquaint themselves with the uses and varieties of measuring techniques, so that their own use of tests and measurement will show an objective and intelligent understanding of what measurement means and how it can best be made to improve teaching and learning.

There is no doubt that classroom teachers and supervisors with a limited knowledge of tests and measurement have misused measuring materials heretofore, and there is equally little doubt that the administrator or supervisor who casually accepts and uses carelessly standardized tests will encounter difficulties. Measuring is a scientific process, and it should be reserved for those adequately trained to use tests and measurement properly and to interpret results correctly.

Misuses of Test Results

The conduct of an elaborate testing program is no guarantee that the school in which the tests are given has a superior educational program. Tests give significant information, but information from tests may be neglected or misused. Some misuses of tests are the following:

1. One of the common errors in the use of tests is that of giving a series of tests with no clear-cut purpose and then doing nothing except compiling the results for a report to parents. Testing without a definite purpose is likely to secure meager returns.

2. Other serious errors can arise from failure to realize the limitations of a single application of a test and of the test itself. Too many persons think they know a child's intelligence from a single reading test. In education we gain in the kinds of information at hand by giving different tests.

3. Another misuse of test results is found in using the tests to do things, which should not be done on the basis of any information, that are educationally unsound. It is important that existing weakness in all testing techniques be recognized by everyone who uses them.

4. The tendency to regard norms as standards to be attained rather than the simple measure of present conditions is another misuse of test results. Norms are frequently misused. Norms carry no implications that pupils should be retarded or promoted to fit average conditions.

Suggestions for Improving the Essay-Type of Examination

The criteria for a good test construction do not vary greatly between the new-type test and the essay examination. The following principles are suggested:

1. The content of the essay type of examination should be made to conform to the criteria of the standardized tests as far as possible.   This type of examination can be made as valid as any other forms of testing if care is exercised to make it so.

2. Some of the rules followed in constructing the objective type of test should be applied likewise in the construction of the essay type of examination. The emphasis upon subject-matter as the basis for examination for the selection of items to be tested, is as important a principle in the essay type as in the other types of tests.

3. The content of the examination should be based on its purpose or aim. The fundamental purpose of essay examination should be centered on thought, selection, organization,

generalization, and on other types of mental activity.

4.   The characteristics of good questions should be considered in constructing an essay type of examination. It is desirable for the teacher to make a study of the questions best adapted to the essay examination. If this is done, the objectivity and the reliability of the test are certain to be increased.

5.   The responses made by the pupils should be evaluated according to definite standards. The scoring of the examination papers should be done as fairly and as objectively as possible. A list of possible answers or important idea with acceptable procedures in answering will prove an excellent guide to more equitable scoring of tests. Special criteria for particular items in the test will tend to narrow the elements of subjectivity in scoring.

Improving the Techniques of Evaluating Students' Growth and Development

To many teachers, appraisal is synonymous with the giving of written examinations. From this point of view, in evaluating the results of education, it is only necessary to give some paper-and-pencil tests. Written examinations may be relied upon to furnish evidence of the information which students have acquired, and to reveal their various verbal reactions. A comprehensive program of appraisal should show the degree to which these important desired results of education are actually being realized. The more frequent and objective the measure of educational products, the greater are the possibilities of determining and putting into effect improved educational procedures. To achieve these desired results, the following suggestions are hereby presented for consideration:

1.   *Develop a method of appraisal that will facilitate rather than hinder the desired learning of students.* Some appraisal programs focus the attention of the students upon examinations to such a degree that a good number of them work only to pass these tests. Doing well in the tests becomes the prime motiva-

tion of the students rather than experiencing the satisfaction of learning. In some cases emphasis upon tests has resulted in intense emotional strain on the part of the students. Instead of finding education an interesting and enjoyable experience, the students are constantly harrassed by the grim nightmare of the impending tests or examinations. Some react to current appraisal programs by cramming. Others attempt to memorize a large mass of information which mean nothing to them, for the purpose of giving these data back in examinations; only to forget many of these isolated and meaningless facts after the examinations are over. Appraisal programs that encourage such an attitude seriously hinder effective learning.

The difficulty can be overcome, however, by changing the character of the examinations and by changing their use. To reduce unnecessary cramming on the part of the students, the program of evaluation may be expanded to include a wide variety of types of evidence of student growth instead of limiting it to information tests. By replacing the monthly, semi-semestral, or semestral examinations with a continuous and cumulative collection of evidence, an appraisal program which is an integral part of the normal learning experience can change enormously the attitude of the students toward learning. Testing no longer becomes an ordeal but a normal part of their daily work which helps them to evaluate their own efforts.

2. *Obtain sufficient examples of the student's reactions from which to judge his growth and development.* It is not uncommon for teachers to draw conclusion from one or two of the students' reactions. Sometimes the answers to five or ten questions in a written examination are made the bases for judging the student's development during a quarter or semester. These are obviously inadequate samples of the student's reactions with which to appraise his development. An appraisal program must involve frequent observation and recording of behaviour so that the samples from which judgments are drawn are large enough to give teachers a fair picture of each student's reactions during a month or a semester.

3. *Obtain methods of appraisal which will reveal changes in students taking place over a short period of time.* If we modify instructional materials and procedures to meet the needs and difficulties of individual students, it is imperative that we discover these needs and difficulties before it is too late to make necessary modifications. Hence, we need means of evaluation which are sufficiently refine to reveal some changes in time to modify the course or procedure accordingly. The difficulty can be met by more frequent evaluation and by learning how incipient changes of various sorts are revealed.

4. *Give adequate consideration of the student's individual pattern of desirable educational goals.* The objective of each subject in the curriculum do not represent points to be reached by all students but rather directions toward which students may progress. When objectives are conceived as uniform goals to be attained by all students, teaching tends to become an attempt to maintain a lock-step march to these goals. It is an established fact that students differ, not only in rate and methods of learning, but also in interests, needs, and potential abilities. How far each student may be expected to progress toward any objective varies with his needs, interests, abilities which are involved in his progress.

Pupil's Ratings or School Grades

The discussion of the evaluation of results of teaching and learning is incomplete without a consideration of the real importance of test scores once they have been obtained. However, teachers and students must not consider evaluation solely as a means of obtaining grades. Basically, there are but two grading systems in use at present in this country. All other types of grading system are variations of these two. The first of these is called the Garrett Plan or the Percentage System; the other, the Missouri Plan or the Normal-Curve System.

1. *The Garrett Plan or the Percentage System*—The percentage system of grading assumes an absolute standard. The grades have some subjective concept of perfect performance for

the particular exercise being graded. To this perfection standard he assigns the value of 100 per cent or 100-point scale. The exercite is then judged against this 100 per cent standard. This system is applied to examinations, test, and any other means used to measure the results of teaching and learning. If the outcome of the examination or test shows that three-fourths of the quantity or quality of the perfect exercise is covered satisfactorily, it is given a grade of 75 per cent; if it reaches nine-tenths of the way towards the perfection goal, it is assigned a grade of 90 per cent. The percentage system is used in all public elementary and secondary schools and some private school, college, and universities in the Philippines. The University of Santo Tomas and Far Eastern University use this system of grading.

As noted in the preceding illustration, the percentage system assumes a range of grades from 0 to 100. In other words, it is assumed that a teacher is able to distinguish 101 levels of achievement or ability. Psychology tells us, however, that the human mind, is rarely able to distinguish more than five to seven classes in any situation. We would all probably confirm this idea if we had experience in grading test papers. Those who advocate the curve system for grading purposes take cognizance of this fact inasmuch as they recommend that somewhere between three and seven grade distinction should be made.

A second serious mathematical formula that would apply to this situation is wherein a relatively small proportion of a class will receive grades scattered all along the way from 0 to 70, let us, say, and the much larger section of the class receives grades in the relatively smaller range of 30 points, from 70 to 100.

2. *The Missouri Plan or the Letter-System based on Normal-Curve*—The letters-system based on Normal-curve uses an entirely different point of reference. It is a system of distributing grades based on the normal probability formula and the law of chance. The average achievement or ability of

the particular class taking the test is used as a standard against which each individual's performance is judged. The individual's test performance is graded in proportion to its distance from the average score. The group of scores clustering around the average score is given the middle grade symbol; the scores better than the average, another symbol; those lower than the average, another symbol; and so on out as far as the particular school system demands. This plan is based upon relative values, and marks are determined according to the rank or order of the merit. The distribution of grade is determined by some arbitrary scheme, such as the normal curve or some percentage distribution. Grades under such conditions are usually in letters or numbers, and the scales ordinarily used have four or five divisions. The University of the Philippines and Silliman University use this system of grading.

The real difference between these two systems is that the Percentage or Garrett Plan assumes that the standard of judgment can be applied reliably and validly by the teacher, while the Normal-Curve or Missouri Plan recognized that test vary in difficulty and that judgments vary in the marking; hence, marks can and should show relative ability only. According to Ruch,[11] "marks cannot be reduced into an absolute scale such as the percentage scale because no one knows what 100% means." However, reducing relative marks into percentage still persists in the Philippines and in America.

The normal-curve system, on the other hand, originates from the basic mathematical laws of chance, and is constructed according to the binomial expansion theorem. With such mathematical precision, one can face the grading problem with greater confidence that the results will be reliable.

A marking system based upon the normal probability curve indicated by the five letters with their corresponding areas computed on the bases of the M (median) and 6 (S.D.).

---

11.   G.M. Ruch, *The Objective or New-Type-Examination* (Chicago: Scott, Foresman and Company, 1929), pp. 369-402.

In a five-letter system based upon M and 6 or S.D., the areas representing the various letters are described as follows:

> A is 1.50 or more above the Mean.
> B is between +.50 and +1.50.
> C is between —.50 and +.50,
> D is between —.50 and —1.50.
> E is 1.50 or more below the Mean.

The normal-curve pictures accurately what actually happens when a large, unselected group is measured for educational achievement and the results are presented graphically. Since this is what happens under controlled conditions, it gives us a guide as to what we might expect in a particular testing situation; hence, it might be called the expectancy curve. When the results of the particular test that we administer do not take the form of the curve, we are challenged to answer the question "Why?" Has the instruction been faulty? Has the test been properly constructed? Has the subject-matter been too easy or too hard? Just what has happened?

Basic Principles of Good Marking System[12]

Regardless of which type of grading is used by a school, it seems desirable to determine principles that are fundamental to good marking system. The following are suggested as basic principles:

1. *A marking system should be clear and definite so that it can be easily comprehended by the pupils, teachers, and parents.* If a five-point letter scale, as A, B, C, D, and F, is adopted, the letters should be interpreted for what they actually mean. In other words, the grades should be defined so that the standard for each grade is clear and definite. There is need for a briefer description of the various letters in report cards, catalogs, etc. This description should bring out both qualitative and quantita-

12.   H.C. Gregorio, *Principles of Education* (Manila: R.P. Garcia Publishing Company, 1950), pp. 234-236.

tive aspects of the grades.

2. *A marking system should be realistic, reasonable, and as true to human life patterns as possible.* Grades should be as realistic as we can make them. They must make sense. When a teacher gives 50 per cent of his 100 students an A, he says, in effect, that 50 of the 100 students are "excellent" (according to our definition of A.). Or again, when a teacher gives no grades below C, we might wonder how he derives his average, and what average might mean in these days.

3. *A marking system should provide sufficient range of grades so that various degrees of attainment can be indicated reliably.* If grades are used only to indicate the accomplishment of definite goals which have been designated, these goals should be arranged according to relative importance so that grades will indicate relative accomplishment. The final grade of a student in a course should be the average of the comparable relative grades obtained in the course.

4. *A marking system should be based on objective measures or standards that can be checked objectively or rated consistently with a high degree of reliability.* Standards will give the teacher a clear picture of the growth achieved by the pupils. The results should be expressed in point scores that can be easily converted into grades in conformity with the grading system used by the school. Reliability can only be obtained by using objective types of tests.

5. *A marking system should utilize statistical procedure in converting scores into grades.* However, a too complicated statistical procedure should be avoided by the teacher. The normal-curve system of grading is commendable for this purpose.

6. *A marking system must be used as a means to an end and not as an end in itself.* It should be used to guide the pupil in his learning, to guide the teacher in determining the effectiveness of his teaching, and to guide the parents in evaluating

what changes take place in the lives of their children.

Principles to be Observed in Evaluating Teaching and Learning

Evaluation, to be effective, must be based on the following general principles:

1. *Evaluation must be based on the clear concept of the aims of education outlined in our Constitution, of the school, and of the course of study.* Evaluation of the work of a school is made in terms of the philosophy of the school and the objectives which the school is expected to accomplish. The aims of the course of study must be formulated in terms of child growth and development. The ultimate purpose of evaluation is to improve the educational program of the school and to make it more effective.

2. *Evaluation should be comprehensive.* It should not be limited to isolated goals, or educational objectives, but should include all the major objectives of instruction. It is concerned with all the aspects of pupil behaviour and with all the objectives which the school and society hope to achieve. In other words, it should include all factors involved in the total teaching-learning situation.

3. *Evaluation should be continuous and must be made an integral part of all teaching and learning.* While the usual program of evaluation in this country is periodic; on the order hand, evaluation in the modern program permeates the program of improvement, and is continuous. Gradual and continuous change is recognized as desirable and characteristic of a modern educational program. Evaluation, to be of value, must run parallel to education which is considered by John Dewey as life, growth, and reconstruction of human experiences. If we consider education as directed growth, or a continuous modification of behaviour, only then can a continuous appraisal be adequate.

4. *Evaluation should be functional.* Evaluation, which is

part and parcel of the total teaching-learning situation, cannot help being functional. Evaluation of the teaching-learning situation, to be of value to all members of the teaching personnel, must improve the existing situation and the conditions that affect them. The purpose of any program of evaluation is to discover the needs of the individual being evaluated and then to design learning experiences that will solve these needs.

5. *Evaluation should be cooperative.* If evaluation is to be based on all aspects of the program of teaching and learning, it is only reasonable to suggest that all persons in the program should participate in it cooperatively. Cooperative action by the teaching personnel and staff should be the outcome of evaluation.

6. *Evaluation should be based on accepted criteria or standard...* The criteria which are used in the evaluation should be consistent with the accepted educational philosophy and objectives of education. Of several types of criteria to be used, those concerned with the pupil growth and development and the factors that affect such growth should receive first consideration.

7. *Evaluation should be diagnostic.* Evaluation, to be of value, should serve as a guide to the teacher and as an enlightenment to the learner. When a pupil makes an error, the teacher must determine how to direct the thinking of the student in order to build up a correct reaction in place of the incorrect one. It is important that the teacher must be able to measure the extent and the degree of learning that results from study and teaching in order to note weaknesses and defects, as measured by the desired level of mastery.

8. *Evaluation should be based on the accepted principles of validity, reliability, objectivity, practicability, and appropriateness in the particular situation to be appraised.* To observe the above-mentioned principles, such devices as check lists, rating scales, tests of different aspects of teaching ability, interviews, and questionnaires should be utilized. Through the use of such

devices, much valuable data may be gathered relative to many of the important aspects of teaching and learning.

9. *Evaluation should be considered as basic to guidance.* This means that the evaluation system should be closely related to the guidance program of the school. An effective evaluation program provides information basic to the effective guidance of all pupils in school and adjustment to the needs and abilities of the individual pupil. Evaluation familiarizes the teacher with the nature of pupil learning, development, and progress. Evaluating, as well as guidance, operates as a part of the complete learning process.

10. *Evaluation should foster creativity.* Effective evaluation is dynamic and should be used to stimulate creative teaching it stimulates, as well as, measures growth. The ultimate worth of evaluation depends upon the coordination of the creative forces of teaching and learning, and the articulation of the activities of the teacher and pupils. Evaluation, to be creative, should be made an integral part of the regular teaching procedure. Evaluation should serve to stimulate creative teaching and learning.

11. *Evaluation must be conceived in terms of the educational purpose of teaching and learning.* If the purpose of teaching and learning is to promote pupil-growth-and-development, evaluation must concern itself with ascertaining the extent to which such growth is being affected. Evaluation familiarizes the teacher with the nature of pupil-learning, development and progress. Evaluation, likewise, appraises the effectiveness of the teaching methods and techniques. In other words, evaluation is essential to the improvement of teaching and learning.

12. *Evaluation must consider all aspects of school and community life that affect the growth of each pupil.* If we are to appraise the educational growth of the pupil, we must evaluate his school life, home life, community life, instructional materials, the physical equipment of the school, his relation to his teacher, his relationship with other pupils, and the general

and specific objectives of education. A complete evaluation will require the use of many techniques rather than using a single check list. Evaluation, to be effective, must be comprehensive.

GUIDE TO OBSERVATION ASSIGNMENT AND REPORT

Assignment for Observation

Aims:

1. To acquaint the prospective teachers with the importance of evaluation in teaching.
2. To acquaint the prospective teachers with the correct procedure in administering classroom test.
3. To develop an appreciation of the educational values of measurement and evaluation in teaching.

The importance of evaluation in teaching cannot be denied. The growth and development of the pupils and the effectiveness of the teaching procedure can only be measured by the results obtained through evaluation. Testing or examination should be considered an essential method of instruction, for a proper integration of tests with teaching procedures, brings results. In order to have educational value, the results of the test must be evaluated in terms of their true functions.

Class or Grade————Section———— Date —————

Teacher observed—————-—Observer————————

Observe a class where a written check-up is given on the lesson just taught. Examine the test used and the results of the test. Make a report based upon the following questions:

1. What types of examination questions were given in the test and for what purposes were those types intended?
2. Were the several purposes of testing recognized?
3. Were the results tabulated and transmuted to per-

centages or marks for classification purposes or for determining the growth of development of the pupils?

4. Did a large number of the teacher's mark approach the normal curve?

5. Were the rules given in your textbook observed in the construction and administration of the test? Give the principles violated.

6. Is the evaluation used by the teacher limited to the educational objectives?

7. What other achievement of the pupils are not measured by the written test or examination?

8. What are your comments and suggestions?

SUGGESTED EXERCISES FOR STUDY AND DISCUSSION

I. Indicate whether these sentences are true or false (verify):

———— 1. Measurement, as used in teaching, has a wider scope and extension than evaluation.

———— 2. A fixed norm or standard is an important characteristic of a teacher-made test.

———— 3. Dr. Rice is considered the Father of the Mental Test or the Intelligence Test.

———— 4. A test is considered valid when it measures what it intends to measure or to be measured.

———— 5. If a test possesses marked validity it will have a dissatisfactorily low reliability.

———— 6. Evaluation is comprehensive when it measures all factors in the teaching-learning situation.

———— 7. General intelligence, as the term implies, is a measure of achievement.

———— 8. Standardized educational tests tend to produce mediocrity in teaching.

————9. All educational tests have a diagnostic purpose or function.

————10. Ease of administration refers to economy of efforts in giving and in scoring the test.

— — —11. Examination can be used with good effect to motivate learning.

— — —12. The emphasis in evaluation is placed on subject-matter achievement or on specific skills and abilities.

— — —13. For the purpose of comparing schools or classes, non-standard tests are utilized.

— — —14. The development of mental and achievement testing has led to the formulation of several types of examination.

— — —15. Evaluation, to be effective, must be functional and continuous.

— — —16. The best known individual test is the Stanford Revision of the Binet test, first offered in its present form in 1937.

— — —17. The non-standardized test is one with a fixed norm and it is conducted by means of rigidly prescribed rules.

— — —18. The teacher-made test is a good example of a standardized educational test.

— — —19. Evaluation, to be effective, must be made an integral part of every teaching method or procedure.

— — —20. Standardization of tests in all subjects includes uniformity in testing and in scoring.

— — —21. Norm should be regarded as an educational objective for the individual pupil.

— — —22. Measurement is focused on isolated points; evaluation is focused on the whole child in his environment.

— — —23. Prognostic tests may also be regarded as a type of mental test in that they attempt to measure the capacity for a special subject.

— — —24. Survey tests are tests which are useful chiefly in measuring the achievement of the pupil, class or school.

———25. The utilization of a standard measurement is in itself a complete teaching act.

———26. Measurement implies the use of educational tests which are expressed in qualitative terms.

———27. Examinations make possible the setting up of specific objectives.

———28. Reliability is most frequently expressed by the use of the co-efficient of correlation.

———29. Educational tests have as their primary purpose the measurement of ability to learn.

———30. Evaluation and measurement as used in teaching supplement and implement each other.

———31. The use of standard educational tests was introduced in the Philippine Public School system in 1924.

———32. Tests have no teaching value unless the results are interpreted and applied.

———33. Silliman University and the University of the Philippines are using the Garret Plan of grading.

———34. In the Percentage System of grading, the central point of reference is the median or the norm.

———35. The essay type of questions or examinations help students to gain facility in the generalization and expression of ideas.

———36. In the Philippine Normal College, intelligence test is given as an entrance requirement for admission.

———37. A test is objective when personal opinion is eliminated from administering and scoring.

———38. The Missouri Plan of grading is based on the normal probability formula or law of chance.

———39. The Normal-Curve system of garding assumes an absolute standard.

———40. The program of evaluation is comprehensive when the appraisal covers the total growth of the child.

GUIDE QUESTIONS FOR STUDY

1. Why is it necessary to measure mathematically the efficiency of teaching and learning?

2. In what respect is an achievement test essentially different from an intelligence test?

3. Why are the pupil's achievement and the teacher's success in teaching closely related?

4. What are the advantages of the objective types of test over the essay type of examinations?

5. Why are reliability and objectivity considered important considerations in the evaluation of tests?

6. What are the advantages of teacher-made objective tests over the standardized tests?

7. What means are suggested to make the scoring of the essay examination more uniform and reliable?

8. What is your attitude toward the grading system used by the Bureau of Public Schools? Support your side.

9. What are the basic principles of a good marking system?

10. State some of the outstanding principles to be observed in evaluating teaching and learning. Evaluate each principle.

References

Adams, H.P. and F.G. Dickey, *Basic Principles of Supervision.* New York: American Book Company, 1953. Chapter 12.

Adams, G.A. and T.L. Torgerson, *Measurement and Evaluation for the Secondary Teacher.* New York: The dryden Press, Inc., 1956. Chapter 11.

Bernard, H.W., *Psychology of Learning and Training.* New York: McGraw-Hill Book Company, Inc., 1954. Chapter 21.

Brueckner, L.L., and G.L. Bond, *The Diagnosis and Treatment of Learning Difficulties.* New York: Appleton-Century Crofts, Inc., 1955. Chapter 2.

Cronback, L.J., *Essentials of Psychological Testing.* New York: Henry Holt and Co., Inc., 1950.

Greene, H.A. and others, *Measurement and Evaluation in the Elementary Schools.* New York: Longmans, Green and Company, 1953. Chapter 2.

Johnson, E., and R.E. Michael, *Principles of Teaching*. Boston: Allyn and Bacon Inc., 1958. Chapter 14.

Ross, C.C., and J.C. Stanley, *Measurement in Today's Schools*. 3rd ed. New York: Prentice Hall. Inc., 1954. Chapter 12.

Travers, R.M., *How to Make Achievement Tests*. New York: The Odyssey Press, 1950.

Wrightstone, J.W., and others, *Evaluation in Modern Education*. New York: American Book Company, 1956.

6

Principles Underlying Classroom Management and Discipline

Aims of the Chapter:

1. To provide the students with a proper concept of the purpose of routine and to acquaint them with the effective means of establishing a desirable routine.
2. To develop the power to appreciate methods of discipline and the ideals of discipline.

Meaning and Importance of Classroom Management

Classroom management and discipline are two important factors that have a decided influence upon the character and efficiency of the teaching and learning situations. Classroom management refers to the operation and control of classroom activities. It is relatively confined to the more mechanical aspects of teaching activity. Much of the discussion of classroom management assumes that its sole purpose is to save time and energy. Some of the things a teacher should consider in planning classroom management are regulations on seating and attendance, the handling of instructional materials and equipment, and the control of activities during the class period. The success or failure of teaching is determined often by the way the class is organized and managed. Unless the details

of the classroom procedure are carefully worked out, much
time will be wasted and little will be accomplished.   Therefore,
the teacher should thoroughly routinize the details of the daily
practice in conducting classroom work or activities.   However,
the teacher must guard against a too automatic sequence of
movement from one phase of work to another, least a sense of
monotony develops.   Spontaneity and freedom for the unexpected must always be present to challenge alertness on the
part of the pupils.   A thorough mechanization of classroom
procedure may destroy the spirit of spontaneity.

A well-managed classroom will give the pupil rich opportunities for mental growth and development.   Good classroom
management produces favorable working conditions conducive
to good learning and makes school work enjoyable and interesting.   The teacher, in the real sense of the word, is the custodian
of the learning opportunities of the pupil.   Progressive education
is concerned with providing every pupil with the facilities that
encourage learning and opens the avenue for it.   The school is
looked upon as the agency of society to provide these opportunities.   Anything the teacher may do to inhibit these opportunities violates his trust.   A well-managed classroom also makes
the pupil apprecia e the value of time upon which his future
success depends.   Thus, effective teaching and learning are
possible only in a well-managed classroom.

The Activities to be Routinized

Since school activities are social activities, we must look
into the routine found in adult society as a guide in laying the
basis for routine in classroom organization and control.   Much
of the details of providing a good work space can be routinized.
There should be a place where to put things out of the way,
and everyone in the room should know where each thing goes.
Routine should merely aid, in setting before the pupils, opportunities for educational experience.   The ability to set up routine
and to conform properly to it is in itself a worthwhile and
necessary outcome of education.

The complexity of the modern school system calls for more routinization of our classroom procedure. It is, therefore, exceedingly important for the teacher to determine what classroom activities should be routinized and made into habits. The teacher will find the task much easier if the pupils are brought to see understand fully the value of routine. Likewise, he should make it a point to present to his pupils the reasonableness of every phase of routine he wishes to develop. Certain classroom activities should be conducted in the most effective way to allow more time for essential learning activities. It is, therefore, necessary that daily activities can be turned into habits to facilitate speed and avoid waste of time. This is time-and-nerve-saving, and it is also good education. Routinizing certain activities has a further value in that it prevents confusion and saves time. Confusion reduces the effectiveness of learning activities. Routinizing also aids in keeping the attention of the pupils upon their work. The following should make up routine activity:

1. *Seating*—In a small class, designated seats are not necessary. However, members of larger classes should be assigned definite seats, even if the seats are movable. This is a fundamental principle of classroom economy. Confusion can be avoided by assigning definite seats to the pupils. In doing this, however, consideration should be given to those with physical defects or needs that warrant special attention. Nearsighted pupils or pupils hard of hearing should be seated near the front of the room. Most seating, however, is done alphabetically. The arrangement enables the teacher to become acquainted with the pupils in a very short time. It also makes it convenient to return class-papers, notebooks, and other instructional materials that the teacher may pass and collect. This also makes it possible for the teacher to check up on the attendance quickly. In a small class, designated seats are ordinarily not necessary.

2. *Class Roll*—The class roll should be carefully kept. A definite way of checking should be adopted and followed by the

teacher with the aim to save time. An effective device for checking up on attendance will save time for more essential learning activities. The teacher should find a way to do this to minimize class distraction. A cardboard diagram of the seating arrangement in squares with names for each square and the use of a monitor will facilitate the roll-call. An alphabetical arrangement will also help in checking up attendance. It is also necessary that the teacher should make it a routine detail to check up the roll at the beginning of the class period. Roll-call at the end of the hour should be discouraged. The teacher should, likewise, learn the names of each pupil. Knowing the names of each pupil will help in the prevention of disciplinary problems.

3. *Entering and leaving the room*—Entering and leaving the room should be in an orderly manner. These movements should be so orgnized that there is no confusion and loss of time. Unorganized movements lead to congestion and encourage loitering and disorder. Passing to and from the classroom should be informal, yet successful informality can be achieved only by insisting upon the observance of certain prescribed rules of conduct that become part of the routine of the school.

4. *Distributing, collecting, and handling of materials*—More time is often wasted in using ineffective methods of distributing, collecting, and handling materials than in any other single activity. A well-routinized procedure enables the pupils to get the materials before them with the least possible loss of time and energy. The plan most commonly used in distributing and collecting materials is to have the light materials passed to the end of the rows or forward, depending upon the seating arrangement. Books and other heavy materials should be distributed by pupils assigned to the task. In the lower grades the employment of monitors will help solve the problem. Instructional materials should be collected before the beginning of the period and they should be placed within the reach of the teacher. Pupils should be taught how to distribute and collect all materials carefully and quietly. Much time would be

saved and classroom interest preserved if this work is well routinized.

5. *Use of blackboard*—Routine must be established for the use of the blackboard if the class is expected to make much use of it. A well-routinized procedure must be set up to avoid confusion and loss of time. If biackboards are used frequently for practice exercises, pupils should be assigned to their regular places of work each time. Confusion and loss of time are prevented if pupils know where to go immediately without being directed by the teacher. Those who are in their seats should likewise, be told to work on the problems.

6. *Use of laboratory equipment*—If laboratory equipment are used frequently, the class should be accustomed to uniform routine for the handling of those equipment. The teacher must see to it that all the laboratory equipment to be used in the class period are carefully checked in advance and conveniently arranged so that the class procedure may go forward with a minimum of confusion, loss of time, and misdirected energy. There should be a place where to put all laboratory equipment out of the way, and every pupil should know where the equipment will go. The teacher and the pupils should do the job of returning the equipment if no laboratory assistant is hired for the purpose. Such responsibility is educational to the pupils.

Principles Underlying Classroom Management

1. *The teacher should bear in mind that the plan in handling classroom activities should be adapted to the classroom conditions.* The size of the class, the arrangement of the classroom equipment, and the materials in teaching must be well considered by the teacher.

2. *The teacher should bear in mind that regulations on absence and tardiness should be handled according to administrative requirements.* Attendance should be checked up at the beginning of the period. The pupils should be required to pre-

sent their excuse slips for absences before the class period begins. Tardy pupils should also be required to have admission slips which would be collected at the close of the period.

3. *The teacher should bear in mind that the handling of instructional materials should be routinized to save time and avoid confusion.* Routine has its place only when it contributes to thie end. The teacher must decide what rules should be applied in his classroom to effect this end.

4. *The nature and needs of the pupils should be borne in mind in making the seating arrangement.* Seats and seating should be adjusted to the needs of the pupils and should be arranged in an orderly and efficient way. Seats should be of the right size and type to give comfort to the pupils.

5. *It should be borne in mind that effective teaching and efficient learning are possible only when the classroom condition is normal.* The teacher should know the working conditions essential to good teaching, learning, and proper behaviour. His chief responsibility lies in making the best of his conditions and utilizing what good features are at his disposal.

6. *The teacher should bear in mind that the positive approach to classroom management and control is more effective than the negative approach.* A positive approach to classroom management and control really means looking for favorable, constructive conduct and commending pupils for it, and in most occasions, ignoring conduct that is not acceptable. A positive approach to classroom management and control is based on self-motivation and control.

School Discipline

Every phase of school management is closely related to school discipline. A well-ordered classroom is likely to be free from disciplinary problems. According to Hansen,[1] "discipline becomes a problem when students are not productively busy." Discipline must not be confused with stupid forms of punishment. Discipline is associated with wholesome class conduct. Discipline is always connected with a goal. The attainment of a goal whlch is bigger than that which can be reached immediately by the individual involves discipline. Thus, discipline may be thought of as an organization of one's impulses for the attainment of a goal. Modern educators think of discipline as primarily concerned with meeting the causes of maladjustments in the school so that right thinking and right conduct may be firmly established. Often-times, disciplinary problems grow out of poor classroom procedures and the teacher's weak personality. Thc teacher who really teaches will generally be able to maintain a fairly good order, and one may be quite certain that continuous disorder is the result of faulty organization and technique in the treatment of the lesson. Studies have shown that one chief cause of the teacher's failure is his inability to maintain order in the classroom.

According to Mueller,[2] "discipline means preparing boys and girls for life in a democratic society." He further states that the purpose of discipline is to help the individual to acquire knowledge, power, habits, interests, and ideals which are designed for the well-being of himself and his fellows; that discipline is a matter of education. Classroom discipline seeks to bring about desirable behavior on the part of all pupils.

Good teaching is made possible by good discipline. Likewise, Grim and Michaelis[3] state that "good discipline is a result of good teaching, a by-product, as it were." Good discipline

1. K. H. Hansen, *High School Teaching* (New Jersey: Prentice-Hall, Inc., 1957), p. 360.
2. A. D. Mueller, *Teaching in the Secondary School.* (New York: The Century Company, 1928), p. 48
3. P. R. Grim and J. U. Michaelis, *The Student-Teacher in the Secondary School* (New York: Prentice-Hall, Inc., 1954), p. 261.

implies obedience on the part of every pupil to classroom rules
and regulations with the aim of achieving success in learning.
It has been said that discipline is best when it is least in
evidence. Ability to secure good discipline is one of the qualities
of a good teacher. Psychological studies have revealed that
poor discipline is one of the causes of failure in teaching. The
correct techniques of management and method must be regarded
as the principal agency of good discipline within the school.
Good discipline is enforced not merely for regulative purposes;
it has also important educational values inherent in itself.

Modern Conception of Discipline

The modern conception of discipline is that it is both regulative and educative wherein the attention of the teacher is
directed to the development of constructive attitudes and habits
of conduct, rather than to regulations of control negative in
nature. It is regulative because without quiet and order,
effective teaching on one hand, and profitable learning on the
other, are not possible. Pupils doing group work require a
quiet and regulative classroom atmosphere in other that they
may derive the maximum benefit from the exercises. The true
function of classroom discipline is to create and maintain classroom conditions favorable to effective teaching and learning,
or to create a desire to help establish and maintain good
working conditions to further the accomplishment of the
objectives for which the teacher and the pupils are working.
The ideal conditions for teaching and learning depend largely
upon the attitude of the learner, classroom conditions conducive
to good teaching and learning, and the teaching skill of the
teacher in setting the stage for learning.

The real purpose of modern discipline in school is to guide
social development and adjustment. The problems of classroom
discipline are problems for guidance and for education, not for
coercion and punishment. And of course, the kind of guidance
we give depends on what the teacher wants to produce. It
has not been long since most parents and teachers sought
implicit obedience—unquestioning docility and conformity as

evidence of successful discipline. But unfortunately this criterion is rapidly giving way to the idea that initiative, self-direction, and social conscience are the normal indications of wholesome development.

The modern concept of discipline is based on rational approach. In a rational approach to discipline, mere compliance is subordinate to understanding. The pupils must be made to understand why certain modes of behavior are to be followed, to question the reasonableness of things, to have the habits of finding out about things, and to make up their own minds. They must grow up as people who have had much practice in planing for the welfare of themselves and their communities. The teachers must see to it that discipline of the home and the school does not interfere with that development by inculcating an attitude of subservience to the ideas and demands of the older generation. The discipline of both the home and the school should recognize the dignity of each individual and his right to seek recognition and to direct his own activities. Modern discipline must be viewed with new insight and understanding.

The modern concept of discipline is based on the following democratic principles:

1. Discipline based on devotion to humanitarian principles and ideals such as freedom, justice, and equality for all rather than discipline based on a narrower and more egoistic affiliation.

2. Discipline which recognizes the inherent dignity and rights of every human being, rather than discipline attained through humiliation.

3. Discipline which develops self-direction, self-discipline rather than discipline based on compulsion and obedience.

4. Discipline based on understanding of the goal in view rather than discipline based on high authority.

It can be said that modern concept of discipline is based on democratic principles. Discipline is not coercion through force but it is a spirit. And a spirit cannot be ordered, or punished into or regimented for. Demoratic discipline is based on admiration and love of an ideal or good and the love of this goal must be so great that sacrifice for the attainment of this goal ceases to be sacrifices and becomes incidentals of a process. Those persons who complain about the softness of the modern schools and who demand that the school use "Army methods," do not understand the methods of education for a democracy. The teachers must bear in mind that democracy is built on respect, on confidence in each other and on cooperation. True discipline is based on willing cooperation, which springs from knowledge, idealism, and a sense of service.

One great task of the teacher in a democracy is to understand and accept principles of democratic discipline. However, by understanding and accepting the principles of democratic discipline does not mean that all disciplinary problems are solved, or will-disappear. The other great task which confronts the classroom teacher on his job is to translate the principles of democratic discipline into daily action in his classroom. It is with this idea in mind that the principles governing the handling of disciplinary problems are discussed in this Chapter.

Causes of Disciplinary Problems

The teacher will do well to become familiar with the causes of violations of discipline in order that such causes may be minimized, if not prevented, and offenses may be more satisfactorily diagnosed and treated. The fundamental causes of disciplinary problems may be summarized under the following classifications:

1. *The teacher's personal factor*—The teacher's poor personality is oftentimes the cause of poor discipline. This factor refers to lack of knowledge of the subject-matter, constant nagging and scolding, lack of sympathy, temper, poor decision, harsh treatment of the pupils, poor methods of instruction, and

lack of knowledge of the nature of the children. The petty, fault-finding, and nagging teacher is oftentimes disliked and resented by young students. The teacher's lack of training and lack of knowledge of children may have a psychological basis. From this deficiency originates many disciplinary problems. A teacher with such a personality keeps his pupils unhappy and produces poor teaching results. The study by Lee[4] reveals this fact. According to Lee's study, good teachers possess personal appearance, poise, tact, cheerfulness, self-control, cooperativeness, consideration, alertness and adaptability, dependability, and discretion; while poor teachers possess a considerable number of negative personality traits.

2. *Physical factors*—These refer to health and physiological elements that determine adolescent characteristics. Educational studies recognize the importance of health to school discipline. Pupils with poor health or who labor under physical handicaps inevitably complicate the problems of discipline. A bad health condition often leads to irritability, restlessness, or sullenness. Abnormal glandular action may develop a phlegmatic, nervous, or irritable individual. The physical elements that determine adolescent characteristics are closely related to health factors. Rapid bodily growth makes the adolescent self-conscious, restless, and emotional. The growth factor often lead to general mischief and sensitiveness to the teacher's influence.

3. *Individual factors*—These factors are classified under egotism, immaturity of judgment, low mentality, and self-consciousness. Other factors underlying the behaviour of the individual are the desire for mastery and dominance, desire for activities and adventures, a sense of superiority, and conflicts and repression. From these individual factors flow all types of disciplinary problems. Pupils who are self-centered have no regard for what others are doing or what others may be

4. G. C. Lee, *An Introduction to Education in Modern America* (New York: Henry Holt and Co., 1957), pp. 322-323.

thinking of their behavior. They are oftentimes defiant toward those in authority and want to have their own way among their fellow members of the class. It is the responsibility of the teacher to help the pupil overcome self-conceit, whatever may be the cause. Pupils may continue to misbehave because they cannot see the bad effect of their behavior. This failure to analyze and to look ahead may be caused either by lack of mental ability or by immaturity. Lack of mental ability and immaturity of judgment often causes embarrassment and trouble that are more far-reaching than may have been anticipated.

4. *Social factors*—Social factors, like individual factors, are also variously classified, the more important of which are: desire for social approval, desire for sensationalism, desire to be well known to everybody in school, and resentment to control. The youth, to gain recognition or the attention which a developing inferiority complex demands, often indulges in sensational behavior.

In direct contract to the preceding types of pupils, many pupils dislike nothing so much as to be considered different. They desire to be like the majority. Older pupils would stubbornly resist any limitation upon their personal right. A study made by Morehouse[5] revealed that approximately twenty-two per cent of the disciplinary problems in the high school may be classified as problems arising from antagonism to imposed control. However, although young people seem to resent control, they usually recognize the need of some supervision of their behavior by the trained teacher.

5. *Emotional factors*—All learning has emotional correlates. In other words, emotions are involved in the whole business of teaching and learning. Emotional factors refer to individual friendships or personal relations and tensions. These

5. F. M. Morehouse, "Discipline of the School," in N. L. Bossing, *Progressive Methods of Teaching in Secondary Schools.* Chicago: Houghton Mifflin Company, 194?, p. 162.

also include patterns of interpersonal relationships as they existed in the classrooms. Hostility, apathy, cliquishness, overt disturbances—all are manifestations of qualities of interpersonal relationships in the classroom. Conflicts arising from personal relations will reflect themselves in the shape of discipline problems. Strong friendship among pupils sometimes produces stubborness against the intrusion of the teacher through criticism or blame. Likewise, vehement antipathies, hatreds, and animosities between pupils may encourage individual feelings to supersede reasonable adjustments to teacher demands. Many fights and many instances of undesirable behavior are sidelines of individual or group tensions.

6. *School factors*—These factors refer to the unattractive schoolroom, an unhygienic room condition, and the lack of organization of classroom routine. These factors should not be overlooked though some of them are beyond the teacher's control. Poor school conditions have a depressing and detrimental effect on pupils. The pupils cannot develop a natural respect for an unattractive room. On the other hand, a cheerful atmosphere serves to arouse the pupil's spirits and to stimulate in them a desire to achieve. Poorly ventilated rooms are likely to make the pupils restless or depressed. In school the attractiveness of the classroom, the adequacy of the heat, the light, and the ventilation are important because they affect the behavior of the pupils.

7. *Lack of training*—Lack of training is often the cause of disciplinary trouble. The very nature of the child is such that he cannot be expected to behave like a well-trained and cultured adult. An individual who lacks proper training cannot distinguish between right and wrong until he is taught. Too often a breach of discipline is committed through ignorance. Discipline disintegrates when pupils do not know what to do, do not understand what is expected of them.

8. *Work factors*—Work factors refer to subject-matter, methods, procedures, assignments, and other learning activities. Poor subject-matter planning or bad teaching automatically

increases the number of discipline problems. Too difficult or too easy subject-matter, methods or procedures too much on a merely verbal level, type of work too advanced or too infantile, load of assignment too heavy or too light, work or activities badly scheduled, are sources of discipline problems. When too much of the work or activities of the pupils remain unchallenged, they search for other outlets.

Creating Favorable Teaching·Learning Situation for Good Discipline

The basic ways of creating a favorable learning situation for discipline are in reality the same basic steps in good teaching. Classroom discipline is a product of the teaching and of the learning processes. The basic ways of creating a good learning situation for discipline are in reality the same basic steps in good teaching. Disciplinary problems are like teaching and learning difficulties for they need diagnosis, direction, prevention, and treatment. It cannot be denied that most of the disciplinary problems in the classrooms can be prevented or greatly minimized with a favorable teaching-learning situation. Ideal conditions for learning depend upon environmental conditions conducive to learning and the skill of the teacher in setting the stage of learning which includes teaching skill itself. Poor teaching and unproductive learning are important causes of poor discipline in the classroom. In other words, good teaching and effective learning are often free from disciplinary problems. According to Crow and Crow,[6] "good teaching is the best alleviator of classroom tension." Good discipline is a product of favorable environment and good teaching.

There is no better way of assuring good classroom discipline than through good planning of the teaching-learning process, clear and achievable aims and objectives, realistic and appropriate program of studies, and direct methods and meaningful activities. When the teacher lacks planning of the daily

6. L. D. Crow and A. Crow, *Introduction to Education* (New York: American Book Company, 1947), p. 311.

activities, when the aims and objectives are not clear and unachievable, when the program of studies are subjective and inappropriate, and when the methods and activities are unrealistic and meaningless, classroom discipline is inevitable. On the other hand, if the pupils are engaged in objective, realistic, understood, achievable, and meaningful activities or learning situations, the problem of discipline is minimized. There is no better way of assuring good discipline in the classroom than to keep the pupils busy throughout the whole period. Busy pupils will have little or no time to do mischief, or to create disturbance; hence, discipline problem is minimized. An active class rarely has persistent problems of discipline. When pupils find nothing interesting and meaningful to do, discipline problems are sure to appear. Favorable teaching-learning situation is conducive to good classroom discipline.

In creating a favorable teaching-learning situation for good discipline, the following points are suggested for its accomplishment:

1. The teacher should create an environment that is socially and emotionally pleasant, satisfying, and stimulating. Social and emotional environment is an important factor in learning.

2. The teacher should create an attitude or atmosphere that is conducive to learning. The ideal conditions for learning depend largely upon the attitude of the learner toward the educational programs and activities.

3. The teacher should create goals for the work of the pupils—goals which are meaningful and achievable. It is an accepted fact that meaningful goals beget motivation and bring about the desired behavior.

4. The teacher should create meaning in the materials and the activities the pupils will undertake. The most effective learning comes when the learners find meaning in the subject-matter they study and the activities they undertake.

Improving Classroom Discipline

In improving classroom discipline, it is well to keep in mind the saying that "an ounce of prevention is better than a pound of cure." The prevention of misconduct is certainly to be preferred to the correction of it. The former insures the smooth running of the school as well as the efficient learning of the pupils. The following preventive measures are suggested:

1. *Providing interesting activity for the pupils*—Interesting activity is the key-note to proper school discipline and it is undoubtedly the most important element in good teaching and learning. A pupil who is interested in his work has little or no time for idleness and mischief. Activities based on the pupil's experiences and interests should be introduced. Pupils enjoy activities in which they can participate with a hope of successful achievement. An active class or pupil rarely has serious or persistent problems of discipline. When pupils find nothing useful or interesting to do, problems of discipline are sure to appear.

2. *Providing proper motivation*—Sometimes, mental and physical fatigue many reach such a point as to neutralize temporarily a pupil's interest in his work. When such point is reached, the teacher can help keep every pupil mentally alert through proper motivation. The term motivation does not mean spectacular method of approach, but it does imply that the interests and abilities of the learner will be challenged. Teaching should be adjusted to the mental maturity of the learners, and each learner should be brought into the discussion of the lesson. To secure mental alertness the following incentives may be employed:

(a) Keeping every member of the class busy. Busy hands generally cause little trouble. It is believed that idleness breeds conduct difficulties.

(b) Holding every member of the class responsible for all the things taught in the classroom

3. *Making use of personality and personal influence and maintaining proper personal attitude*—We often see a teacher who seems to be endowed with some magic power for maintaining excellent discipline in the classroom. Teachers with pleasant personalities control their classes, not by physical force, but by the power of their personalities. A teacher's good personality may include his mastery of his subject; his confidence in his own ability; his faith and confidence in the good intentions of his pupils; his cheerful, pleasant, sympathetic attitude; a courteous and friendly treatment of his pupils coupled with fairness of judgment. Most often, the personal influence of the teacher over particular pupils is a powerful factor in controlling their conduct. Such is the example act by a few teachers of exceptional merit and ability, who have the power of inspiring loyalty and admiration among their pupils.

4. *Building up a school spirit*—Another way of securing good school discipline is to build up a school spirit. The essential characteristic of a good school spirit is an attitude of goodwill and cooperation. Pupil participation in class management and discipline has been much advocated as the best means of securing a feeling of responsibility on the part of the pupils for the welfare of the whole group, as well as for the exercise of self-control. The development of an attitude of goodwill and cooperation should be the goal of every classroom activity. To develop such an attitude, the teacher should turn the classroom into a workshop where the pupils have a good opportunity to work together under the wise guidance of the teacher.

5. *Conference with the pupil*—This means talking matters over with the pupil. A quiet, serious conference with the pupils, in which the wise teacher asks well-directed questions that lead the pupil to discover for himself the seriousness of his behavior, is the most effective way of correcting a fault constructively. Such a method will give the pupil a chance to explain his side of the case and will unable the teachers to understand the real nature of the offense; hence, establishing personal relations which should bring about mutual under-

standing. The open admission of one's guilt is in itself a wholesome corrective.

6. *Stimulation of group responsibility*—With older pupils, right conduct should be the result of group attitudes of approval and disapproval instead of being a primitive fear reaction. The teacher should direct the attention of the group to the necessity for cooperation among all if each one is to get the best results. When group offenses are committed, they may give excellent opportunities for the consideration of the problems of schoolroom ethics. Since rules are usually made for the good of the group, it might be well for young people to participate in the formulation of codes of behavior for the school. A school code worked out by the pupils under the wise guidance of the teacher is likely to be obeyed. A sort of cooperative government among pupils will also stimulate group responsibility.

7. *Correct attitude on the part of the teacher*—To be successful in discipline, a teacher must take the correct attitude toward the school situation. He should always look at problems objectively. Thus, he should not take an offence as a personal insult. The teacher who evinces genuine faith in the good intentions of the pupil will find that faith rewarded. The teacher should never administer punishment in the spirit of revenge, because he would thus violate a fundamental principle. Virtues, such as justice, sympathy, patience, and tact, that make up the ideal character, are valuable to the teacher. A study of the literature on this subject shows unanimity regarding the value of kindness and sympathy in the correction of undesirable behavior.

8. *Providing proper routine*—A teacher who provides the proper routine avoids many disciplinary problems. When the proper procedure has been outlined, there is little temptation to indulge in anything out of the way. Routine is frequently prescribed by means of rules. Rules should be few as possible and should all be based on the fundamental rule that whatever is done in school aim primarily to promote the welfare of the

school and of the class as a whole. To develop certain habits that grow into routine in the lives of the school children is satisfying not only to the teacher, but to the pupils, as well.

9. *Giving individual assignments* —Many disciplinary problems arise from the misconduct of the bright pupils who have completed the regular work assigned, Psychological findings reveal that bright pupils learn faster than the dull ones. Not having anything to do, they try to find something to do for the rest of the period. A teacher may give individual assignments to these pupils to keep them busy and, thereby, prevent the waste resulting from misdirected energy. Provision may be made for the bright pupils by placing a shelf of suitable books at their disposal. When they have completed their assigned task, they may reach for these books and read them. Children need both mental and physical activity. They become restless if they are denied the activity their developing bodies require.

Discipline in Relation to Good Teaching

Good discipline is closely related to good teaching. Rigid control of behavior is, by its very nature, wholly antagonistic to good teaching. Similar control in learning requires that everybody learns the same thing at the same time. In many classrooms, pupils sit where they are told, ask permission to speak or to move, and spend the class hour following the teacher's directions and answering his questions. Too often discipline is concerned with the means of compelling children to act in certain ways, to the neglect of a psychological analysis of the process and its effects. This sort of classroom discipline, this fettering of both mind and body, is out of place in the education of free men. Free men will not really be free if they are gullible and unquestinoingly obedient. Citizens who believe and do as they are told are especially susceptible to exploitation by economical and political vultures. Competent citizenship requires an alertness to personal justice and a concern for the general welfare, that should be exercised from the earliest years.

Many of the difficulties which teachers have with discipline are due to conflict between the psychological needs of pupils and unwise provisions or requirement in the classroom. Most prominent among these needs are the need for recognition and the need for activity that challenges the interest and ability of the pupil. It is therefore necessary that the discipline of both the home and the school should recognize the dignity of each individual and his right to seek recognition and direct his own activities. The problems of inappropriate responses are problems for guidance, for education, for coercion and punishment. The goal is not the person who will faithfully do as he is told, but the individual who is in the habit of seeking his own success, directing his own destiny and cooperation in improving the general welfare.

Keeping discipline in the classroom is a matter of directing and guiding the pupil's interest and energy. The keeping of order is a function of the teacher's ability to utilize fully the energy of the pupils. They should be kept busy all the time. The teacher's task is that of directing and guiding this energy into proper channels. He should not attempt to suppress its flow. If the pupils do not react to stimuli, they are not teachable. Instead of looking upon this manifestation of life and energy as something inimical to teaching, the teacher should look upon it as its opportunity. Of course, it is not easy to keep all pupils busy all the time. Even though the lesson is being taught perfectly, there will be exceptional instances in which pupils will disturb the class. There is the dull pupil who will not be interested in what is going on, because he does not understand. On the ether hand, there is the bright pupil who will have seen through the problem long in advance of the rest and who is likely to be the center of mischief. To meet the problem, extra work can be assigned to the bright pupils, but during the recitation most of the discussion must fit the capacities of the average students or the large middle group. Hence, disciplinary devices other than good teaching must be brought into play.

Corrective Measures Prescribed by the Bureau of Public Schools

The Bureau of Public Schools suggests an outline of approach for dealing with disciplinary cases.[7] Likewise, the Service Manual provides specific punishment for specific cases of breach of discipline as well as the ways of dealing with students facing disciplinary action.

1. *Suspension or Expulsion*—The Civil Service Manual of the Bureau of Public Schools gives the principal, the division superintendent of schools, and the Director of Public Schools, the power to suspend or expel pupils for serious misbehavior. The principal has the power to suspend a pupil for a period not exceeding three days without the prior approval of the division superintendent of schools, if the offense is committed for the first time and is not serious in character. Suspension of the pupil for more than 3 days, but not exceeding 30 days, requires the [approval] of the Superintendent. Suspension for a year or for the remainder of the school year is generally given for such offenses as : "theft, persistent cheating in class work, insubordination, the forging of school records, assaulting other pupils, gross indecency of language or conduct, or incorrigible misbehavior." Expulsion is ordinarily the punishment for such offenses as assaulting a teacher, participating in school strikes, gross immorality, or injuring other pupils with knives or other dangerous weapons.

2. *Corporal Punishment Prohibited*—While Filipino teachers are given ample power to enforce corrective discipline, they are, nevertheless, strictly prohibited from inflicting any form of corporal punishment. Any form of punishment such as slapping, pushing pupils about, imposing manual work as punishment, reducing scholarship ratings for bad conduct, subjecting a pupil to unnecessary ridicule, using expressions tending to destroy the pupil's self-respect, and the

7. *Bureau of Education, Bulletin No. 6, s.* 1947, "Suggested Outline of Procedure for the Study of Disciplinary Cases."

permanent confiscation of personal belongings of pupils, is strictly prohibited. Correctional punishment less severe than suspension is sometimes desirable and necessary for minor offenses.

In this country, school strike is considered a serious offense, and, therefore, strikers are given a heavy penalty. Pupils who take part in, or encourage school strikes, cannot be readmitted to school nor permitted to participate in any school activities without prior approval of the Director of the Bureau of Public Schools. The strikers, are however, given the privilege to present their petition to the school authorities concerned.

3. *Withdrawal of Privileges*—The Service Manual of the Bureau of public Schools recognizes as a corrective measure, apart from suspension or expulsion, the withdrawal from the pupil, temporarily or permanently, of the privilege of holding a position of honor or trust, of joining athletic competitions, and of participating in any school drama or play, or of being a member of any school clubs or societies. Only pupils who have good records and are well behaved are allowed to join such extra-curricular activities.

Thorndike, likewise, found by scientific means the effect of punishment in his extensive experiments on human learning. He found out that the result demonstrated a strong positive effect of reward, but not comparable negative effect of punishment. Thorndike, accordingly, revised his law of effect by assigning much greater weight to reward than to punishment.

Principles Governing the Handling of Disciplinary Problems

Experiences and a knowledge of the psychology of human reactions have led to some generally accepted principles that should govern the use of measures to correct undesirable behavior. There are no scientific studies available that have determined beyond doubt the values of various forms of corrective devices. The teacher must bear in mind that a corrective measure which may fit one particular situation perfectly may be inadequate in another situation. The effectiveness depends upon both the fitness of the measure and its wise use. The teacher should select from the devices recommended on the basis of his own experience.

1. *The teacher should be responsible for his own task of disciplining pupils.* Correction must not be done by proxy. It is a general practice of some teachers to refer their disciplinary problems to the principal. The teacher must assume his share of responsibility. His ability to settle his own disciplinary problems is an index of his efficiency. The more the teacher refers cases of discipline to his principal, the more he reveals his own weakness. The teacher should be careful not to send the offender to the principal until he has exhausted all of his own resources. Only disciplinary problems affecting the whole school should be referred to the principal, such as violation of school rules or regulations, destruction of school property, theft, and forging of the school records.

2. *The teacher should cooperate with the school administration in upholding and enforcing school regulations, and in maintaining siandards affecting disciplinary problems.* Disciplinary problems affecting the whole school system must not be ignored by the teacher. The teacher should cooperate with the principal or supervisor. In this way, both principal and teacher will understand each other better in the adjustment of school problems and can assist each other in carrying out a program of guidance aimed at the improvement of the pupils.

Likewise, the mutual cooperation between the parents and the teacher is desirable. The teacher should work cooperatively with parents. In this way, both the teacher and the parents can assist one another in carrying out a program of guidance aimed at the improvement of the individual concerned.

3. *The teacher should not punish the whole class for the wrong done by one pupil.* It is an unsound practice in a democratic society to punish all members of the group for the error made by a member of the group. It is a well-recognized fact in the field of jurisprudence that to shield the criminal makes the innocent an actual participant in the crime. In the confusion of the group, the individual who is the cause of it can be singled out.

4. *The teacher should approach disciplinary problems positively, not negatively.* The teacher should cultivate the habit of looking for, and emphasizing the brighter side of things. The teacher should not be extravagant with scolding nor should be stingy with praise when it is needed. A practice that should be carefully avoided is that of directing the pupils' attention to the bad behavior and by scolding the offender in their presence. This is detrimental to the total welfare as well as to the individual. The teacher should hold up good things for all to see, and maintain the pupils' respect through a pattern of justice and fair play. A pat on the back in the form recognition of the task well done will go a long way to sustain a pupil's self-respect. It may be well for every teacher to calculate his daily ratio of positive versus negative comments. It can be said that the teacher who takes an optimistic, friendly, and positive outlook toward life in general and life in the classroom in particular, has also taken a step to prevent some of the most basic and most persistent discipline problems.

5. *The teacher should not make the correction within the hearing of the other pupils.* Corrections must be made privately whenever practicable. Never humiliate a pupil in the presence of his equals when it can be avoided. When censure is necessary, it must be administered privately. It must be made outside the classroom. It is a sound educational practice to have a private conference with the pupil over matters that need correction. The teacher must always remember that individual transformation is the fundamental objective of discipline whenever misdeeds are considered. Correction

must be confidential. This concept is based on democratic principles. Shaming a pupil before the class will destroy respect for authority and will ruin the morale of the individual and of the group.

6. *The teacher should not attempt to settle any problem of discipline at the height of his anger.* When punishments have to be administered, they should be delayed until passion has subsided. No immediate corrective action should be taken under the stress of emotion as the result is oftentimes ineffective. The more tense the situation is, the more need there is for calmness on the part of the teacher. Anger must never be used as a means of control. The teacher should consider carefully the best means of dealing with the pupil. Recent studies in psychology reveal that emotion inhibits clarity of thought. Experience has shown that mistaken punishment often has its origin in the administering of punishment at the height of anger. Psychologically, anger is a sign of weakness that pupils detect and fear.

7. *The teacher should endeavor through a talk with the pupil to make clear to him the need for correction.* It is generally accepted that the most effective technique of behavior adjustment is the personal talk. The pupil's point of view is most important. The teacher will do well to stimulate the pupil to do as much of the talking as possible. It is necessary for the teacher to talk over with the pupil all phases of misdeeds so that the seriousness of the offense may be perfectly understood. By directing his attention to the cause of the trouble, the teacher gets an opportunity to correct the problem and to help the pupil to understand himself. The reason for his conviction should be made apparent to the offender. If possible, the pupil should be made to admit the need for correction. On the other hand, the teacher should keep in mind in all phases of disciplinary actions that the recognition of the fault and the admission of the need for its correction is a prime educational objective in character development.

8. *The teacher should treat the offender in terms of his*

social and economic states. A pupil with poor social and economic background, most often, cannot adjust with other pupils. The teacher should make it his business to know the name, habits, peculiarities, and social and economic background of everyone in his class. A pupil may have done mischief because he is just hungry. The pupil who is always in want finds it difficult to understand why he cannot have what he needs. Theft often begins when wants are so strong as to overcome any moral standards that approach the problem better. The teacher must explore every possible reason for the classroom behavior that steams at least indirectly from his social adjustments in and out of school.

9. *The teacher should adjust the correction to the nature of the offense and to the pupil concerned.* Behavior that carries serious implications affecting the well-being of society should be treated differently from behavior that is harmful but not serious. In the language of Bossing,[8] "an eye for an eye theory is, in some measure, necessary and desirable." In this case, a careful study of the case is essential. In making corrections, the nature of the individual must be taken into consideration. According to James, there are tough-minded and tender-minded individuals. Tender-minded individuals should be treated with patience and care.

10. *The teacher should never use corporal punishment as a solution to any disciplinary problem.* In the Philippine public schools, corporal punishment is strictly prohibited. We may say that it is desirable that an individual suffers for his misdeeds, but this does not imply that the form of punishment need cause physical pain. To average pupils, mental pain is more effective than physical pain as a corrective measure. The law of effect operates here. Every individual has a strong tendency to refrain from doing an act which is annoying and to repeat that which is satisfying.

8. Nelson L. Bossing, *Progressive Methods of Teaching in Secondary Schools*, Vol. I, Chicago: Houghton Mifflin Company, 1942. p. 140.

11. *The teacher, in handling disciplinary problems in and out of the classrooms, should always bear in mind the limitations on disciplinary impositions* upon the culprit as embodied in the Service Manual and in the various circulars issued by the Bureau of Public Schools. The teacher should know the existing rules and regulations which relate to discipline, and be governed by them.

12. *The teacher should be able to guide the pupils in setting up rules of conduct, and after the rules have been adopted, he should guide and direct the pupils in their observance.* The rules of conduct worked out by the pupils themselves under the wise guidance of the teacher are likely to be obeyed. Through their experience in formulating rules of conduct, the pupils find outlets for their youthful energy and learn to recognize the reason for the observance of school rules and regulations. The pupils thus receive worthwhile training in desirable citizenship in a democracy. The value of the procedure lies in the fact that the pupils become voluntarily disposed to adhere to the rules. This is utilizing the idea that the best kind of discipline is one that emanates from the pupils themselves.

13. *The teacher should show respect and kindness during the investigation.* Pupils have rights which should be respected and honored by the teacher or investigator. Pupils resent being treated with disrespect or being treated like criminals. The courteous and self-respecting teacher retains his dignity as he conducts an investigation. Sarcasm must be avoided in talking to the pupils. To gain respect, the teacher should talk with a kind, soft, and understanding voice. He gets more cooperative response when he appears calm, unperturbed, and casual, with a soft and kind voice that draws pupils to him. After the guilt has been established, the guilty must be treated respectfully and must be shown positive consideration. Self-respect must be maintained at all costs.

14. *The teacher should consider self-control as an ultimate*

goal of teaching. Self-control can be taught like the other subjects in the school curriculum. It is achieved through positive experience. A pupil who desires to be honest, respectful, courageous, dependable, and constructive, must acquire the ability to control himself. Self-control is taught and practised by those who would acquire it. The pupils should be given opportunity to practice self-control in the classroom and in out-of-school. To develop self-control, the pupils should be encouraged to take responsibility for doing things and to make them feel proud of their achievements.

15. *The teacher should see that punishment is reasonable and constructive.* The prohibitive types of punishment are prescribed in the Service Manual of the Bureau of Public Schools. Ii cannot be denied that it is most questionable whether any form of punishment in school is reasonable or constructive. The teacher should however, decide cases on the basis of things reasonable or constructive. Punishment is reasonable when it implies the use of good judgement based on facts, or harmonizing cause and effect of the offense committed. Constructive punishment is one that has educational value to the child. The teacher must conceive of discipline as constructive and as concerned with the development of those habits and attitudes that contribute to the social being of the pupil and the effective achievement of the aims and objetives of the school. Reasonableness and constructiveness are related to all types of punishment in school.

16. *The teacher should see to it that friendship with the offender is maintained.* It can be denied that correction of any kind represents an unfortunate situation, yet at the same time, both the teacher and the offender should recognize certain penalties for breach of established order. Likewise, both should maintain impersonal attitudes toward each other. As soon as the issue is settled the teacher should take the first step to reinstate the offender to good sanding by giving him something to do with the aim to restore former relationship. The teacher should try to set him at ease and put him

back in full standing with his classmates. The offender will admire the teacher for being sport, friendly, and kind. The spirit of sportsmanship and belongingness must be manifested by the teacher to set as example to the young.

GUIDE TO OBSERVATION ASSIGNMENT AND REPORT

Assignment for Observation

Aims :

1. To understand the problems of classroom management and discipline with particular reference to teaching.

2. To become acquainted with the principles governing classroom management and discipline.

Classroom management and discipline have different meanings but both have a decided influence upon teaching and learning situations. The success or failure of teaching is often determined by the way classroom management and discipline are handled. A well-managed classroom and a well-disciplined class will give the pupils rich opportunities for mental, physical, social, and moral growth. It must be remembered that effective teaching and learning are possible only in a well-managed classroom.

Class or Grade— — — — — Section — — — Date— — — —

Teacher observed— — — — — — — —Observer— — — — —

Go to the classroom assigned to you and observe the seating arrangement, the movement of the pupils to and from the classroom, and the collection of instructional materials. Note also the behavior of the pupils. As a result of your observation, be able to answer the following questions :

1. Were the instructional materials and other materials

passed to the pupils according to the routinized procedure ?

2. Were the pupils assigned to seats ? Outline a plan of checking up and correcting the seating arrangements in the room you visited.

3. List the additional routine you observed. Did the routine established by the teacher fit the present needs of the class ?

4. Did the teacher command the attention of the entire class ? Did you notice any sign of irritation on the part of the teacher during the recitation ?

5. Did you notice any specific device used by the teacher in classroom discipline ? Were the pupils free to talk with their classmates during the recitation ?

6. Did you notice any situations created by the teacher in which pupils were taught the following:

   (a) Cooperation

   (b) Respect for the opinions of others

   (c) Giving suggestions without hurting the feelings of others.

   (d) Utilizing criticisms effectively

7. What are your criticisms and suggestions for improvements?

SUGGESTED EXERCISES FOR STUDY AND DISCUSSIONS

Indicate whether these sentences are true or false (verify):

—— 1. Routine affairs in the school are important in classroom management and control.

—— 2. The monitorial system of management is undemocratic.

—— 3. For economy of time, it is well to routinize the passing of books and supplies.

—— 4. Good character traits can be developed through good classroom management and control.

—— 5. Classroom management is merely a matter of keeping order, and nothing more.

—— 6. In a democracy, it is desirable that all children's activities be put under rigid control.

—— 7. The teaching personality of the teacher has a weak influence in classroom control.

—— 8. Economical and effective management is essential to good teaching and learning.

—— 9. The function of classroom management is to set the stage for effective teaching and learning.

——10. Good classroom management is often the cause of disciplinary problems.

——11. Corporal punishment, scolding, and isolation are modern corrective devices for bad conduct.

——12. The teacher should be responsible for his own task of disciplining pupils.

——13. Discipline for the individual comes largely from without rather than from within.

——14. That he who governs least governs best is an unsound statement.

——15. To be effective, corporal punishment should be administered when one is angry.

——16. The psychological basis of routinizing activities is habit-formation.

——17. Constant nagging and harsh treatment of pupils lead to perfect control of the class.

——18. Effective classroom control needs a proper emotional setting.

——19. All activities in the classroom should be routinized for all children.

——20. In a democratic country, discipline should be made synonymous with character education.

——21. There are more problems of classroom management in small classes than in big classes.

——22. A feeling of inferiority leads a child to maladjustment.

——23. The primary purpose of classroom management is to eliminate waste of effort.

——24. A conference with pupils is recommended as an effective method of administering punishment

——25. Effective punishment is that which is already related to the offense committed.

——26. Making the child rewrite his lesson ten times is a good form of punishment.

——27. It is much better to have attention focused upon cause than upon effect.

——28. It is a wise practice to punish the class for the wrong done by the individual pupil.

——29. To be effective, corrective measures must be understood by all the pupils.

——30. Poor discipline is the greatest single cause of failure among new teachers.

——31. Reducing the grades of the pupil because of poor conduct is a sound educational practice.

——32. Mental pain, a punishment, is oftentimes more effective than physical pain.

——33. All disciplinary problems must be referred to the principal.

——34. Classroom management refers to the operation and control of classroom activities.

——35. Effective teaching and learning are possible only in a well-managed classroom.

——36. The complexity of our school system calls for routinization of classroom activities.

——37. Calling the names of the pupils is the most economical way of checking up on the class attendance.

——38. Modern discipline in the classroom is more regulative and less educative.

——39. Physical and mental defects complicate the problem of classroom discipline.

GUIDE QUESTIONS FOR STUDY

1. In what way do classroom management and discipline affect the teaching and learning process?

2. What are some advantages of routinizing classroom procedures?

3. What are the dangers of too much control in the classroom?

4. In this country, what are the main causes of poor discipline in the classroom?

5. What are some physical factors that bring about the disciplinary problems of the classroom?

6. In your opinion, what are the contributing causes of the disciplinary problems in the elementary schools? In the high schools?

7. Enumerate some principles that can be applied in handling disciplinary problems in the light of the modern conception of discipline.

8. What do you think are some of the corrective methods that can be used in disciplinary cases?

9. What should a teacher do to maintain a discipline that will interest the pupils and make them happy?

10. Do you believe in the use of corporal punishment in school? Support your answer.

REFERENCES FOR READING AND STUDY

Bossing, N.L., *Progressive Methods of Teaching in Secondary Schools.* Boston: Houghton Mifflin Company, 1942. Chapters 5 and 6.

Burton, W.H., *The Guidance of Learning Activities,* 2nd ed. New York: Appleton-Century Crofts, Inc., 1952. Chapter 22.

Bureau of Public Schools. *Circular No. 40, s. 1945, Circular No. 4, s. 1950.*

Crow, L.D., and A. Crow, *Introduction to Education.* New York: American Book Company, 1947. Chapter 13.

Douglas, H.R., *The Organization and Administration of Secondary Schools,* rev. ed. Boston: Ginn and Company, 1945. Chapter 11.

Grambs, J.D., and W.J. Iverson, *Modern Methods in Secondary Education.* New York: The Dryden Press, 1952. pp. 248-259.

Johnson, E.A., and R.E. Michael, *Principles of Teaching.* Boston: Allyn and Bacon Inc., 1958. Chapter 13.

Hymes, J.1.., Jr., *Behavior and Misbehavior.* New Jersey: Prentice-Hall, Inc., 1955.

Michaelis, J.U., and P.R. Grim, *The Student-Teacher in the Elementary School.* New Jersey: Prentice-Hall, Inc., 1953. pp. 150-170.

7
Teacher Status

Of all the different factors which influence the quality of education and its contribution to national development, the quality, competence and character of teachers are undoubtedly the most significant. Nothing is more important than securing a sufficient supply of high quality recruits to the teaching profession, providing them with the best possible professional preparation and creating satisfactory conditions of work in which they can be fully effective. In view of the rapid expansion of educational facilities expected during the next three Plans, and specially in view of the urgent need to raise standards to the highest level and to keep them continually improving, these problems have now acquired unprecedented importance and urgency.

A programme of high priority in the proposed educational reconstruction, therefore, is to feed back a significant proportion of the talented men and women from schools and colleges into the educational system. For this purpose, it is necessary to make an intensive and continuous effort to raise the economic, social and professional status of teachers in order to attract young men and women of ability to the profession, and to retain them in it as dedicated, enthusiastic and contented workers. This can be done, to a very limited extent only, through appealing to motives such as love of children or of teaching, interest in academic work or research, idealism and desire for social service, which attract a small proportion of able young persons to the teaching profession. There can, however, be no doubt that the provision of adequate remuneration, opportunities for professional advancement, and favourable conditions of service and work, are the major programmes which will help to initiate and maintain this 'feedback' process. We propose to discuss some important aspects of these programmes in the course of this chapter and the next.

Remuneration

The Post-Independence Period. In the post-Independence period, continuous efforts have been made to improve the remuneration of teachers at all levels and schemes for this purpose have figured prominently in all the Plans. But the net results achieved have not been adequate, particularly in respect of primary school teachers. This will be seen form Table 1.

It will be seen that the increase in the remuneration of the different categories of teachers is far from uniform. The largest proportional increase has taken place in the salaries of teachers in primary schools. But owing to the very low levels of remuneration which obtained in 1950-51, these are still far from satisfactory. The improvement in the salaries of teachers in the universities, vocational schools and colleges in also noticeable. But in the colleges of arts and science and in secondary schools, there has been an actual decrease in remuneration in real terms. The picture is worst at the per-primary stage because the salaries in pre-primary schools are governed, not so much by departmental regulations, as by 'market conditions. This is because most of the pre-school institutions are unaided and located in urban areas where an over-abundant supply of women teachers is available.

It will also be noted that a good deal of the effect of the increase in remuneration at all stages has been offset by the rise in the cost of living which has taken place during this period—the remunerations in the various types of institutions have risen by 18 to 92 per cent while the cost of living has risen by 65 per cent. It is only in four types of

TABLE 1

Average Annual Salaries of Teachers in India
(1950-51 to 1965-66)

Type of institutions	Average Annual salary of teachers (at current prices) in				Average annual salary in 1965-66 at 1950-51 prices
	1950-51	1953-55	1960-61	1965-66	
1	*2*	*3*	*4*	*5*	*6*
A. Higher Education					
1. University departments	3,759 (100)	5,456 (145)	5,475 (146)	6,500 (173)	3,939 (105)
2. Colleges of arts and science	2,696 (100)	3,070 (114)	3,659 (136)	4,000 (148)	2,424 (90)
3. Professional colleges	3,948 (100)	3,861 (98)	4,237 (10.)	6,410 (162)	3,885 (98)

B. Schools

4. Secondary schools	1,258 (100)	1,427 (113)	1,681 (134)	1,959 (156)	1,187 (94)
5. Higher primary schools	682 (100)	809 (119)	1,058 (155)	1,228 (180)	741 (109)
6. Lower primary schools	145 (100)	652 (120)	873 (160)	1,046 (192)	634 (116)
7. Pre-primary schools	914 (100)	770 (84)	925 (101)	1,083 (118)	656 (72)
8. Vocational schools	1,705 (100)	1,569 (92)	2,041 (120)	2,887 (169)	1,750 (103)
All Teachers	769 (100)	919 (120)	1,218 (158)	1,476 (192)	895 (116)
9. Cost of living index for working classes	100	95	123	165	

(Contd.)

TABLE 1 (*Contd.*)

1	2	3	4	5	6
10. National income per head of population (at current prices)	267 (100)	255 (96)	326 (122)	424 (159)	

Source: Ministry of Education, From A. The figures for 1965-66 are estimates made in the Commission Secretariat.

N.B. The figures within brackets give the index of growth on the basis of 1950-51=100.

institutions—vocational schools (69 per, cent), universities (73 per cent), higher primary schools (80 per cent) and lower primary schools (92 per cent) that the rise in remuneration has exceeded that in the cost of living. In some sectors, e.g., pre-primary, the increase in the cost of living has been greater than that in remuneration. On the whole, there was some improvement in the remuneration of teachers in real terms up to 1960-61. This has since been almost completely neutralized by the sharp increase in prices that has taken place in the last two or three years. This has, we are afraid, adversely affected the morale of teachers. In our opinion, the most urgent need is to upgrade the remuneration of teachers substantially, particularly at the school stage.

The Commission made a study of the remuneration of teachers in all the States and Union Territories. It revealed two major weaknesses:

(1) *Inter-State Differences.* There are substantial differences in the remuneration of teachers from State to State, particularly at the school stage; and

(2) *Intra-State Differences.* Even within a State, there are variations in remuneration. At the university stage, salaries vary from faculty to faculty. The teachers in affiliated colleges do not have the same scales of pay as those in universities. At the school stage, there are often substantial differences in the remuneration of teachers working in institutions under different managements.

There has been a strong demand for the abolition of these variations. It has been suggested that the first type of variation can be eliminated or reduced to the minimum by adopting national scales of pay with adjustment in allowances for inevitable local variations in the cost of living and that the second should be offest by adopting the principle of parity. Both these proposals need a closer examination.

National Scales of Pay. The demand for the introduction of national scales of pay for all categories of teachers is supported unanimously by teachers' organizations. We found that the proposal had a ready acceptance in higher education because of the developments in the post-Independence period. The University Education Commission recommended that the multiplicity of scales of pay which them existed in the universities and colleges should be reduced to the minimum and that an attempt should be made to adopt national scales of pay for teachers in higher education. This recommendation was broadly accepted and some action to implement it has since been taken. The UGC is attempting to introduce common scales of pay for different categories of teachers in the universities and similar scales of pay for teachers in affiliated colleges. Attempts for the introduction of common scales of pay are also being made, with a fair amount of success, in respect of engineering institutions. It is true that, in spite of all that has been done during the last ten years, there are still considerable variations in the scales of pay of teachers in higher education. But the important point is that the general principle of adopting national scales of pay has been broadly accepted; and all that is needed is to make a more determined effort to move forward on the lines already set. This is a comparatively simpler issue.

At the school stage, however, the problem is more difficult because the desirability of introducing national scales of pay at this stage is itself challenged. It is argued, for instance, that as the cost of living varies from one part of the country to another, a common national scale of pay would really imply unequal payment and cause considerable hardship to school teachers with lower levels of income. It is also pointed out that the supply and demand position for the different categories of teachers varies considerably from one part of the country to another. Women teachers, for instance, are readily available in some areas and are very difficult to obtain in others. Under these circumstances, it is pointed out that a common scale of pay would make it more difficult to recruit them in just those areas where they are most needed. There is some force in these arguments. But in our opinion, they only make out a case for providing local allowances in addition to basic national scales of pay rather than disprove the need to adopt minimum national scales of pay to reduce the large disparities that now exist in the salaries of school teachers in different States. We, therefore, recommend that, at the school stage, the Government of India should lay down the minimum scales of pay for school teachers. The States and Union Territories should then adopt equivalent or higher scales of pay to suit their local conditions.

The Principle of Parity. With regard to the intra-State differences, we recommend that the remuneration of teachers working under different managements should also be the same and that all teachers having the same qualifications and the same responsibilities should have the same, or at least similar, remuneration and conditions of work and service. The problem will have to be discussed separately for higher and school education.

(1) *Higher Education.* There is a good deal of disparity in the remuneration of teachers of different categories in higher education. For instance, the remuneration of teachers in different faculties is not the same: the teachers in the faculties of engineering and medicine are paid higher than those in the humanities. There is also a difference, in most parts of the country, between the salaries given to teachers in universities and those given to teachers in affiliated colleges. In many States, teachers in government colleges do not get the scales of pay given to university teachers, although their remuneration is often much better than that of teachers in affiliated colleges. We recommend that these differences should be reduced to the minimum and efforts made to eliminate them gradually.

(2) *School Teachers.* We recommend that the scales of pay of school teachers belonging to the same category but working under different managements such as government, local bodies or private organizations, should be the same. The existing variations are purely historical in origin. The administrative

authorities under the British did not wish to reduce the salaries of government servants; at the same time, they were anxious to keep salary costs down to a level which the economy could afford. Hence the salaries of teachers in local authority schools were deliberately fixed at a point lower than that for government teachers and those for teachers in private schools were fixed at a still lower point. This 'policy has had two unfortunate results: it has lowered the average wage for teachers in general, as teachers in government service were a very small minority; it has also introduced an undesirable 'caste' system among them. It is time to eliminate these relics of the past.

We are happy to note that a move in this direction has already been initiated and is well on the way. The principle of parity has been accepted at all levels of school education in seven States (Andhra Pradesh, Kerala, Madhya Pradesh, Madras, Mysore, Punjab and Rajasthan). In three States (Assam, Gujarat and Maharashtra) it has been accepted at the primary level, bat not at the secondary for all categories of teachers. In five States (Bihar, Jammu and Kashmir, Orissa, Uttar Pradesh and West Bengal) it has not been accepted at any stage and the scales of pay prescribed for teachers in non-government schools are different and much lower. Some illustrations of this are given in Table 2.

It will be seen that, in some cases, the differences are marginal while in others, they are serious and glaring.

Three main arguments are put forward for retaining this disparity in remuneration. The first is that the teachers in non-government schools are not well-qualified and not properly selected. We cannot accept this contention. Instead of perpetuating unequal remuneration on these grounds, it is essential to adopt the principle of parity in remuneration, and simultaneously to prescribe the same qualifications for teachers in all types of schools and to introduce a similar machinery for their recruitment. The second is that teachers in government service have certain handicaps such as liability to transfer, application of conduct and discipline rules, etc., and that

TABLE 2

Pay Scales for Teachers in Government and Non-Government Schools in Some States

State and category of teachers	Government institutions	Non-government institutions
1	*2*	*3*
Assam		
1. Principal of a higher secondary school	Rs. 350—1000 (starting salary of Rs. 450)	Rs. 250—600 (starting salary of Rs. 390)
2. Assistant teacher in high school (trained graduate)	Rs. 250—700	Rs. 125—270 (starting salary of Rs. 140)

(Contd.)

TABLE 2 (*Contd.*)

1	2	3
Bihar		
Matriculate trained teacher in a primary school	Rs. 115—200 (D.A. Rs. 5)	Rs. 50—90 (D.A. Rs. 30)
Orissa		
Assistant teacher (trained graduate) in a secondary school	Rs. 185—325	Rs. 175—300
West Bengal		
1. Headmaster of secondary school	Rs. 325—1000	Rs. 350—525
2. Assistant teacher in a secondary school with M.A./M.Sc./M. Com. & B.T.	Rs. 225—475	Rs. 210—450
3. Assistant teacher in a secondary school with B.A./B Sc., & B.T.	Rs. 175—325	Rs. 160—295

parity in remuneration would tilt the balance materially in favour of teachers in private schools. We do not agree with this view either. We are opposed to the idea of frequent transfers in government schools and have recommended that their teachers should, as for as possible, be localized. We do not support the restrictions on the academic freedom of teachers in government educational institutions and instead of compensating them for it in monetary terms, we have recommended the grant of academic freedom. There are bound to be some differences in conditions of service in government and non-government institutions. For instance, private educational institutions can provide a more satisfying experience to certain persons while teachers in government schools have better prospects of promotion. But in the proposals formulated by us, these ᵣdifferences have been reduced to the minimum and there is, therefore, no justification to continue the existing disparity of remuneration. The third argument put forward is financial and it is said that the funds needed to upgrade the salaries of teachers in local authority and private schools to the level of those in government schools are not readily available. We recognize the force of this argument and recommend that the principle of parity should be accepted as a State policy forthwith but that its full implementation should be spread over a phased programme of about five years.

Revision of Salaries. In making our proposals for the revision of the remuneration of teachers, we have kept the following principles in view:

(1) At the university stage, the remuneration of teachers should be broadly comparable with that of the senior services of the Government so that a fair proportion of the top talent in the country is attracted to the profession of teaching and research. What is important here is that the salary of a vice-chancellor should be about the same as that of a Secretary to the Union Government; the maximum salary of a university professor should be the same as the maximum in the senior scale of the IAS; and for outstanding professors, higher

salaries comparable to super-time scales of pay of the IAS should be available.

(2) The scales of pay of primary teachers should be comparable to those of public servants with similar qualifications and responsibilities. But they should have a higher basic pay in recognition of the two years of professional training which they have received.

(3) Since teaching is a unified profession, requiring common attitudes of devotion and dedication and since teachers at every stage are entrusted with the responsibility of educating the younger generation, the differences in the remuneration of the teachers at the different levels—primary, secondary and university—should be reduced to the minimum. For example, the minimum salaries of primary, secondary and university teachers should be in the ratio of 1 : 2 : 3. At present, the starting salary of a primary teacher can be as low as Rs. 60—80, which is about one-twelfth to one-sixteenth of the starting salary of a professor.

(4) In order to induce better qualified teachers to teach at the lower stages—the raising of educational standards will ultimately depend upon this—it is essential to adopt a policy under which the scales of pay of teachers at the school stage will be based only on qualifications and be made independent of the sub-stage—pre-primary, lower primary, higher primary, lower secondary or higher secondary—in which they might be serving. While we accept this idea in principle, it may not be possible, on financial grounds, to adopt it immediately *in toto*. We have, however, taken the view that at least the headmasters of all large lower primary schools (say, with an enrolment of about 200) and of all higher primary schools should be trained graduates and should have the same scale of pay as that of trained graduate teachers in secondary schools. Similarly, a certain proportion of the teachers at the secondary

stage should have the same qualifications and the same scales of junior lecturers in affiliated colleges.

(5) The improvement in salary scales should not be entirely automatic: it should be linked with the improvement in qualifications and quality.

Salaries of Teachers. In the light of these general principles, we propose the following scales of pay in Table 3.

We shall now turn to a discussion of these scales in some detail.

Reform at the University Stage. As a result of the recommendations of the University Education Commission and the work done by the UGC during the last ten years, considerable improvement has been made in regard to the scales of pay of teachers at the university stage. The multiplicity of scales which existed in the past has been reduced and the new scales adopted are more comparable to those in the senior administrative services of the Government of India. National scales of pay have been suggested for teachers in universities and in affiliated colleges and these are being increasingly adopted by the institutions concerned. We also welcome the recent decision of the Government of India, on the recommendation of the UGC, to sanction the new scales of pay for university teachers, which have been indicated above. The main points to be considered in this context, therefore, are two: (a) implementation of these proposals; and (b) relating them to improvement in quality and qualifications of teachers.

To facilitate the introduction of these scales at an early date, and especially in private institutions which are so numerous, we recommend that assistance from the Centre be provided to meet the additional expenditure on a sharing basis of 80 per cent from the Central funds and 20 per cent by the State Government and that, in the case of private colleges, the Central assistance may even be provided on a 100 per cent basis. Such assistance should continue during the Fourth Plan period; and, in the meanwhile, steps may be taken by the State Governments to devise an appropriate system of grant-in-aid for placing the revised scales on a permanent basis. Our proposals on this subject have been discussed elsewhere.

TABLE 3

Recommended Pay Scales for School Teachers

Teachers	Remuneration	Rs.
1	2	3
(1) Teachers who have completed the secondary course and have received two years of professional training	Minimum for trained teacher	150
	Maximum salary (to be reached in a period of about 20 years)	250
	Selection grade (for about 15 per cent of the cadre)	250—300

N.B. The minimum salary of a primary teacher who has completed the secondary course should be immediately raised to Rs. 100; and in a period of five years, it should be raised to Rs. 125. Similarly, the minimum pay of a teacher, who has received two years of training, should be raised immediately to Rs. 125; and it should be raised to Rs. 150 in a period of five years. Untrained persons with the requisite academic qualifications should work on the starting salary until they are trained and become eligible for the scale.

(2) Graduates who have received one year of professional training — Minimum for trained graduate — 220

Maximum salary (to be reached in a period of 20 years) — 400

Selection grade (for about 15 per cent of the cadre) — 400—500

N.B. Untrained graduates should remain on their starting, salary of Rs. 200 p.m. until they are trained and become eligible for the scale.

(3) Teacher working in secondary schools and having postgraduate qualifications — 300—600

N.B. On being trained, they should get one additional increment.

(4) Heads of secondary schools — Depending upon the size and quality of the school and also on their qualifications, the headmasters should have one or other of the scales of pay for teachers in affiliated colleges recommended below.

(Contd.)

TABLE 3 (*Contd.*)

1	2	3
(5) Teachers in affiliated colleges	Lecturer—Junior scale Senior scale	300—25— 600 400—30— 640 —40— 800
	Senior Lecturer/Reader I II III Principal	700— 40—1100 700— 40—1100 800— 50—1250 1000—50—1500

N.B. The Proportion of lecturers in the senior scale to those in the junior scale should be progressively improved. By the end of the Fith Plan, this proportion should be raised to about 75% on an average.

1	2	3
(6) Teachers in university departments	Lecturer	400—40—800— 50— 950
	Reader Professor	700—50—1250 1100—50—1300 —60—1600

N.B. (1) The proportion of junior to senior posts (i.e. Readers to Professors) is about 3 : 1 at present in the universities (the corresponding ratio for affiliated colleges is 5 : 1). We should gradually move in the direction of raising it to 2 : 1.

(2) One-third of the professors should be in the senior scale of Rs. 1600—1800. Special scales should be introduced for exceptionally meritorious persons and in selected Centres of Advanced Studies.

Note :

(a) The above scales of pay for school teachers are at the current price level and include the existing dearness allowance. Suitable increases will, however, have to be made for rise in prices from time to time. For this purpose, there should be parity in dearness allowance, i.e., the dearness allowance in any given year should be the same as it is paid to government servants drawing the same salary.

(b) All scales of pay should be periodically reviewed and revised at least once in five years.

(c) Compensatory cost of living allowance given in cities, house-rent allowance or other allowances are *not* included. These will be in addition to the salary recommended above and should be given on a basis of parity.

(d) The scale of pay are to be integrally related to the programmes of qualitative improvement of teachers through improved methods of selection, and improvement in general and professional education.

(e) The scales are to be given to all teachers - government, local authority or private.

(1) *Teachers in Universities.* In regard to the qualifications and selection procedures for university teachers, we agree with the recommendations made by the Model Act Committee which we quote for ready reference:

The standard and quality of work of a university depends very largely on the quality of its teachers. It is most important that every care is exercised by the authorities concerned so that teachers of the highest competency are recruited by the universities. Also the conditions of service and opportunities for professional advancement should be such as would attract and retain in the service of the universities men of outstanding ability. The power to appoint teachers must be vested in the Executive Council, but all the teaching appointments should be made by the Executive Council only on the recommendation of a properly constituted Selection Committee. The Selection Committee should consist, besides the Vice-Chancellor and the Head of the Department concerned, of a certain number of experts. This number may vary in accordance with the category of teachers to be appointed. For a professor, it should be necessary to have two or even three outside experts. It may be an advantage to have one nominee of the Chancellor/Visitor on the Selection Committee. The Court of the Academic Council should not select a representative to the Selection Committee. It should be a clear rule that the Executive Council should accept the selection unanimously recommended by the Selection Committee. In rare cases; if for good reasons for Executive Council is unable to accept the recommendation of the Selection Committee, efforts for a better selection may be renewed in the following year. A great deal of what is described as university politics or interference of outside politics in universities arises in connection with appointments. Universities must have the freedom to make their own appoints; but they must be steadfast in their desire to make right appointments.[1]

1. *Report of the Committee on Model Act for Universities,* Ministry of Education, Government of India, 1964, pp. 23-4.

(2) Our attention has been drawn to the fact that, in most universities, candidates for appointment as professors are called for interview before a selection committee. Each candidate is interviewed by the committee for 10 to 15 minutes. We are definitely of the view that, in the case of such high level appointments, interviews have hardly any meaning, and, in fact, tend to discourage first-rate men from offering for such appointments. Professors should be persons of standing in the subjects and should be known to the experts by reputation in the fields of their work. It should, therefore, be possible for a selection committee to make a selection on the basis of a careful consideration of the information supplied by the candidates and other relevant data which may be available to the committee. If considered necessary, candidates who have been found suitable for appointment by the selection committee may be invited by the vice-chancellor for a personal discussion before making a formal offer of appointment.

(3) *Teachers in Affiliated Colleges.* The procedure described above will also apply to university colleges. Problems do not generally arise with regard to government colleges where recruitment is done through a Public Service Commission. In private affiliated colleges, however, the situation needs considerable improvement on the following lines:

(a) The qualifications of teachers in these colleges should be prescribed by the universities and should be similar to those prescribed in university departments.

(b) Each post should be advertised and selection committees should be formed on the lines recommended above for the universities.

(c) On the advice of the selection committee, the appointment should be made by the managing committee constituted for the college. As recommended by the Model Act Committee, the managing committee should be a compact body consisting of about 10 members. The composition of this body should be prescribed by the university. The principal of the college should be a member of this body and in addition there should be provision for one or more teachers to be on it, preferably by some method of rotation rather than by election. The university should nominate to the governing body two representatives who should normally be teachers of experience.[2]

(d) If any exemption is to be given at all from the possession of the prescribed qualifications, it should not be for more than a year or two. Even when circumstances demand that the exemption should last for a longer period, such exemption given for a temporary period should not lapse into permanent exemption. It is unfair to admit students to a course unless there are qualified teachers.[3]

(e) While the right to make appointments should vest in the colleges, it should be open to the university to withhold 'recognition' of colleges, if persons with high qualifications are rejected without adequate reasons and others with lower qualifications, even though satisfying the minimum requirements, are appointed. In some of these cases this happens because the institution is, either openly or without avowing it, a narrowly denominational institution. In other cases it may just be a case of improper exercise of patronage by the managing body or it may be due to extraneous pressures.[4]

(f) We further recommend that it would be desirable to adopt a discriminating approach between one private management and another. Where good standards are maintained and the management has shown its

2. *Report of the Committee on Model Act for Universities*, Ministry of Education, Government of India, 1964, p. 28.
3. *Ibid.*, p. 28.
4. *Ibid.*, p. 28.

competence to conduct the institution satisfactorily, greater freedom should be given to it in the choice of its teachers. Where the management is not satisfactory, greater control should be exercised.

Pay Scales for School Stage.   As compared to higher education the problem of improving the remuneration of teachers at the school stage is more complex and difficult.   It is also far more urgent.   This urgency has increased because Government has recently sanctioned new scales of pay for teachers in higher education and thus increased the gap, which was already large, between their salaries and those of the school teachers.

Our first proposal is that the existing multiplicity of scales of pay should be reduced and that there should be three main scales of pay for school teachers:

(1) A scale of pay for teachers who have completed the secondary course and are trained and who would form the vast bulk of teachers at the primary stage;

(2) A scale of pay for trained graduates who would form a small proportion of teachers at the primary stage but the vast bulk of teachers at the lower secondary stage;

(3) A scale of pay for teachers with postgraduate qualifications who would form a small proportion of teachers at the lower secondary stage, but the bulk of teachers at the higher secondary stage.

Incentives to teachers of special subjects or to teachers with additional qualifications can be given in the form of advance increments or special allowance.   The scales of pay of special teachers (i.e. for drawing, craft, physical education, etc.) can also be related to these three basic scales in some suitable manner. The scales of pay for librarians should also be related to those for teachers in a suitable manner.

Scales of Pay of Teacher Who Have Completed the Secondary

Course. With regard to this category of teachers, we make the following recommendations :

(1) There should be no teacher at the primary stage who has not completed the secondary school course and has not had two years of professional education.[5]

(2) In so far as teachers who have completed the secondary school course are concerned, we recommend the following scales of pay :

(a) The minimum pay of a primary school teacher who has completed the secondary school course should be Rs. 100. This minimum should be given effect to immediately; and within a period of five years, it should be raised to Rs. 125.

(b) The minimum pay of primary school teachers who have completed the secondary school course and are trained, should be Rs. 125; and within a period of five years, it should be raised to Rs. 150.

(c) The following scales of pay should be adopted, as soon as practicable and at any rate not later than the first year of the Fifth Plan, for all primary school teachers who have completed the secondary school course and are trained :

Starting salary	Rs. 150
Maximum salary (to be reached in a period of 20 years)	Rs. 250

5. There is one exception to this rule. As stated already, the head-masters of all higher primary schools and of lower primary schools with an enrolment of more than about 200 should be trained graduates. The salaries of trained graduates working in the above posts at the primary stage should be the same at those of trained graduates working in secondary schools. This will be discussed in the following section.

Selection grade available for 15 per
cent of the cadre   Rs. 250
                                          to 300

Note

(i) The scale should be the same for all qualified and
trained teachers working at all the sub-stages—pre-
primary, lower primary or higher primary—and, in
accordance with the principle of parity, should also
be given to teachers in local authority and private
schools.

(ii) Only the scales of pay of qualified and trained primary
teachers are to be upgraded substantially. The scales
of pay of the other categories of primary teachers need
not be upgraded to the same extent. It should be
an objective of administrative policy to keep them substantially lower so that the teachers would have an
adequate incentive to improve their general and professional qualifications.

(iii) To expression 'trained' should be interpreted to mean
teachers who have had two years of professional
education.

In other words, these improvements in remuneration will
be linked with improvement in the quality and qualifications
of primary teachers. The principal method to be adopted to
raise the average remuneration of primary teachers will be to
organize an intensive programme of raising the qualifications
of teachers in service, as described in the next chapter, and to
eliminate, in a phased programme spread over a period of
about ten years, all teachers other than those who are qualified
and trained.

(3) Our attention has been drawn to an anomaly which
must be removed as early as possible. Several States restrict,
on financial grounds, the number of posts which carry the

salary scale of trained teachers who have completed the secondary school course. The remaining posts are usually assigned to lower scales of pay sanctioned for teachers with lower qualifications. Not infrequently, persons with lower qualifications are recruited to these posts even when qualified and trained teachers are available. This is bad enough; but what is worse, even trained and qualified teachers who are recruited against the posts are given, *not* the salaries of qualified and trained teachers to which they are entitled, but the lower salaries meant for these posts. As the completion of secondary school course and two years of professional training are accepted as the minimum qualification for a primary teacher, this practice should be abandoned as early as possible and the principle adopted that every trained teacher who has completed the secondary school course receives the scale of pay sanctioned for such teachers. This will remove an injustice now being done to a large number of teachers in service, and create an incentive for unqualified or untrained teachers to become qualified and trained.

Scales of Pay of Teachers in Secondary Schools. At present, the scales of pay of teachers at the secondary stage are fixed in a rather haphazard manner and scales of remuneration do not always show a clearly integrated picture from primary school to the university. Some definite principles in fixing their pay scales and relating them to the scales of pay of primary school teachers on the one hand and those of the university teachers on the other must be followed. In this context, we suggest the following :

(1) The scales of pay fixed for headmasters of lower and higher secondary schools should have a definite relationship with those of the teachers an affiliated colleges or even in universities. Depending upon the quality, size and function of the school and the qualifications of the person concerned, the salary scales of the headmasters of lower secondary schools should be the same as those of junior or senior lecturers or readers. In the higher secondary schools, the principals

or headmasters should be entitled to the scales of pay of a reader and, in some selected institutions, even to that of a professor. This would help to lessen the gap between salaries at the school and university levels.

(2) On the basis of their general education, the assistant teachers in secondary schools can be divided into two categories: graduates and those with postgraduate qualifications. The relative proportions of these two categories should be definitely prescribed. We recommended that, depending upon the size, function and quality of school, the proportion of teachers with postgraduate qualifications should vary from about 10 to 30 per cent. It may be pointed out that by 'postgraduate' qualifications we mean the same type and level of qualifications as are prescribed for junior lecturers in affiliated colleges. Teachers with other postgraduate qualifications should be fitted in the scale of pay for graduate teachers in a suitable manner.

(3) The scales of pay of trained graduate teachers should have a minimum of Rs. 220 rising to Rs. 400 in a period of about 20 years. There should be a selection grade which would rise to Rs. 500 and be available to about 15 per cent of the cadre.

(4) Teachers with postgraduate qualifications in higher secondary schools should have the same pay scales as those of junior lecturers, i.e., Rs. 300 – 600, since their academic qualifications will be the same. They should be given one increment when trained.

(5) Teachers with first or second class in B.A./B.Sc. or M.A./M.Sc. should be given advance increments in the above scale. An advance increment should also be given to those who are M.Eds.

(6) Professional training should be obligatory for all

secondary school teachers. It should preferably be taken before first employment. Exceptions may be made in the case of teachers with postgraduate qualifications and of first and second class graduates. They may be untrained at the time of appointment but should take professional training within three years. All untrained teachers, however, shall remain on their own starting salary and be integrated into the regular scale of pay only after professional training.

The effect of these proposals can be appreciated in relation to the existing situation. The Commission carried out a study of the emoluments of school teachers in 29 districts (out of a total of 312) and its relevant findings are shown in Table 4.

TABLE 4

Emoluments of School Teachers in 29 Districts (1965)

	Percentage of Teachers		
Emoluments per month	*Lower primary*	*Higher primary*	*Secondary*
1	2	3	4
Rs. 60 and less	2.2	2.3	
60–80	15.7	4.9	
81—100	29.9	14.1	4.3*
101—120	25.4	19.3	9.1
121—140	22.1	31.1	13.2
141—160	2.9	13.0	17.6
161—180	1.2	6.0	11.7
181—200	0.3	6.5	9.7
201—220	0.3*	1.2	6.5
221—240		1.0	6.3

1	2	3	3
241—260		0.5	5.2
261—280		0.2	4.7
281—300		0.1	4.4
301- 320		0.1*	1.9
321—340			1.7
341—360			1.1
361—380			0.7
381—400			0.5
401—420			0.8
421—440			0.2
441—460			0.2
461—480			0.0
481—500			0.1
Above 500			0.1
	(100.0)	(100.0)	(100.0)
n	94,434	30,624	17,707
N	1,329,544	431,158	249,298

*The figures represent 'Rs. 201 and above' in the case of lower primary teachers; 'Rs. 301 and above' in the case of higher primary teachers; and 'Rs. 100 and less' in the case of secondary teachers.
'n' indicates the number of teachers included in this study.
'N' represents the total number of teachers in the category concerned.

Recruitment of School Teachers. As at the university stage, the improvement in the salaries of school teachers must be linked with an improvement in their qualifications and methods of recruitment. The responsibility for this will be on the State

Education Departments. The qualifications of teachers will have to be prescribed by the State Board of School Education and the Education Departments would have to devise proper procedures for their recruitment. Our recommendations regarding the qualifications of school teachers have been given above. In the light of these and in view of local conditions, we trust that the State Board of School Education would prescribe the qualifications for primary and secondary teachers in all schools—government, local authority or private. With regard to methods of recruitment, we make the following suggestions :

(1) *Government Schools.* The existing methods of recruitment are satisfactory.

(2) *Local Authority Schools.* With regard to local authority shools, we recommended in Chapter X the constitution of district school boards which will remain in charge of all school education within a district. They will recruit the teachers required for their schools through selection committees consisting of a representative of the district school board, the District Education Officer or his representative, and a panel of two or four persons as may be prescribed by Government.

(3) With regard to *private schools*, the existing position leaves much to be desired and the recruitment procedures will have to be tightened on the lines recommended earlier for affiliated colleges. Every school recognized and aided by the State Education Department should be required to have a managing committee on which there would be representatives of the Department. The Department should also prescribe the qualifications for teachers which should be similar to those in government institutions. Every post to be filled should be adequately advertised and interviews should be held by a selection committee duly constituted by the managing committee and having on it one or more experts, depending upon the importance of

the post. A report on the applications received, interviews held and final selection made should be submitted to the Department for approval. As in the case of private affiliated colleges, it will be necessary to leave the authority to appoint teachers with the managing committees of the schools. But unless a teacher is appointed after the procedure prescribed above is followed and approval is obtained, no grant-in-aid should be paid on his salary, and there should be no hesitation in withholding such approval. A discriminating approach will have to be adopted and greater freedom in these matters should be allowed to good and efficient managements while those which fail to maintain standards or leave room for malpractices should be controlled more rigorously.

Promotional Prospects. Unfortunately, promotional prospects for teachers are poor at almost all stages, and it is this aspect, rather than the scales of pay as such, that often deters talented persons from joining the profession. Steps should therefore be taken to see that good promotional prospects are provided at all stages of education, not only for improving qualifications, but for rewarding good teaching. For this, we make the following proposals :

(1) *School Stage.*

(a) Qualified and trained teachers in primary schools should be considered for promotions to higher posts as headmasters or inspectors of schools, ordinarily meant for trained graduate teachers. About ten to fifteen per cent of these posts should be reserved for such promotions.

(b) Similarly, trained graduate teachers who have done outstanding work as teachers should be eligible for promotion to ten to fifteen per cent of the posts carrying salaries of teachers with postgraduate qualifications.

(c) It should be made possible for school teachers who show the necessary aptitude and competence to be appointed as university teachers. To help in this, the UGC should give *ad hoc* grants to outstanding school teachers to do research into problems of interest to them and incidentally to qualify themselves for work at the universities.

(d) Scales of pay spread over twenty years cover too long a period. It would be desirable to introduce a system under which teachers obtain advance increments for outstanding work. About 5 per cent of teachers should be able to reach the top of the scale in about ten years, and another 5 per cent in about 15 years.

(2) *University Stage.* The following measures may be considered :

(a) An *ad hoc* temporary post in the higher grade should be created for a lecturer or a reader who has done outstanding work and who cannot be given his well-earned promotion because no suitable posts are vacant. He should then be absorbed against an appropriate permanent post as soon as it becomes available. Before such promotions are made, the work of the persons concerned should be evaluated by a specially constituted expert committee and the approval of the UGC obtained. An arrangement of this type already exists in rhe CSIR and ICAR.

(b) In some departments where outstanding work is done, the number of posts at the professor's level should be determined on the requirements of the department and should not be arbitrarily restricted to one.

(c) If the services of an outstanding person are to be retained or obtained at the professorial level, it should be open to the university concerned, in consultation with the UGC, to offer a suitable remuneration even beyond the special scale of Rs. 1,600—1,800. Each case should be considered on its merits and considerable elasticity should be permitted in fixing salaries.

Relating Salaries to Costs of Living. Two other points which have often been raised in the discussions with us, deserve notice. The first of these relates to the adjustment in salaries consequent upon a rise in prices. It has been suggested that, after salaries have been revised adequately in line with present price-levels, a mechanical formula should be adopted to adjust them to future movements in the cost of living, as has been done, for instance, in the case of industrial workers. While we realize the need to link salaries with the cost of living we think that this can be better done through the principle of parity. We have recommended that all salaries of teachers should be reviewed every five years; and we have also recommended the principle of parity under which the dearness allowance to be paid to all teachers should be related to that of government servants. This will ensure adequate adjustments of salaries and allowances to movements in cost of living.

Welfare Services. A large number of suggestions have been put forward with a view to providing certain welfare services to teachers such as grant of free housing, free education for children, and free or subsidized medical facilities. While suggestions of this kind may serve as transitional measures until adequate salary scales are adopted, we do not think that an emphasis on such marginal benefits is the right approach to an equitable solution of the problem. The best course would be to pay to the teachers adequately so that no special benefits of this type need be offered.

One important proposal, however, needs consideration. This relates to the need to organize a general programme of welfare services for all school teachers in each State or Union Territory. The funds for this programme should be jointly raised, teachers contibuting 1½ per cent of their salaries and the State contributing an equal amount. The entire amount thus raised should be administered by committees consisting of representatives of teachers and Government. There should be a State level committee to decide a broad policy, and district level committees to operate the fund in accordance with the general policies laid down. The fund could be utilized for grants for purchase of books and equipment, travel grants, scholarships for education of children, suitable assistance in case of serious sickness or disaster, and such other unforeseen calamities. When such a general welfare fund is created for each State or Union Territory, the existing teachers' welfare fund set up by the Government of India may be advantageously merged with it.[6]

Financial Implications. An obvious objection to these proposals for improvement of remuneration can be taken on financial grounds. It may be argued that, at the present and proposed levels of expansion of education, the country does not have the resources to adopt these scales of pay. We realize that the increase recommended by us will lead to a substantial increase in educational expenditure. But unless the salaries are upgraded to these or even better levels and unless a feedback process is properly initiated and maintained, it will not be possible to improve standards, and education would be unable to make a significant contribution to national development. The future of education and consequently of the nation is at stake and the price must be paid. We believe that we can and should find the funds needed.

A study of the salary structure in educationally advanced countries reveals some interesting points. In some countries, e.g., the USSR, teaching is among the best professions. In most of them, a wage comparable with other professions is assured. Salaries at the university level are generally high

6. We recommended that these services should also be extended to university teachers. From this point of view, they should be permitted to join a common programme to be organized for all teachers on a State basis. In the alternative, each university may organize a welfare fund for its teachers on the above lines.

enough to attract a reasonable proportion of the best talent in the country. The gap between the salaries of university and school teachers is narrow. Even the highest salaries show a reasonable relationship to the national dividend; and the salary is related, not so much to the institution in which the teacher works, as to his qualifications. It is because of these factors that these countries can support a large expansion of education and also attract a fair proportion of talented persons to the teaching profession.

The recognization of the salary structure for teachers on these lines is not generally feasible in a developing country where the general situation is exactly the opposite. For instance,

—the salaries of teachers are high with reference to the national dividend;

—the salaries of teachers compare unfavourably with those of other public servants which are even higher; and

—there are wide differences between the salaries of teachers at different levels.

The basic reason for this situation is that the salaries of the superior ranks in government service are fixed very high and without any reference to the economic capacity of the people. The origin of this is often purely historical, as in our own country. Under the imperial regime, the salaries of the superior government servants were fixed, not in relation to the national dividend of the Indian people, but with reference to salaries prevailing in England. Consequently salaries of the superior government servants (who were mostly Englishmen) came to be far above the economic capacity of the Indian people. Even when Indians were recruited to government services, these salaries were not reduced because it was not politically expedient to make any marked distinction between them and the expatriate officers. Hence the salaries of government servants as a class came to be fixed at a much higher level than what the country could afford. This position did not create any difficulties so long as the total volume of governmental services was limited. But it soon became the main bottleneck preventing the proper development of all social services in general and of education in particular. A solution was, therefore, attempted by the adoption of three questionable devices :

— Even in government service, the teachers were paid lower than other categories of employees who had the same (or even inferior) qualifications and responsibilities;

— The bulk of the educational enterprise was placed, not in the public or State sector, but under local bodies and in the private sector;

— The principle of parity was rejected and teachers in local authority and private schools were paid at lower rates.

We have recommended that these devious methods should be given up forthwith. If this is done and all teachers are to be paid adequately and on the basis of parity, there are only two ways in which the problem can be solved : either the salaries of all government servants should be reduced—which cannot be done unless all incomes are regulated—or the expansion of education will have to be restricted. Since the latter is neither desirable nor possible, the basic dilemma becomes clear : the State is not able to regulate all incomes and reduce the salaries of other public servants, and it does not have the money to give justice to teachers by raising their salaries to a level comparable to that of other Government servants.

The only rational way out of the situation would be to revise all salaries and base them, not on the historical legacies of the past, but on our needs for services and the economic capacity of our society to bear the financial burden. This would imply a substantial downgrading of many salaries and a drastic levelling down of other incomes. If such attempts were made, teachers would be ready to play their part, although they resist, and rightly so, any attempt to keep their salaries only at a lower level.

Need for Central Assistance. Before leaving this subject, we would like to stress two points. The first is the urgency of the problem. The need for improving the salaries of the school teachers in a big way is justified fully on its own merits and has become urgent, partly because of the programme of educational improvement we have in view and partly because of the rise in the cost of living. This urgency has been heightened by the recent revision of the salaries of university teachers which has widened the existing disparities even further. We, therefore, recommend that the proposals made by us regarding the improvement of salaries of school teachers should be given effect to immediately. The second point relates to central assistance. During the first three Plans, almost every State Government revised the salaries of teachers more than once and the assistance of the Central Government was made available, in some form or other, for most of these revisions because the expenditure on these programmes was always treated as a 'plan outlay'. The salaries of teachers are very much on the low side at present and the effort needed to raise them to satisfactory levels is huge, partly because of the size of the increment and partly because of the numbers involved. We are afraid that the State Governments will not be able to deal with this very significant problem quickly and adequately unless Central assistance is made available on a generous basis. We, therefore, recommend that liberal Central assistance should be given to State Governments for improving the salaries of school teachers as recommended by us. Whether this assistance is given to them through the Plans or outside the Plans is not really an important issue, although we are of the view that the existing practice of including this expenditure within the Plan should preferably be continued.

Retirement Benefits

Principle of Uniformity. Of the various schemes for retirement benefits now in force, probably the best is that provided by the Government of India for its employees. This includes a death-cum-retirement gratuity, pension or gratuity, depending upon the length of service performed, and a family pension. State Governments are now adopting it with certain modifications for their own employees but there are various differences between the benefits given to employees of the Central Government and those given to the employees of the State Governments. Similarly, no attempt is being made to extend the scheme to teachers in local authority and private schools. We see no justification for these variations and recommend that the system of retirement benefits to teachers should be based on the principles of uniformity and parity. The principle of uniformity implies that retirement benefits should be uniform for all government servants— Central and State; and the principle of parity implies that retirement benefits given to teachers working in educational institutions conducted by local authorities and private organizations. The introduction of such uniformity and parity would not involve any large increase in expenditure and would be easier to adopt than even parity in remuneration.

Retirement Benefits for School Teachers, Interim Measures : While this is the ideal towards which administrations should move, some alternative transitional solutions to the problem may have to be adopted. With regard to school teachers, we make the following recommendations :

(1) *Age of Retirement.* For government teachers, the age of retirement is 58 years in some cases, 55 years (with provision for extension up to 58) in others and in one State (West Bengal), 60 years. The same rules generally apply to teachers in local authority schools. For private school teachers, the age of retirement varies, from area to area, from 55 to 58 years and even to 60 years. In

Bihar it is 62 years. In Orissa, there is no age limit for retirement and a person can work as long as he is physically fit. Until provision for adequate pension is made, it is desirable to provide for a higher age limit for retirement. We recommend that the normal retirement age for teachers should be 60 years; and there should be provision for extension up to 65 years provided the person is physically fit and mentally alert to discharge his duties efficiently.

(2) *Retirement Benefits*. The teachers in government schools are provided with pension, gratuity and family pension in most States. In others, provision is made for provident fund and insurance. The Union Territories generally offer the same benefits as are given to the employees of the Central Government.

With regard to teachers working in non-government schools; most of the States provide a contributory provident fund only. Recently, however, the Triple-Benefit Scheme, which provides for provident fund, pension and insurance, is becoming popular. Originally introduced in Madras, it has now been adopted in Andhra Pradesh (without insurance), Assam, Bihar, Kerala, Mysore and Uttar Pradesh. In addition, Kerala offers the same retirement benefits for teachers in non-government schools as are given to teachers in government schools, provided the former opt for the conduct and discipline rules applicable to government servants and renounce the right to participate in elections. West Bengal provides only provident fund and gratuity. The Ministry of Education has drawn up a Triple-Benefit Scheme for teachers in non-government schools which is now being adopted in the Union Territories. In view of the progress already made, we recommend that, as an interim measure, the Triple-Benefit Scheme should be adopted for all teachers in non-government schools in all States and Union Territories.

The interest on the provident fund amounts of school teachers is now generally paid at 4 per cent per year. It should be much higher. There are also some other problems connected with its administration. We shall discuss these in some detail in the next section with reference to teachers in higher education.. The same recommendations should be extended, *mutatis mutandis,* to the provident fund of the school teachers also.

Retirement Benefits for Teachers in Higher Education : *Interim Measures.* The retirement age for teachers in higher education is ordinarily 60 years, with provision for extension generally up to 65 years. and in a few cases, even up to 70 years. Most of the universities offer a contributory provident fund only. The rate of contribution is generally 8⅓ per cent of the basic pay. Some universities permit the teacher to contribute up to 15 per cent of his pay and their own contribution is credited, depending upon the salary, at 8 to 12 per cent. Some provide for gratuity in addition to contributory provident fund. In Madras, the Triple-Benefit Scheme has been extended to university and college teachers. A decision to the same effect has also been taken by the Central universities and the details of the proposal are being worked out. We recommend that it would be desirable to adopt the Triple-Benefit Scheme for all university and college teachers.

Where a scheme of provident fund is in operation— whether for school or college teachers,—we suggest the following changes :

(1) At present, a teacher begins to contribute to the provident fund only afrer he becomes permanent. In our opinion, the contribution to the provident fund, which is a compulsory form of saving, should begin right from the first day of a teacher's career. We, therefore, recommend that all teachers, whether temporary or permanent, should be required to contribute to the provident fund.

(2) The contribution of the employers to the provident fund of a teacher should be paid from month to

month and the present rule that the teacher is not entitled to get employer's contribution if he leaves the service within five years, should be rescinded. It serves no useful purpose and is patently unfair to the teachers.

(3) At present, the amounts of the contributory provident funds of teachers are generally invested in the Postal Savings Bank where a separate account is maintained for each teacher. This has obvious administrative advantages. But financially, it is a very disadvantageous procedure. The rate of interest on deposits in Postal Savings Bank is only four per cent, though for long-term deposits like provident funds, the rate of interest should be six per cent or more. There is thus a considerable loss to teachers and we recommend that a more equitable system of investing provident fund amounts should be devised.

Conditions of Work and Service

Conditions of Work. In creative work like teaching or research, the provision of stimulating conditions of work and adequate opportunities for professional advancement are extremely important and can play a very significant role in attracting and retaining the right type of persons in the profession The conditions of work in educational institutions should be such as to enable teachers to function at their highest level of efficiency. This would imply the provision of certain minimum facilities in the classroom essential teaching aids, library and laboratory facilities, and the maintenance of a manageable pupil-teacher ratio. It will also imply a system which encourages initiative, experimentation and creativity and gives adequate freedom to teachers in the organization of their coures and in the use of methods and techniques they consider most suitable. The hours of work should be similar to those of other public servants, account being taken, not only of actual classroom teaching, but also of other work connected with it, such as study and preparation, correction of exercises, evaluation, organization of co-curricular and extra-curricular activities, tutorials, seminars and other programmes of student guidance. Adequate facilities should also be provided for professional growth through seminars, summer institutes, grants for the purchase of books or conduct of research, liberal facilities for study and sabbatical leave for self-renewal, and adequate prospects for promotion to higher cadres. We also recommend that a scheme should be drawn up under which every teacher should get a concessional railway pass to any part of India once in five years on payment of a reasonable contribution related to his salary.

Parity in the Terms and Conditions of Service. The terms and conditions of service of teachers in government and local authority service are fairly satisfactory, except in one major particular : that the academic and civic freedom of these teachers is often severely restricted. The conduct and discipline rules applicable to teachers in government service (and these are generally extended to teachers in local authority service as well) are the same as for all other government employees. There is no reason why this should be so. Each profession should have separate conditions of service; and the conduct and discipline rules for teachers should provide academic freedom which is essential to enable them to function efficiently. Moreover, existing conduct and discipline rules were mainly framed under a foreign regime when control of the political views of teachers was a major objective of official policy. Unfortunately, these rules, which have long become obsolete, are still substantially in force. It would, therefore, be desirable to frame separate and new conduct and discipline rules for teachers in government service, which would ensure them the freedom required for professional efficiency and advancement.

In so far as private schools are concerned, the difficulties are of two kinds : several private managements have not framed proper terms and conditions of service; and not infrequently, the services of teachers are terminated on inadequate grounds and without regard to fairness and justice. To meet the first of these difficulties, we recommend the adoption of the principle of parity and suggest that the terms and conditions of service of teachers in government and private schools should be the same. This will confer some material benefits on the teachers in private schools and give greater academic freedom to teachers in government schools. We feel that, as a general practice, the services of a teacher should be terminated only after the prescribed procedure is followed and he is given adequate opportunity to defend himself. In all cases, there should be an appeal to an arbitration tribunal consisting of a representative of the teacher, a representative of the management and a representative of the Department.

Residential Accomodation. The probelm of residential accommodatiion is of great importance. Difficulties often arise in the rural areas when no residential accommodation is available locally and the teacher is compelled to stay in another locality. This interferes with the efficiency of his work and prevents him from building up proper contacts with parents or undertaking programmes of adult education. These and such other problems would be eliminated if it were possible to provide reasonable residential accommodation for teachers in the locality ltself. We recommend, therefore, that every effort should be made to increase residential accommodation for teachers in rural areas. It should be regarded as a responsibility of the local community to provide such accommodation. Wherever necessary and possible. State subsidies should be made available for the programme. In urban areas, and particularly in big cities, the problem is sometimes easier and sometimes more difficult than in villages. A programme of building construction and grant of adequate house-rent allowances in all big cities to enable teachers to obtain decent housing facilities is needed. Cooperative housing schemes for teachers should be encouraged and loans for construction of houses should be made available on favourable terms.

In the universities and affiliated colleges, it is neces-

sary to provide residential accommodation. General experienc
has been that universities which provide residential accommodation to teachers have been able to obtain the services of
eminent teachers and to retain them. The target to be reached
over the next 20 years should be to provide residential
accommodation to about 50 per cent of the teachers in the
universities and to 20 per cent in affiliated colleges.

Additional Earnings. The problem of additional
earnings of teachers, over and above their salaries, deserves
consideration. At the school stage, the chief source of additional earnings to teachers is private tuitions. This practice
prevails largely in urban areas and, in many places, complaints
are made that it has become almost a scandal. We realize
that some children (these may be gifted children preparing
to excel in examinations or backward ones who may need
special aid to come up to the ordinary level) will need extra
assistance from the teachers. In our opinion, such assistance
should be provided, on an institutional basis, by the school
itself. The teachers concerned should be adequately remu-
nerated and the cost should be met partly by charging
special fees and partly from school funds. At the university
stage, the chief source of additional remuneration is part-
time consultancy to government or industry, or remuneration from additional work, such as research carried out
by the department, or fees for evaluating examination
scripts. Such additional earnings should be permitted,
though care should be exercised to see that the concession is
not abused and that the work of the department does not
suffer. The existing practice under which a teacher is required
to pay a part of his earnings to the employing authority is,
in our opinion, unfair. We think that such payment should
not be required where the earnings do not exceed 50 per cent
of the salary. If they exceed this amount, a progressive
reduction may be made.

Civic Rights. We attach great importance to the civic
freedom of teachers. We consider the participation of teachers
in social and public life to be highly desirable in the interest
of the profession and the educational service as a whole, and

that such participation will enrich the social and political life of the country. Teachers should be free to exercise all civic rights enjoyed by citizens and should be eligible for public officers at the local, district, State or national levels. No legal restriction should be placed on their participation in elections. When they do so, they should be expected to pro- ceed on leave during the election campaign and to relinquish temporarily their teaching duties if the requirements of public office interefere with their proper discharge. Such partici- pation should be in a purely personal capacity and care should be taken to see that the institution which the teacher serves or his students are not involved in it.

Women Teachers. Some disscussion is needed regarding two important categories of teachers with special problems— women teachers, especially for rural areas, and teachers for tribal localities. At present, women teachers form the majority at the pre-primary stage. At other stages, the proportion of women teachers has been continually increasing in the post-Independence period as the statistics in Table 5 will show.

It will be seen that the number of women teachers in lower primary schools has increased from 82,000 to 200,000 or from 18 to 24 per 100 men teachers. In the higher primary schools, where the demand for women teachers is great, espe- cially in rural areas, their number has increased from 13,000 to 140,000 or from 18 to 37 per 100 men teachers. In secon- dary schools and colleges or arts and science, the increase is not so large, but shows steady progress. It is only in voca- tional schools and colleges—and this is not unexpected— that their number is still very limited.

It is necessary to emphasize the need for the employment of women teachers in increasing proportions. At the lower primary stage, they make good teachers; and in many rural areas, the presence of a woman teacher will bring more girls to schools. At the higher primary stage, the employment of women teachers and the conduct of special schools for girls will be necessary for some years to come in most of our rural areas. In secondary schools and colleges of arts and science, the proportion of institutions for girls is continually increasing. These are mostly staffed by women teachers. Even in the remaining institutions, a large majority are really mixed institutions with some proportion of girls attending. In all of them, it should be a rule to have at least one woman teacher on the staff and where the number of girls is large, at least one woman teacher for every 30 girls. Girls are also increasingly attending vocational schools and this emphasizes the need for the employment of more women teachers in them.

TABLE 5

Women Teachers (1950-65)

Item	1950-51	1955-56	1960-61	1965-66 (estimated)
1	2	3	4	5
1. *Women teachers in lower primary schools*				
Total No. of women teachers	82,281 (18)	117,067 (20)	126,788 (21)	200,000 (24)
2. *Women teachers in higher primary schools*				
Total No. of women teachers	12,887 (18)	23,844 (19)	83,532 (32)	140,000 (37)
3. *Women teachers in secondary schools*				
Total No. of women teachers	19,982 (19)	35,085 (23)	62,347 (27)	95,000 (28)

	1	*2*	*3*	*4*	*5*

4. *Women teachers in schools for vocational education*

Total No. of women teachers	2,131	2,966	3,948	6,200	
	(23)	(22)	(17)	(17)	

5. *Women teachers in institutions for higher education (arts and science)*

Total No. of women teachers	1,716	3,136	5,645	8,512	
	(10)	(13)	(16)	(17)	

6. *Women teachers in colleges for professional education*

Total No. of women teachers	334	666	1,865	2,750	
	(7)	(8)	(12)	(11)	

Source: Ministry of Education, Form A.

N.B.　　Figures in parentheses show the number of women teachers for every 100 men teachers.

This problem was examined in detail by the National Committee on Women's Education which has made a number of useful recommendations on the subject. We support them fully. For convenience of reference, however, we would highlight the following recommendations:

(1) The employment of women teachers should be encouraged at all stages and in all sectors of education.

(2) Opportunities for part-time employment of women teachers should be provided on a large scale in order to enable married women to look after their homes in addition to teaching.

(3) Residential accommodation should be provided for

women ?teachers, particularly in rural areas, on a priority basis.

(4) In order to get women teachers to work in rural areas in adequate numbers, the scheme of condensed courses for adult women which is now being implemented by the CSWB should be expanded. Promising girls from rural areas should be given scholarships to educate and train themselves to become teachers.

(5) Many?women cannot remain away from their homes for long periods as is often required in courses of professional training or of further general education. They will, however, be greatly benefited by private study and correspondence education. These facilities should be specially provided for them.

(6) Wherever necessary, special allowances may be given to women teachers working in rural areas.

Teachers for Tribal Areas. Equally important is the need to secure the services of good teachers for tribal areas. It will be necessary to give special allowances to such teachers because they have to live under very trying conditions. Assistance may also have to be provided for the education of their grown-up children. Residential accommodation is very often a must as no rented buildings are available in places where the tribals live.

It is also desirable to provide some special training to teachers who are going to work in tribal areas. This should include a study of the tribal language or languages and of tribal culture. In States where there is a large tribal population, special institutions will have to be set up to provide orientation courses to teachers posted to tribal localities. Encouragement should also be given to tribal young men and women to become teachers in the schools of these areas.

Teachers' Organizations. Teachers' organizations in all parts of the world have following an almost identical pattern of growth: starting as 'trade unions' designed to fight for material benefits and gradually becoming bodies concerned with many aspects for their members' lives. The National of Union of Teachers in the UK, for instance, was founded in 1870 because of a desperate need to improve salaries and conditions of work. Since then it has broadened its functions enormously, though it still continues to be active and increasingly successful in negotiating material benefits for its members. In India also, teachers' organizations are developing on the same broad lines. Most of them are currently engaged, and rightly so, in securing better salaries and conditions of work for teachers. But some of them have already started other programmes of academic work and are conducting research, organizing in-service education and producing literature needed by teachers. On the whole, however, the teachers' organizations have still a long way to go, especially in the development of their academic programmes. While the States can assist in this undertaking, it is essentially a task for the teachers themselves.

Some of the functions of teachers' organizations will be

—to secure for their members, individually and collectively, their rightful status—social, economic and professional;

—to safeguard their professional interests and to secure satisfactory conditions of work and service;

—to secure the professional growth of teachers through refresher courses, seminars, publications, library service and research;

—to work for the improvement of education in response to the challenge of the ever-changing socio-economic situation;

—to improve the teaching of subjects through the establishment of subject-teachers' associations; and

—to establish a professional code of conduct for teachers and to ensure that it is followed by members.

Professional organizations of teachers fulfilling the above functions and having a responsible and representative body of members should be recognized by the Central and State Governments. Such recognition should entitle them to the right of being consulted on all matters relating to school education, general and professional education of teachers, and their salaries and conditions of work and service.

Joint Teachers Councils. On the lines of the scheme recently approved by the Government of India for joint consultative machinery and compulsory arbitration for Central Government employees, we recommend the constitution of joint teachers' councils in each State and Union Territory. These councils should consist of representatives from teachers' organizations and officers of the Education Departments, with the Secretary, Education Department, as chairman. These would meet as often as necessary but at least once in six months. Their scope and functions will include all matters relating to conditions of service and work, welfare service of teachers of all categories, and general programmes for the improvement of education.[7] The councils will be advisory bodies; but there would be a convention that, subject to the final authority of the State Cabinet, agreements reached at the council shall become operative. If there is a total failure of negotiations, compulsory arbitration should be provided for in respect of matters of pay and allowances, hours of work and leave. The joint teachers' councils will create a forum where the officers of the Department will meet the representatives of teachers' organizations at a sufficiently high level. We trust that this would help to build good relations between teachers and the State Governments and promote the cause of education by smoothening the innumerable administrative problems which are not promptly dealt with and which, by causing much avoidable suffering and inconvenience to teachers, have an adverse effect on educational standards.

7. With regard to recruitment, promotion and discipline, the councils will deal with matters of general principles only and not with individual cases.

Social Status and Morale. The efficiency of the teaching profession and its contribution to national development in general and educational improvement in particular, will depend largely on its social status and morale. This will, in its turn, depend upon two inter-related factors: economic status and civic rights of teachers, and their professional competence, character and sense of dedication. Throughout the world, the general experience has been that, as the material rewards of teachers are elevated, it becomes possible to recruit into the profession individuals of a continually improving quality and with more extended professional training; and in proportion as the competence, integrity and dedication of teachers has increased, society has been increasingly willing—and justifiably so—to give greater recognition to their material and economic status. We visualize a similar development in India over the next twenty years.

National Awards for School Teachers. For some years past, the Ministry of Education has been operaring a scheme of national awards for school teachers.[8] The principal object of the scheme is to grant recognition to school teachers who have done outstanding work and helped to raise the status of the teaching profession. By and large, the scheme has worked fairly well. We would, however, reqnest the Ministry of Education to examine the following suggestions which were made to us regarding this scheme and which, in our opinion, will improve its effectiveness.

(1) The number of awards is very small at present. In our opinion, there should be about 500 awards. As the primary stage, it is very difficult to compare the merits of teachers working under entirely different conditions. We, therefore, suggest that, broadly speaking, an award should be given every year to a primary teacher from each district. For secondary teachers there should be about 200 awards in all, given on a State-basis as at present.

8. Similars schemes have also been in operation in some States.

(2) In order to minimize the influence of non-educational considerations such as politics of caste, it is desirable to strengthen the selection committees for the awards at all levels. With the committees at the State level, some outstanding non-official educationists and teachers known for their integrity and public status should be associated, and to the extent possible, this should also be done in the district-level committees.

(3) The travelling allowance given to the teachers receiving awards should be on the same basis as for Class 1 officers of the Government of India. The arrangements for their stay in Delhi should be comfortable and generous.

SUMMARY

1.   Intensive and continuous efforts are necessary to raise the economic, social and professional status of teachers and to feed back talented young persons into the profession.

2.   *Remuneration.* The most urgent need is to upgrade the remuneration of teachers substantially, particularly at the school stage.

(1) The Government of India should lay down for the school stage minimum scales of pay for teachers and assist the States and Union Territories to adopt equivalent or higher scales to suit their conditions.

(2) Scales of pay of school teachers belonging to the same category but working under different managements such as government, local bodies or private managements should be the same. This principle of parity should be adopted forthwith. But its full implementation may, if necessary, be phased over a programme of five years.

(3) The Commission proposes the following scales of pay:

Teachers	Remuneration
	Rs.
(1) Teachers who have completed the secondary course and have received two years of professional training.	Minimum for trained teachers 150
	Minimum salary (to be reached in a period of about 20 years) 250
	Selection grade (for about 15 p.c. of the cadre) 250—300

N.B. The minimum salary of a primary teacher who has completed the secondary course should be immediately raised to Rs. 100; and in a period of five years, it should be raised to Rs. 125. Similarly, the minimum pay of a teacher, who has received two years of training, should be raised immediately to Rs. 125; and it should be raised to Rs. 150 in a period of five years. Untrained persons with the requisite academic qualifications should work on the starting salary until they are trained and become eligible for the scale.

(2) Graduates who have received one year's professional training.	Minimum for trained graduates 220
	Maximum salary (to be reached in a period of 20 years) 400
	Selection grade (for about 15 p.c. of the cadre) 300—500

(*Contd.*)

N.B. Untrained graduates should remain on their starting salary of Rs. 220 p.m. until they are trained and become eligible for the scale.

(3) Teachers working in secondary schools and having postgraduate qualifications. 300—600

N.B. On being trained, they should get one additional increment.

(4) Heads of secondary schools. Depending upon the size and quality of the school and also on their qualifications, the headmasters should have one or other of the scales of pay for affiliated colleges recommended below.

(5) Teachers in affiliated colleges.

Lecturer: Junior scale	300—25—600
Senior scale	ʼ00—30—640
	—40—800
Senior Lecturer/ Reader	700—40—1100
Principal I	700—40—1100
II	800—50—1500
III	1000—50—1500

N.B. The proportion of lecturers in the senior scale to those in the junior scale should be progressively improved. By the end of the Fifth Plan, this proportion should be raised to about 75 per cent on an average.

(6) Teachers in university departments.

Lecturer	500—40—800
	—50—950
Reader	700—50—1250
Professor	1000—50—
	1300—60—
	1600

N.B. (1) One-third of the professors to be in the senior scale of Rs. 1500—1800. Scales comparable to the supertime scales in IAS to be introduced for exceptionally meritorious persons and in selected Centres of Advanced Studies.

(2) The proportion of junior (lecturers) staff to senior (readers/professors) staff in the universities which is now about 3:1 should be gradually changed to 2:1.

Notes—(*a*) The above scales of pay for school teachers are at the current price level and include the existing dearness allowances. Suitable increases will, however, have to be made for rises in prices from time to time.

(*b*) Compensatory cost of living allowance given in cities, house-rent allowance or other allowances are *not* included. These will be in addition to the salary recommended about and should be given on a basis of parity.

(*c*) The scale of pay are to be integrally related to the programmes of quantitative improvement of teachers through improved methods of selection, and improvement in general and professional education.

(*d*) The scale are to be given to all teachers—government, local authority or private—on the basis of parity.

3. *Implementation of Scales at the University Stage.*

(1) The scales proposed above for teachers in higher education have already been approved by Government. To facilitate their introduction, assistance from the Central should be provided to meet additional expenditure on a sharing basis of 80 per cent from Central and 20 per cent from State funds. In the case of private

colleges, Central assistance may even be provided on a 100 per cent basis.

(2) The introduction of these scales of pay should be linked with improvement in the qualifications of teachers and improvement in the selection procedures for their appointment. This should be done on the lines of recommendations of the Committee on Model Act for Universities. For the recruitment of professors, a slightly different procedure has been suggested.

(3) The qualifications of teachers in affiliated colleges should be the same as those for teachers in the universities. The method of recruitment for them should also be similar. A discriminating approach should be adopted, in regard to these, for privately managed colleges. Good institutions should be allowed greater freedom in the choice of their teachers and stricter control should be exercised where the management is not satisfactory.

4. *Implementation of Scales for School Teachers.*

(1) Three main scales of pay should be recognized for school teachers: (a) for teachers who have completed the secondary school stage and are trained; (b) for trained graduates; (c) for teachers with postgraduate qualifications.

(2) There should be no teacher at the primary stage who has not completed the secondary school course and has not had two years of professional training.

(3) Headmasters of higher primary and lower primary schools with enrolments of more than 200 should be trained graduates. Their salaries should be the same as those of trained graduate teachers in secondary schools.

(4) The practice of creating posts in lower scales of pay

and recruiting to these either teachers with lower qualifications when qualified teachers are available or recruiting qualified teachers to these posts and paying them at lower scales, should be abandoned.

(5) Scales of pay of secondary school teachers should be related to scales of pay for teachers in affiliated colleges and universities on the one hand and to those of primary teachers on the other.

(6) Scales of pay for headmasters of lower and higher secondary schools should have a definite relationship with those of teachers in affiliated colleges or even universities. That is to say, the scale of pay for headmasters should be the same as that for lecturers, readers, or even professors, depending upon the size, function and quality of the school.

(7) The proportion of teachers with postgraduate qualification in lower secondary schools should vary from 10 to 30 per cent, depending upon the size, function and quality of the school.

(8) Teachers with first or second class B.A./B.Sc. or M.A./ M.Sc. or with M. Ed. degree should be given advance increments in the scale.

(9) Professional training should be obligatory for all secondary school teachers.

(10) State Boards of School Education and the State Education Departments should prescribe qualifications of teachers and lay down proper procedures for selections, not only for government schools, but also for those conducted by local authorities and private managements.

(11) Every private school recognized and aided by State Education Departments should be required to have a Managing Committee with representatives from the

Department; the Department should prescribe the qualifications for teachers similar to those in government institutions; every post to be filled should be adequately advertised and interviews held by duly constituted selection committees; and no grant-in-aid should be paid for the salary of a teacher appointed outside the rules.

5. *Promotional Prospects.* It is necessary to improve promotional prospects in the teaching profession in order to attract and retain men of talent. From this point of view, the following suggestions are made:

(1) *School Stage.* Qualified and trained teachers in primary schools should be considered for promotion as headmasters or inspectors of schools.

(2) Trained graduate teachers in secondary schools who have done outstanding work should be eligible for promotion to posts carrying salaries of teachers with postgraduate qualifications.

(3) Secondary school teachers with the necessary aptitude and competence could be enabled to become university and college teachers. The UGC should give *ad hoc* grants to outstanding teachers to do research into problems to encourage them and incidentally to qualify themselves for work at the universities.

(4) Advance increments for teachers doing outstanding work should be made possible. Normally, a teacher reaches the maximum of his scale in a period of 20 years. It should be possible for about five per cent of the teachers to reach the top of the scale in about ten years and for another five per cent of teachers to reach the same in about fifteen years.

(5) *University Stage.* *Ad hoc* temporary posts in a higher grade should be created for a lecturer or reader who

has done outstanding work and who cannot be given promotion for non-availability of a suitable post.

(6) In Departments doing postgraduate work, the number of posts at professorial level should be determined on the basis of requirements.

(7) It should be open to a university in consultation with UGC to offer remuneration, even beyond the special scale of Rs. 1600-1800 to outstanding persons.

6. *Relating Salaries to Costs of Living.* All teachers' salaries should be reviewed every five years and the dearness allowance paid to teachers should be the same as that paid to government servants with the same salary.

7. *Welfare Services.* A general programme of welfare services for all school teachers should be organized in each State and Union Territory, the funds being contributed by teachers (at 1½ per cent of the salaries) and an equal amount being given by the State. The fund should be administered by joint committees of representatives of teachers and government. When such a fund is organized, the existing teachers' welfare fund set up by the Government of India may be advantageously merged in it.

8. *Need for Central Assistance.* The proposals for the improvement of salaries of school teachers should be given effect to immediately. Generous Central assistance should be made available to State Governments for this purpose.

9. *Retirement Benefits.* (1) The system of retirement benefits to teachers should also be reorganized on the principles of uniformity and parity. This is to say, the retirement benefits given to employees of the Government of India should be extended automatically to teachers in the service of the State Governments in the first instance and then to teachers working under local authorities and private management.

(2) As an interim measure, the triple-benefit scheme should be more widely adopted both for teachers in local authority and private schools as well as for the university and college teachers.

(3) The normal retirement age for teachers in schools, colleges and universities should be made 60 years with provision for extension up to 65 years.

(4) A higher rate of interest should be given to teachers on their provident fund and for this purpose, a better system of investing these funds should be devised.

10. *Conditions of Work and Service.* (1) The conditions of work in educational institutions should be such as to enable teachers to function at their highest level of efficiency.

(2) The minimum facilities required for efficient work should be provided in all educational institutions.

(3) Adequate facilities for professional advancement should be provided to all teachers.

(4) In fixing the hours of work, not only actual classroom teaching, but all other work a teacher has to do should be taken into consideration.

(5) A scheme should also be drawn up under which every teacher will get a concessional railways pass to any part of India once in five years on payment of a reasonable contribution related to his salary.

(6) New conduct and discipline rules suitable for the teaching profession should be framed for teachers in government service.

(7) The terms and conditions of service of teachers in private schools should be the same as for government schools.

(8) The provision of residential accommodation for

teachers is extremely important. For this purpose, it is suggested that—

(a) every effort should be made to increase residential accommodation for teachers in rural areas and State subsidies should be made available for the purpose;

(b) a programme of building construction and grant of adequate house rent allowance should be adopted in all big cities;

(c) cooperative housing schemes for teachers should be encouraged and loans on favourable terms should be made available for construction of houses; and

(d) in universities and colleges, the target should be to provide residential accommodation to about 50 per per cent of the teachers in the university and 20 per cent of them in affiliated colleges.

(9) Private tuitions should be discouraged and controlled. Special coaching for children who need it should be provided on an institutional basis.

(10) At the university stage, part-time consultancy or additional work, such as research by teachers in higher education should be permitted; and no payment should be required to be made to the institution if the earnings do not exceed 50 per cent of the salary.

(11) Teachers should be free to exertise all civic rights and should be eligible for public office at the local, district, State or national level. No legel restriction should be placed on their participation in elections, but when they do so, they should be expected to proceed on leave.

11. *Women Teachers.* (1) The employment of women teachers should be encouraged at all stages and in all sectors

of education. Opportunities for part-time employment should be provided for them on a large scale.

(2) Adequate provision should be made for residential accommodation particularly in rural areas.

(3) The condensed courses for adult women operated by the Central Social Welfare Board should be expanded.

(4) Increasing facilities should be provided for education through correspondence courses.

(5) Wherever necessary, special allowances should be given to women teachers working in rural areas.

12. *Teachers for Tribal Areas.* (1) Teachers for tribal areas should be given special allowances, assistance for the education of their children and residential accommodation.

(2) Provision should be made for giving special training to teachers who are to work in tribal areas.

13. *Teachers' Organizations* (1) Professional organizations of teachers which carry out work for the improvement of the profession and of education should be recognized by the Central and State Governments and consulted on matters relaing so school education, general and professional education of teachers and their salaries and conditions of work.

(2) Joint Teachers' Council should be constituted in each State and Union Territory to discuss all matters relating to teachers' salaries, conditions of work and service and welfare service. These should consist of representatives of teachers' organizations and officers of the State Education Department. Conventions should be developed to the effect that unanimous recommendations of the Council would be accepted by Government. In certain matters, there should be provision for arbitration when negotiations fail.

14. *National Awards.* The Ministry of Education should consider the following suggestions:

—the number of national awards should be increased;

—The selection committees should be strengthened; and

—Travelling allowance given to the awardees should be similar to that sanctioned for Class I officers of Government.

8

Teaching Methods, Guidance and Evaluation

The need for a continual deepening of the school curricula which we examined in the preceding chapter is intimately related to the equally urgent need for a continual improvement in teaching methods and evaluation (inclusive of guidance). We shall devote this chapter to the consideration of some of the important aspects of this programme.

Teaching Methods: Discovery and Diffusion

Scope of the Discussion. A good deal of attention has been directed in recent years to the techniques of revitalizing classroom teaching in Indian schools. Basic education was intended to revolutionize all life and activity in the primary school and draw out 'the best in the child—body, mind and spirit. The Secondary Education Commission devoted an entire chapter in its report to dynamic methods of teaching, discussing the objectives of the right techniques, the values of various activity methods and the different ways in which these methods and techniques could be adapted to suit different levels of intelligence. Considerable efforts have been made during the last decade through seminars, workshops, refresher courses and summer institutes to introduce the teacher, especially at the secondary stage, to new techniques of instruction. The use of audio-visual aids has been on the increase in urban schools.

and even television has been brought into the service of class-room teaching in Delhi. And yet it will be generally agreed that the impact of these activities on teaching practices in the vast majority of our schools has not been very significant. The picture is particularly dismal in the rural areas, and especially in the primary schools. In the average school today, instruction still conforms to a mechanical routine, continues to be dominated by the old besetting evil of verbalism and therefore remains as dull and uninspiring as before.

Why does this happen? The problem is complex and the answers to it are not easy to give. But in our opinion, the following are the four major factors that impede progress:

(1) *The weakness of the everage teacher.* By and large, the competence of the average teacher is poor; this general education is below standard and his professional preparation unsatisfactory.

(2) *The failure to develop proper educational research on teaching methods.* Little has been done to find out in crucial sectors the methods that are best suited to our conditions and needs. For instance, the best methods teaching beginning reading in a phonetic script like Devanagri have yet to be developed.

(3) *The rigidity of the existing educational system.* Better methods of teaching are discovered, not so much through educational research, as through the adventures of gifted teachers who have the courage to get off the beaten track. Our educational system is not designed to encourage initiative, creativity and experimentation on a large scale and is, therefore, not able to keep itself abreast of the times.

(4) *The failure of the administrative machinery to bring about a diffusion of new and dynamic methods of teaching.* Even assuming that a good method of teaching is discovered and is actually introduced in a

few progressive schools, the problem still remains of diffusing it among the other schools so that it becomes the common practice in the educational system as such. This is a difficult task, and we have yet to find the right techniques for accomplishing it.

The first of these problems has already been discussed in Chapters III and IV and the second is dealt with in broad terms in a subsequent chapter. We do not propose to examine here the methods of teaching different school subjects as there is a good deal of pedagogical literature available on these topics. It is our considered opinion, however, that the failure to modernize our teaching methods is very largely due to the third and fourth factors stated above—the rigidity of the educational system and the administrative failure to diffuse even known and practised methods among the schools. We shall address ourselves mainly to these two problems in the course of this chapter.

Elasticity and Dynamism.   In a modern society where the rate of change and of the growth of knowledge is very rapid, the educational system must be elastic and dynamic. It must gave freedom to its basic units—the individual pupil in a school, the individual teacher among his colleagues, and the individual school (or cluster of schools) within the system to move in a direction or at a pace which is different from that of other similar units within the system without being unduly hampered by the structure of the system as a whole. In this process, the freedom of the teachers is the most vital; it is almost synonymous with the freedom of the school, for the pupils can rarely be freer than the men and women who teach them. It will, therefore, be quite an order to equate the elasticity and dynamism of an educational system basically with the freedom of teachers.

It has to be remembered that advances in classroom practice never occur on a broad front, with all the teachers and all the schools moving forward in unison. In a school system with a large number of untrained or postly trained teachers, there is need for a solid framework of detailed syllabuses, text-books, examinations, frequent inspections and well-defined rules. The average teacher who wants security rather than opportunity for creativity may welcome his support. But the work of the best teachers can be crippled if they are not per-mitted, encouraged and helped to go beyond the departmental prescriptions. The success of an educational reform will depend upon this flexible approach where the good school or the good teacher is able to forge ahead and the necessary supports are provided to the weaker institutions to introduce the reform gradually. The task of the administrator or inspector in such a situation becomes very difficult. He cannot take the easy line of imposing common restrictions on all or be daring enough to give equal freedom to all. We expect him to analyse the strengths and weaknesses of each school and of each school teacher and to help them make the best progress they can. One of the essential conditions for making an edu-cational system elastic and dynamic, therefore, is for the administrator to develop this competence, to discriminate between school and school, between teacher and teacher, and to adopt a flexible mode of treatment for individual or insti-tutions at different levels of development. This alone can help to promote initiative, creativity and experimentation on the part of the teachers.

Certain general conditions are necessary to promote this elasticity and dynamism, some of the more important of which are given below:

(1) The individual teacher is most likely to try bold changes in teaching practice if there is a feeling of reform in the air and if he sees his small contribution as part of a major social revolution.

(2) The experimenting teacher must have much more than the passive acquiescence of the school inspectors. He must feel that officers of the Education Deparment are

personally eager to see experimentation and that they
are willing, within reasonable limits, to accept a proportion of failures as part of the price.

(3) The inspectors are the key figures in any reform of
classroom practice. They are *Authority*, present and
obvious. They should be consulted from the beginning,
should know that their criticism and suggestions carry
weight, and should be made to feel that the proposed
changes are, in some measure, *their* reforms. A school
system can be no more elastic or dynamic than the
inspectors will let it be. This is why the in-service
education of inspecting officers assumes great significance.

(4) The sympahty and support of headmasters and senior
teachers must be won quite early in the programme
if they are not to dampen all youthful ardour to
experiment and explore. They may not want to break
new ground themselves. But if they do not feel they
are being by-passed and that the new system is not
being foisted on them, they can become its patrons,
if not its practitioners. There is also much to be gained
by winning the approval of teachers' organizations to
any movement that increases flexibility in the school
system. Individuals will experiment more readily if
they feel that experimentation has the general support
of the profession.

(5) Anything that breaks down the isolation of the teacher
increases his sense of assurance and makes it easier for
him to adventure. The strengthening of the teacher's
sence of inner security is a purpose common to all the
methods advocated to increase the elasticity or dynamism in a school system. It is the basis of all real
reform in teaching practice. There are occupations
where a mass advance can be achieved by the invention
of new equipment and the issuing of instructions for
its use. No worth-while advance in is possible teaching

method unless the individual teacher understands what he is doing and feels secure enough to take the first new steps beyond the bounds of established practice. It is easier for a teacher to do so in a small group than when he is working alone. The success of 'team teaching' in introducing new teaching techniques into some American schools is based on the fact that it is not the individual but the team that is responsible for the planning and execution of new methods. It is our belief that the proposed organization of a school complex in which the teacher works in a cooperative group is more likely to help flexibility than the present system of isolation.

(6) Nothing reduces a teacher's sense of security or his willingness to take advantage of freedom so seriously as does his ignorance of the subject-matter he has to teach. If he is only a few lessons ahead of his class he dare take no risks, and finds safety in the old routine of rote memorizing. Increasing the teacher's level of general education is, in general, the surest way of ensuring that some of them will adopt livelier and more meaningful methods of teaching. Fortunately, the limiting factors is not so much the absolute amount of knowledge the teacher has but the gap between what he knows and what his pupils know. Consequently, the easiest place to introduce innovations is in classes I and II. There is also a great advantage in taking the lowest classes of the schools as a starting point for reform, since it is at this level that the greatest 'pupil wastage' occurs through repetition and drop-out.

(7) When in doubt, teachers will teach in the way they were taught themselves and not in the way they were told to teach. So, if a school system is to become more flexible and teaching methods more lively and varied, it is essential that these qualities be established very early in the *practice*, as well as in the *theory*, of at least some of the teacher-training institutions. A few trai-

ning institutions at both the primary and the secondary levels should become centres for devising, testing, and adapting methods and materials to be used in the schools.

(8) A teacher or institution will be able introduce innovations more easily if the parents of the pupils know enough about their purpose so as not to have any fear that they will interfere with their children's chances at the final examination. A strong and respected headmaster or teacher can probably best win over the parents by his own efforts; but in most cases, it will be neccessary for the Department to help in convincing parents that changes in methods are desirable and officially approved.

(9) Innovations are more likely to occur if there is a ladder of promotion up which the brigh young teacher can hope to climb by outstanding service.

(10) Obviously, elasticity or dynamism will be increased if there is a reasonable provision of books, teaching materials, and services that will enable some children to undertake part of their work alone or in groups. There is a limit to what can be expected of the most imaginative teacher if all he has is a bare room, a blackboard, a standard textbook, and sixty pupils. The most pressing needs for a teacher who wants to branch out on new methods are, therefore, a good supply of books and paper, and particularly at the lower levels of school education, some simple tools and materials for making equipment. If some teachers in the more poorly equipped schools are to have a real chance to make use of any freedom they are given, it would seem desirable to have at the disposal of the district education officer a sum of money, not too tightly bound up by regulations, that might be used, with discrimination, in providing the minimum facilities and services to certain schools and teachers who show a special

willingness and capacity to adopt new methods and standards of teaching. The amount of such aid should never be so great as to make any experiment expensive, unreral, and incapable of being applied widely. Too many 'pilot projects' are conceived on such an elaborate scale that they irritate teachers in the average schools and are of little value to the system as a whole.

If measures like those described above can be taken, schools and teachers will have opportunities to venture forth on their own and try out new ideas and experiments. Of course, those that will actually utilize this freedom will be few. But it is these few teachers and schools whose work will put dynamism into the system as a whole and help in raising standards, in breaking new ground and in continually adapting the system to the demands of a changing society

The Diffusion of New Methods. Elasticity in a school system is obviously of limited value unless the good practices developed by a few adventurous teachers or schools are spread more widely through the system as a whole. Unfortunately, this is by no means an automatic process in education, where successful experiments frequently die with the men and women who started them, and where the natural rate of spread of even the more viable innovations is measured in decades rather than in years. It takes a great deal of administrative skill and preseverance to get bold new methods understood and accepted by the body of average and below average teachers, even when they have amply proved their value—and firm proofs of success are hard to produce in education. The difficulties are multiplied ten-fold when teachers are expected to accept, not just a new technique for achieving the old ends, but methods that embody in themselves a new concept of the very purpose of education. That is why it is such a long and burdensome task to convert a school system based primarily on memorization into one involving understanding, active thinking, creativity and what has come to be called 'problem solving'. Each step is not a step but a leap into the unknown, and the average teacher needs skilled and detailed help, and—what may seem to be a contradiction in terms—sympathetic goading if he is to make it at all. This is precisely the problem that we have to face and solve during the next ten to twenty years.

How can this be done ? Very little systematic research has been undertaken on the diffusion of classroom practices even in the educationally advanced countries, and practically none in developing countries. The earlier researches of Paul Mort and his colleagues at Columbia University seemed to show that a period of 25 to 40 years was neccessary in the United States for anything like full diffusion of a new practice, but the rapid spread of such innovations as the PSSC[1] Physics course (which started in 1957, and is now taken by about fifty per cent of the high school pupils studying physics in the United States) has shown that, under certain conditions, the period can be greatly reduced. This experience and some others of its type seem to indicate that the educational administrator can encourage and hasten the diffusion of new teaching practices in a number of ways, the more important of which are indicated below:

(1) Almost all the factors which render the system elastic enough for the outstanding teacher to break new ground will also make it easier for the mass of average teachers to follow his example. However, mere permissiveness on the part of the authorities will not do the trick. They will need to play a more active part, with something that comes nearer to persuasion than to pressure but which still leaves no noubt in the teachers' minds that the Education Department and its officers favour certain changes. But it must be done with sensitivity and moderation, or the teachers will come to regard the new methods as the Department's latest fad, and may try to apply them, with or without understanding, to the detriment of the normal work.

(2) The main body of teachers will accept new methods

1. Physical Science Study Communittee.

more readily if the immediate goals set before them are limited ones. This means that the methods devised by the brilliant teacher or the subject specialist may have to be approached by stages, and that the stage demanded of each group of teachers may vary with their ability.

(3) The usual devices for in-service training such as refresher courses, workshops, demonstrations, exhibitions of work, and visits of quite long duration (days, not hours) to see the new methods at work in pioneering schools should be adopted on a large scale. Used with discrimination and skill, films, tapes or radio can bring whole lessons to quite isolated schools, though not so much for their effect on the pupils as for their usefulness in providing a model of good teaching for the teachers.

(4) It inerant instructors, specialized in certain subjects and class-levels of techniques, and working under the general direction of the District Education Officer, are even more vital at the stage of diffusing new methods than at the earlier stage of the first experiments.

(5) Probably the quickest and most effective way of having new theories accepted is to embed them in the 'tools' of teaching—textbooks, teachers' guides, and teaching aids of all kinds. Some teaching of theory will, of course, still be essential. But it will spring *from* proposed practices instead of floating airily *above* them. The extent of the theory and the degree of detail with which the practices are set out will vary with the level of general education of the teachers. In the initial stages of development and with weaker schools, it might be necessary for teacher's guides to go into a fair amount of detail on the series of lessons to be arranged throughout the school years, the methods to be used, the teaching aids to be prepared, the activities

to be encouraged, and the tests and techniques of evaluation to be employed.

The technique referred to in the preceding paragraph may
be described as the laying down of 'tramlines' on which the
average teacher can move forward with confidence in his
teaching. This method is different from the traditional practice
under which the teacher is given lectures on general principles
and is then expected to apply them with no more aid than is
given by a mediocre textbook that ofted clashes with the very
principles that are being advocated. It is, of course, the administrator's responsibility to ensure that, while providing 'tramlines' for the mass of the teachers, there is still enough freedom
left for the bold few to travel more freely. But with this pre-
caution, there is no doubt that these 'tramlines' of progress *are*
the techniques that will be particularly effective for diffusing
new methods.

It is obvious that this laying down of tramlines is not a
'once and for all time' business—it requires continuous renewal.
When an administrator lays down a set of tramlines with
immense effort (it takes some years to do so), he generally finds
that his 'progressive' tramlines have become a new 'orthodoxy'
and that he will have to start laying them down once again and
that there will be the same old resistance for breaking away
from the earlier tramlines. But that is an inevitable and peren-
nial problem that every educational reformer must face. The
provisions made to enable the outstanding teachers to leave
the tramlines will help the rest also to leave them in course of
time, while the more adventurous teachers will go still further
ahead to fresh fields and pastures new.

It will be seen that the essence of our recommendation is
that only an elastic and dynamic system of education can provide the needed conditions to encourage initiative, experimentation and creativity among teachers and thereby lay the foun-
dations of educational progress. We firmly believe that the
risks of freedom and trust in teachers that are implied in this
approach are not greater than those of undue restriction and

distrust and they are more worth taking. We should learn to delegate authority, to trust our teachers, to encourage the capacity for leadership amongst them, to treat every institution as having a personality of its own which it should try to develop in an atmosphere of freedom. This would need dynamic leadership at all levels, determined to give education a new deal and to make every teacher, educational officer and administrator put in the best of himself in this great cooperative endeavour.

Textbooks, Teachers' Guides and Teaching Materials

The value of the textbooks as an effective tool of learning and of diffusion of improved teaching methods has been indicated in the preceding section. A good textbook, written by a qualified and competent specialist in the subject, and produced with due regard to quality of printing, illustrations and general get-up, stimulates the pupil's interest and helps the teacher considerably in his work. The provision of quality textbooks, and other teaching and learning materials, can thus be an effective programme for raising standards. The need to emphasize it is all the greater because it requires only a relatively small investment of resources. Moreover, a quality book need not cost appreciably more than the one that is indifferently produced.

Quality of Textbooks. Unfortunately, textbook writing and production have not received the attention they deserve. In most school subjects, there is a proliferation of low quality, sub-standard and badly produced books, particularly in the regional languages. This has been due to a number of factors among which mention may be made of

— the lack of interest shown by top-ranking scholars so that the writing of textbooks has been generally undertaken by persons whose abilities are far from equal to the task;

— the malpractices in the selection and prescription of textbooks which defy control;

—the unscrupulous tactics adopted by several publishers;

—the lack of research in the preparation and production of textbooks: and

—the almost total disregard by private publishers (who are interested only in profits) of the need to bring out ancillary books, such as teachers' guides to accompany textbooks.

State Production of Textbooks. As education began to spread, the textbook industry became one of the very profitable fields for investment and the evils of the type mentioned above became more and more conspicuous. The attention of State Governments was soon drawn to them and it was decided that, in order to eliminate them, the State Governments should take over the production of textbooks. At present, most State Governments have adopted this policy and taken over the production of textbooks. The extent to which this responsibility has been assumed shows considerable variations—some States have produced only a few books at the primary stage while others have produced all books till the end of the secondary stage. In one or two States, not only production but even contribution and sale of textbooks have been taken over by the State.

There have been some definite gains from this policy. Private profiteering has disappeared and prices have been kept low. The malpractices and intrigues which used to be so common a feature of what used to be called the 'textbook racket' have also disappeared. The quality of books has improved in several instances, although the general level of the books still remains poor and their standard does not often come up to that some of the well-established and efficient publishers. The main reason for this failure is that the Education Departments which have taken over the responsibility of textbook production have not adequately organized themselves for it. It is this weakness that is largely responsible for the shortcomings one often sees in the State-produced textbooks, *viz*. failure to revise books for long periods, misprints, poor production, failure to supply books in time, etc. We do not desire to underestimate these deficiencies. What we want to highlight are two points: the first is that these weaknesses do not lead to the conclusion, as some interested parties are ever eager to show, that State-production of textbooks is wrong; and the second is to emphasize the urgency for the Education Departments to organize themselves properly for this great educational responsibility they have undertaken.

State-production of textbooks, it must be noted, is only one step in the direction of improving the quality of textbooks. But by itself, it can achieve little and if adequate steps are not taken in time to organize the activity on right lines, it may even put the clock back. We, therefore, recommend that emphasis should be placed on developing the programme of textbook production on right lines. Some concrete suggestions from this prom of view are made in the paragraphs that follow.

Programme at the National Level. It is essentiat that the best talent available in the country should be brought together to produce the textbooks and other literature needed, both at the school and at the university stages. This can only be done at the national level by agencies set up by the Government of India.

(1) For the university stage, the Ministry of Education is bringing out a series of low-priced and subsidized books in collaboration with appropriate authorities in the USA, the USSR and the UK. This is a useful scheme and its significance has now become even greater. It should be expanded and vigorously developed, along with schemes for books written by Indian authors. We lay great emphasis on the latter schemes. We recommend that as a matter of national policy, nearly all books at the undergraduate state, including those for professional subjects, should be written by Indian authors. In the preparation of these books.

fullest use should, of course, be made of foreign sources. This goal should be capable of realization within 5 to 10 years.

(2) At the school stage, we welcome the steps taken by the NCERT to produce textbooks with the help of scholars available in the country. Some books have already come out; and more will come out soon. These books are meant for use by State Governments who can use them with or without changes. We hope that the State Governments will make full use of this pioneer venture to improve the quality of their books.

(3) The production of textbooks and allied materials at the national level will be greatly facilitated if the Government of India were to establish, in the public sector, an autonomous organization, functioning on commercial lines, for the production of textbooks. We have recommended the establishment of similar organizations at the State level also. But there will be a large number of books, especially in the scientific and technical sector, which can only be produced on a national basis. It would also be desirable to produce several other categories of books at the national level, either for reducing cost or for improving quality or for purposes of national integration. We, therefore, feel that an organization of this type at the national level is urgently needed. We recommend that the Ministry of Education should set up a small committee to work out the details of this project and take all the necessary steps to bring it into existence as early as possible.

Textbooks produced at the national level will have other advantages as well. One of our major recommendations is that we should make an attempt to evolve national standards at the end of the primary, lower secondary and the higher secondary stages. The definition of these standards as well as the organization of a programme for their practical implementation will be greatly facilitated by the production of textbooks at the national level. Such books can indicate the expected standard of attainment far more precisely than any curricula or syllabi; and their practical use in schools is the surest method to raise standards and make the teaching in schools in the different parts of the country fairly comparable. In a subject like mathematics or science, for instance, there is not much scope for local variations and the adoption of common textbooks in all parts of the country is not only feasible, but also desirable from several points of view. The same can be said about a common textbook in citizenship prepared from the point of view of national integration and used in all schools of the country. History is another difficult subject to teach, especially from the point of view of social and national integration; and authoritative well-written books on the subject can be of immense help to all teachers. At present, there is hardly any common book which all the students in India read; and that is one of the reasons why our educational system contributes so little to national integration. On the other hand, if we had, say, a set of 100 books on different topics written by the best of our scholars which would be translated and be available in *every* school and *if* an average student were expected to read them in his school course as a matter of routine, the entire thinking of the rising generation would be different and national integration could be immensely strengthened.

Programme at the State Level. While attempts to improve textbooks at the national level are thus welcome, they cannot be the sole attempts for this crucial reform. Their most effective service is to stimulate other centres into activity and especially to promote similar enterprise at State levels. We recommend that each State should organize an adequately manned expert sections for the production of textbooks for schools. They should make as much use of the work done at the national level as possible. But there is no escape from the fact that each State will have to produce several textbooks in areas where national books will not be available. Even in areas where national books are available, independent attempts by the States will stimulate each other and the Centre itself.

We can hope for the best results only when the national and all the State centres for textbook production are functioning actively and in close collaboration.

The following points should be kept in view by the State Education Departments in organizing their programmes of textbook production :

(1) A separate agency, preferably functioning on an autonomous and commercial basis, should be set up, in close liason with the Education Department for the production of textbooks and teaching aids. It would be extremely difficult, if not impossible, to have within the four walls of usual departmental procedures, the autonomy and freedom which such an undertaking essentially needs.

(2) Production of textbooks is a continuous process. For instance, it takes a year or even more to produce a textbook and a further year for try-out and revision. Within a year of its adoption on a large scale, a process of evaluation has to start; and very soon thereafter, it will be discovered that it needs revision. The machinery set up, therefore, should be adequate to follow all these steps for *every* textbook. It should be an objective of policy to see that a textbook is continuously revised and kept up to date and that a thorough revision takes place at least once in five years, if not oftener. The need for frequent revisions of textbooks is obvious, even if the curricula were to remain unchanged. But we do visualize, as stated in the last chapter, a continual deepening of the curricula. In fact, very often a revision of textbooks will be necessitated, not by a revision of curricula, but as a means of changing and deepening them.

(3) No useful purpose is served by having only one text-book in a subject for a given class—this is almost invariably the position under the existing programmes

of nationalization. It should be an important objective of policy to have at least three or four books in each subject for each class and leave it open to the teachers to choose the book best suited to the school. This is necessary even if there were to be a common syllabus for all the schools. We have recommended, however, that there should be more than one approved syllabus and that each school should be permitted to adopt the syllabus best suited to its own conditions. In such a case, a multiple choice of books should be available for each syllabus.

(4) When Government gets books written, the payment to authors is often so niggardly that the ablest scholars are not generally attracted. This is the one point where private enterprise often scores over State-produced textbooks. It is, therefore, necessary to adopt liberal policies for remuneration, comparable to those of the private trade, and to attract the best people to write books.

(5) State-production of textbooks is not to be used for purposes of earning profits;[2] its sole purpose is to produce the best books and to make them available to the children at the lowest cost. The entire organization should, therefore, be run on a no-profit and no-less basis. The sales of State-produced books, however, are so large and certain, that even when no profits as such is charged and the price is merely rounded off to the nearest five paise, large margins are left over and these are enough to cover the costs of research, overhead establishment and the preparation of ancillary aids like teachers' guides.

(6) The incentive to write books should be encouraged in as many quarters as possible. Apart from commis-

---

2. In one State, we found that 100 per cent profit was charged while fixing the price.

sioning selected persons to write textbooks, which will have to be done in many cases, the Departments should also invite manuscripts, proposals, etc., and be ever on the hunt for new talent. There should be high level committees of professional persons to judge books or proposals submitted; and approved books should be adopted by the Departments and published after making suitable arrangements with the authors.

(7) Special encouragements should be given to teachers to write textbooks. In the USSR, even the highest positions in universities can be obtained by writing outstanding textbooks. Our universities can follow this example. We also suggest that learned societies should give adequate professional recognition to outstanding textbooks.

(8) Good textbooks are not enough; they should be supplemented by teachers' guides and other instructional material. A teachers' guide, as we have mentioned above, should give detailed assistance to teachers. Even for graduate teachers in the United States, some of the new courses being evolved in mathematics, science and social studies contain a great deal of detailed suggestions. The poorly educated and insecure teacher tends to drop into a dreary routine in which every lesson is taught in the same way, and he needs quite detailed suggestions on a variety of methods, which can make his teaching more lively and effective. It is only with the help of such detailed framework of support and guidance that a large number of teachers, particularly in the primary schools, will get off the beaten track.

There are really three aspects to the textbook production programme :

(1) *Academic* aspect which includes the preparation of textbooks, try-out and evaluation;

(2) *Production* aspect which includes all matters relating to printing and publication; and

(3) *Distribution* aspect which includes storage, sales, etc.

The first is the most important aspects, and the responsibility for it will have to be squarely accepted by the State Education Departments on the lines we have recommended above. The second is discretionary. We find that some State Governments have accepted direct responsibility for it and established separate textbook presses. This is the direction in which we should move. The third is really self-continued and is not inseparably linked with the first two. In one State where the State Government had assumed direct responsibility for distribution of textbooks, we found that the precious time of a number of field officers was taken up by sales, accounts and stock-keeping. We recommend that this activity should be promoted through student cooperatives which every educational institution (or group of educational institutions) should be encouraged to establish, and that it should not be assumed directly by the Education Departments.

Provision of Essential Teaching Aids. In assessing the needs of the teacher from the point of view of teaching methods, one is forced to admit that in the majority of schools, particularly at the primary stage, there is still an almost total absence of basic equipment and teaching aids—a good blackboard, a small library, essential maps and charts, simple science apparatus, and necessary display materials. The supply of such basic equipment and teaching aids to every school in the country is essential for the improvement of the quality of teaching. It would indeed bring about an educational revolution in the country. We recommend that lists of minimum teaching aids and equipment needed by each category of schools should be prepared. These may be kept as economical and frugal as possible. But once a certain minimum equipment is considered necessary, steps should be taken to see that it is given to every school on a high priority basis. As in Madras State, the help of the local community could be harnessed in developing this programme. As a first step, we recommend that a good blackboard should be immediately given to all schools.

Several suggestions were made to us to the effect that we should adopt new techniques of teaching which are now coming into use in the advanced countries. These techniques involve the large-scale use of films, radios, tape-recorders and other audio-visual aids, the introduction of open and closed circuit television, and the provision of language laboratories, programmed instructional methods and simple and highly sophisticated forms of teaching machines. With regard to the use of films, filmstrips and other simple audio-visual equipment, it may be possible to make these teaching aids available to every school complex (and through it to every school even in rural areas). In this connection, we invite attention to the Report of a Study Group on Classroom Science Films (their recommendations apply to the teaching of other subjects also) with which we broadly agree. In addition, it should also be possible to equip the majority of upper primary and secondary schools with low cost radio sets. We recommend that Education Departments should work with the All India Radio for the use of radio lessons, supplemented with printed material for the teachers, and, if possible, for the pupils. We also recommend the broadcasting of special radio talks, in the early morning or late evening, specially designed for teachers which will help to deepen their subject knowledge and guide them in lesson preparation. The more sophisticated forms of the newer techniques, however, can be used, generally speaking, as this stage of our educational development only on an experimental basis and in a few schools. It has to be remembered that schools cannot use an equipment which is much beyond the level of technology in the society. Sophisticated equipment given to rural schools, for instance, cannot be maintained and soon falls into disrepair. A few progressive schools may be equipped with new aids like language laboratories and programmed instructional material; but such techniques may preferably be tried out, in the first instance, in the education and training of teachers.

The majority of teachers in our schools will have to rely on inexpensive teaching equipment which are easily available in the locality or are made by them with proper encouragement and little financial assistance. The programmes that will help us most, in the immediate future, in improving the teaching in our schools are, therefore, the following :

(1) The training of teachers in the use and preparation of simple and improvised teaching aids;

(2) The use of the school workshop—and also of programmes of work-experience—to prepare the teaching aids required by the school itself and by other schools in the neighbourhood;

(3) Manufacture of simple equipment on a large scale for reducing cost, and its distribution to schools; and

(4) Sharing the more costly equipment in common by schools in a given neighbourhood. For instance, a group of schools in the neighbourhood may have a projector in common. A good laboratory in one school can be used, according to a carefully prepared plan, by other schools nearby. A group of schools may have a circulating library, and so on.

Class Size

It will be generally agreed that there cannot be a marked improvement in methods of teaching if the teacher is required to teach very large classes as a matter of routine. The phenomenal expansion of primary and secondary education in recent years has resulted in overcrowding in schools, especially in urban areas, where accommodation is not easily available for the extension of the school building or the opening of new sections. The class size sometimes grows to abnormal proportions. A class of sixty children is a common sight in a city. We ourselves have seen, in the course of our tour, classes of sixty and even sixty-five children in a few secondary schools. Quite often, the classroom is not able to accommodate easily such a large number. The problem is solved by pushing the teacher's chair—there is no place for a teachers' desk—into a corner and bringing the front benches almost up to the blackboard ! In conditions like these all talk of creative teaching ceases to have any significance.

Present Position. Tables 1 and 2 show the size of classes at different school stages, on the basis of information supplied by the State Governments for 25 districts selected from eight States in a special study carried out by the Commission.

The tables are very revealing. We find that 11.1 per cent of the teachers at the lower primary stage teach classes of 50-59, 6.5 per cent take classes of 60-69 pupils, and 14.3 per cent have to deal with classes of 70 pupils and more. Some of these classes will be, of course, in single-teacher schools, where one teacher has to take two, three and sometimes even five combined classes. Similarly, at the higher primary and the secondary stages, the position is not much better. The percentage of teachers handling classes of 50 to 70 pupils and above is 13.2 in class VI, 10.2 in class VII, 19.3 in class VIII, 24.1 in class IX, 19.8 in class X, 29.5 in class XI and 36.7 in class XII. It will be seen that the number of teachers handling such large class increases as we go up the educational ladder.

Difficulties of Teaching Large Classes. Methods of teaching in classes of fifty pupils and more cannot be satisfactory. However capable a teacher may be, he cannot pay individual attention to a large number of children, give special assistance to the weaker ones, guide the brighter ones to proceed at a faster pace in an attempt to help one and all to reach the maximum of their capacities. In these circumstances the average teacher will be tempted to resort to rote memorization. Assignments given will generally not be checked and composition exercises will be marked during periods of spasmodic energy. The poor quality of teaching in the ordinary secondary school in urban areas may partly be attributed to overcrowded classrooms.

TABLE 1

Distribution of Teachers in Lower Primary Schools/Sections According to the Number of Pupils they Teach (1965)

State	Below 10	11-19	20-29	30-39	40-49	50-59	60-69	70 and above	Total
	% 2	% 3	% 4	% 5	% 6	% 7	% 8	% 9	% 10
1									
Andhra Pradesh	0.4	6.3	18.5	24.3	21.9	12.5	6.3	9.8	100.0
Kerala	0.2	1.9	31.7	30.8	11.8	4.2	3.4	16.0	100.0
Madhya Pradesh	3.6	14.0	23.8	23.9	15.5	7.9	4.2	7.1	100.0
Mysore	0.7	4.7	13.3	21.5	21.8	13.5	7.7	16.8	100.0
Orissa	1.7	10.4	17.9	30.0	20.1	9.8	4.9	5.2	100.0

Percentage of teachers teaching pupils

(Contd.)

TABLE 1 (Contd.)

1	2	3	4	5	6	7	8	9	10
Punjab	0.2	2.6	10.1	27.3	28.4	18.2	8.4	4.8	100.0
Rajasthan	1.0	7.0	16.6	17.1	11.7	9.2	6.2	31.2	100.0
Uttar Pradesh	1.0	6.5	15.1	20.6	19.9	13.9	8.8	14.2	100.0
All India	0.9	6.1	18.7	23.8	18.6	11.1	6.5	14.3	100.0

TABLE 2

Size of Classes/Sections at Higher Primary and Secondary Stages (1965)

Class	Below 10 %	10-19 %	20-20 %	30-39 %	40-49 %	50-59 %	60-69 %	70 and above %	Total %
VI	9.5	17.1	20.8	23.6	15.8	5.8	2.2	5.2	100.0
VII	9.9	18.9	20.1	26.4	14.5	4.7	1.5	4.0	100.0
VIII	3.9	11.3	15.6	25.7	24.3	11.5	2.5	5.3	100.0
IX	7.8	4.0	10.8	21.8	31.5	13.6	4.7	5.8	100.0
X	0.7	7.4	16.3	25.9	29.9	11.0	2.8	6.0	100.0
XI	2.0	11.8	21.8	19.5	15.4	10.8	6.0	12.7	100.0
XII	0.9	8.0	14.1	15.1	25.2	16.4	8.4	11.9	100.0

We do not, however, support those educational theorists who contend that a class should not have more than twenty or twenty-five pupils. It would be extremely unrealistic for our teachers to think in terms of this ideal. There is indeed no such thing as an ideal class size, and there is no sanctity about the number twenty-five or twenty. In our country, classes of a somewhat larger size than what may be strictly considered as desirable cannot be avoided for a long time to come. Some of the educationally advanced countries are also facing a similar problem. Teachers should reconcile themselves to the acceptance of this inescapable necessity. It is also the responsibility of the training institutions to have a more practical approach to the problem and to evolve methods which would help the teachers to teach classes of this size without a complete abandonment of all pedagogic principles.

Fixing the Maximum Class Size. However, beyond a certain number, it is not possible to extend the class size without doing serious damage to the quality of teaching. This is particulary true at the high school and higher secondary school stages, where individual differences become more marked, requiring special help to be given in many more cases, and where the assignments to be attended to increase in number. We are of the opinion that it is not enough to fix the average pupil-teacher ratio at the different stages of school education. Such a ratio is necessary, of course, to determine the number of teachers required with reference to the enrolments. But it will not necessarily control the class size. We may have a ratio of 40 pupils to one teacher at the primary stage and yet find a class of 10 pupils and another of 80 pupils perhaps in the same district. It is essential that, in addition to the pupil-teacher ratio, the maximum number of pupils to be admitted in a class must also be prescribed, and this maximum should not be allowed to be exceeded in any case. We recommend the following maximum number for the different stages of school education :

Lower Primary		— 50
Higher Primary	)	— 45
Lower Secondary	)	
Higher Secondary		— 40

The class size in classes I and II has a special significance. More than half the enrolment at the primary stage is in these to classes; and very often, they are large classes of 60 or more. In such cases, our first recommendation would be that the requisite number of teachers should be provided and the class size reduced as indicated above. But if this were not possible we would prefer to break this class into two classes of about 30-35 students and engage them only for three hours a day and request the teacher (with payment of a suitable allowance) to engage two such classes per day. This would be a far better method of education than the present system of herding 70 or so pupils in one class and keeping them there for six hours a day.

Multiple-Class Teaching. About 40 per cent of our schools are single-teacher schools and even in other schools, the proportion of big schools where one teacher teaches one class is very small. More than half of our teachers, therefore, have to teach more than one class at a time. This will be seen from Table 3.

In a situation of this type, research in multiple-class teaching is badly needed; and training institutions have to make a special effort in orientating teachers to the special techniques that have to be used under such conditions.

School Buildings

The provision of school buildings is extremely unsatisfactory at present. At the primary stage, only about 30 per cent of the schools are stated to have been housed in satisfactory buildings. The corresponding proportion at the secondary stage is stated to be about 50. This shows the great backlog of unconstructed school buildings which has to

TABLE 3

Distribution of Teachers in Primary Schools/Sections According to the Number of Classes They Teach (1965)

State	One Class %	Two Classes %	Three Classes %	Four Classes %	Five Classes %	Total %
Andhra Pradesh	35.9	27.7	16.9	4.5	15.0	100.0
Kerala	83.5	14.1	0.6	1.8	..	100.0
Madhya Pradesh	30.5	26.1	17.4	8.5	17.5	100.0
Mysore	50.9	21.4	3.7	24.0	..	100.0
Orissa	43.0	29.6	26.2	0.7	0.5	100.0
Punjab	46.4	26.9	14.8	1 1	10.8	100.0

Rajasthan	10.1	20.8	26.2	18.6	24.3	100.0
Uttar Pradesh	36.5	35.9	19.6	2.5	5.5	100.0
Total	43.7	25.6	14.2	8.4	8.1	100.0

Source : State Governments.

Note : The information is based on statistics collected from 25 districts in eight States.

be cleared during the next few years. In addition, buildings will have to be provided for the additional enrolment which will rise with increasing speed. The problem, therefore, has three aspects :

(1) provision of the necessary funds;

(2) reduction of the building costs to the minimum level possible; and

(3) the devising of a suitable machinery which can implement the programme expeditiously and economically.

Funds for School Building. We recommend that the allocations for construction of school buildings in the Central and State budgets should be increased. This is one area where the local community can make a significant contribution. Schemes of grant-in-aid should, therefore, be devised under which assistance from the State will be available to local communities, on a basis of equalization, for the construction of school buildings. Wherever possible, loan programmes for the construction of buildings should be encouraged. Grant-in-aid and loans should also be available to private schools, on a fairly liberal basis, for building construction.[3]

Reduction of Costs. A number of committees have examined this question for both the Central and State Governments, on behalf of the Ministry of Education, the Ministry of Works and the Planning Commission. In addition, the UGC has prepared detailed norms for hostels, staff quarters, libraries, etc., and the Central Building Research Institute at Roorkee and the Indian Standards Institute have made recommendations in this area. The result of all these is that there exist, for most types of school and colleges, space and planning norms and type plans and a good deal of sound advice

---

3. We have used the expression 'school buildings' to include all educational buildings such as classrooms, libraries, laboratories, cycle sheds, hostels and residential quarters for teachers.

that can help in reducing costs. What is required now is a mechanism that will put this information into practice.

In view of the acute shortage of traditional classical building materials and the shortage of accommodation, many schools are today operating in what are classified as temporary constructions' by the PWD and some even in thatched huts. We find that there is a strong prejudice against such structures. In our view this prejudice against the use of 'temporary' buildings or thatched huts for school purposes is totally unjustified. Designed and constructed with a raised floor and high doors and windows with plenty of ventilation, these structures serve more than adequately as school buildings. This should not, however, be misunderstood to imply that *kacha* buildings are always better. This is not so; and some *kacha* buildings prove costlier in the long run because of heavier costs of maintenance. What we wish to emphasize is the need to accept well-planned *kacha* structures as part of our system and to highlight simplicity and utility rather than ostentation in the construction of buildings.

Buildings in Rural Areas. The problem of school buildings needs to be discussed separately for urban and rural areas. In the former case, land values are high; and very often enough land is not available at all. Sophisticated structures are, therefore, necessary, even in order to keep in tune with the immediate environment. In the rural areas on the other hand, land is cheap and readily available; and sophisticated structures often look grotesque in a village atmosphere.

We recommend that everything should be done to encourage local initiative and local contribution in cash, kind or labour for the erection of the schools. A special device that can be of great use is that government should supply only the framework—which can be prefabricated—and the local people should be expected to raise the plinth and fill up the walls. The 'nucleus' approach recommended by the Ministry of Education will be of great help and deserves to be generally adopted.

Buildings in Urban Areas. In urban areas, the following steps should be taken for achieving economy in the construction of educational buildings :

(1) *Judicious Selection of Specifications and Local Materials.* The existing practice of playing safe by adopting conventional specifications is not conducive to economical construction. Economy can be achieved through the selection of locally available materials, use of cheaper materials, omission altogether of certain finishes and acceptance of a lower standard of construction. In all these steps, the governing factors would, however, be the availability of materials, climatic conditions, safety of buildings and recurring costs on maintenance.

(2) *Techniques of Construction.* With careful planning and designing, even the so-called 'temporary' structures can be made to serve a better purpose than many of the rented buildings in which schools are often housed. Such structures should be built, wherever climatic and other conditions permit. If pucka buildings are absolutely necessary, an increasing reliance is needed on the improved techniques of construction such as the use of framed structures, cavity walls, pre-fabricated components, RCC framed for doors and windows and components evolved by the Central Building Research Institute and other research organizations.

Expeditious Construction. In order to expedite the construction of school buildings, the following steps are recommended :

(1) *Rural Areas.* In rural areas, there are no local contractors available. Contractors from urban areas generally charge higher rates when they are required to work in villages. The departmental machinery is also not adequate to reach most of the outlying

villages. For the construction of village school buildings, therefore, we recommend that the agency of the local communities or village panchayats should be utilized to the fullest extent possible.

(2) *Urban Areas.* In urban areas, we recommend that the local agencies like municipalities and corporations should be utilized fully for construction of school buildings. They have the necessary technical staff and can also contribute towards the cost of such buildings. If the responsibility for providing buildings for local schools is placed on municipalities and if a suitable system of grant-in-aid is devised, the progress in this sector would be accelerated.

Supervision and Standardization of School Buildings. For construction of government school buildings, to assist the voluntary organizations for the purpose, to supervise the general programme of construction of school buildings in a State, and to continually introduce improved and economic techniques, we recommend the adoption of the following additional measures :

(1) *Formation of Educational Building Development Groups.* Each State should have an Educational Building Development Group, within the Public Works Department but working in close association with the Education Department, and consisting of an architect, an educationist, an administrator, a civil engineer and a cost accountant, all working on a full time basis (with power to co-opt representatives of special technical skills). The main function of the group would be to improve the planning and construction of government school buildings but its advice should be available for private schools also. There should also be a Building Development Group working at the Centre, for effectively coordinating the working of State-level Groups.

The other functions of the Groups will be (a) to study building requirements in the light of new teaching techniques, (b) to develop in cooperation with manufacturers new building techniques and specifications, (c) to evolve functional and economic type plans for various types of educational buildings, (d) to arrive at a correct assessment of costs of materials and labour required, (e) to conduct field trials, (f) to evaluate the plans, specifications and building techniques already in use, and (g) to study methods of maximizing the use of indigenous materials. The Group at the Centre could profitably bring out a journal highlighting the latest techniques of construction, and researches at home and abroad on conventional buildings.

The State Government should ensure that the recommendations of these Development Groups are followed.

When the Groups in the different States are well established, the possibility of making them function within a rigid framework of maximum cost per place and minimum standards' as is being successfully done in the United Kingdom, should be explored.

(2) To avoid delays in the construction of government buildings a separate unit of PWD should be set up for execution of educational buildings programmes.

(3) *Formation of Educational Building Consortia.* After the Educational Building Development Groups have standardized the plans and the technique of construction, the possibility should be examined of establishing Education Building Consortia (on the lines of similar associations, popularly knows as CLASP, in the UK) to exploit fully the advantages of industrialized buildings.

(4) *Standardization.* Layouts, dimensions, specifications and methods of construction for any particular region should be standardized by the Educational Buildings Development Group mentioned above so that mass production of the different components on a factory scale can be undertaken resulting in economy as well as speed of construction. Considerable work in the field of standardization has been done by organizations like the Indian Standards Institute which could serve as a basis for further studies.

(5) *Buildings for Private Schools.* The economy measures worked out by the Educational Building Development Group in each State for reducing the cost of educational buildings should be made known to the managements of private educational institutions in the State, and the grant-in-aid given to a private management for a buildings should be subject to the upper cost limits worked out.

School Health Services

The provision of school health services (including school meals) is of great importance. The problem has recently been studied by the School Health Committee under the chairmanship of Shrimati Renuka Ray. We broadly agree with the recommendations of the Committee.

Guidance and Counselling

Aim and Scope of Guidance Services. Guidance services have a much wider scope and function than merely that of assisting students in making educational and vocational choices. The aims of guidance are both adjustive and developmental : it helps the student in making the best possible adjustment to the situations in the educational institution and in the home and at the same time facilities the development of all aspects of his personality. Guidance, therefore, should be regarded as an integral part of education and not a special psychological or social service which is peripheral to educational purposes. It is meant for all students, not just for those who deviate from the norm in one direction or the other. It is also a continuous process aimed at assisting the individual to make decisions and adjustments from time to time.

Guidance in primary Education. Guidance should begin from the lowest class of the primary school. It can be used in helping pupils to make a satisfactory transition from home to school; in diagnosing difficulties in the learning of basic educational skills; in identifying pupils in need of special education (e.g., the gifted, the backward, the physically handicapped); in helping potential drop-outs to stay in school; in guiding pupils to develop insight into the world of work and favourable attitudes towards work; and in assisting in plans for their further education or training. Little has been done so far in the shape of guidance services at the primary stage because of the large numbers of institutions involved, the poor qualifications of the teachers and the absence of resources. It would, therefore, be unrealistic for a long time to come to think of providing qualified counsellors in these schools. Some guidance functions can, however, be performed by well-trained primary school teachers. Community resources can also be mobilized to meet some of the guidance needs of the young pupils.

Suggestions for making a begining in guidance in the primary school are outlined below :

(1) The training programme for primary school teachers should include familiarization with simple diagnostic testing, and with the problem of individual differences and their implications for classroom practices

(2) There should be at least one lecturer in the training school who should be able to deal with the subject of principles of guidance and mental hygiene.

(3) Guidance services should be introduced in the training

institutions and in schools attached to the institutions so that the trainees may get first-hand knowledge of the problems involved in their organization.

(4) Wherever possible, short in-service courses in guidance should be provided for primary school teachers.

(5) Simple literature for the occupational orientation of children may be prepared and made available in the regional languages.

(6) At the end of the primary stage, children and parents should be helped in the selection of courses for further education, and the selection should not be based on the examination results alone.

Guidance in Secondary Education. One of the main functions of guidance at the secondary level is to aid in the identification and development of the abilities and interests of adolescent pupils. It helps these pupils to understand their own strengths and limitations and to do scholastic work at the level of their ability to gain information about educational and vocational opportunities and requirements, to make realistic educational and vocational choices and plans based on a consideration of all relevant factors; and to find solutions to their problems of personal and social adjustment the school and the home, Guidance services also help headmasters and teachers to understand their students as individuals and to create situations in which the students can learn more effectively.

Following the recommendations of the Secondary Education Commission, the Ministry of Education set up a Central Bureau of Educational and Vocational Guidance in 1954 to give technical advice and help to the nascent guidance movement in the field of secondary education. Guidance became a Centrally sponsord scheme in the Third Plan and 13 Bureaus have now been set up for the development of guidance services in the States.   These Central and State-level organizations have developed a modest programme of guidance, and services are rendered to the pupils in the schools by trained counsellors and career masters with the help of the teachers.   By the end of the third   plan, the number of schools offering some kind of guidance   was about 3,000, which constitutes only obout 13 per cent of the total number of secondary schools in the country.   Again the majority of these 3,000 schools have only a career master on the staff and offer only an information service.   Very few institutions have a full time or part-time counsellor for giving effective guidance help, including testing and counselling.

It is thus clear that although there is an organized movement for providing guidance services in the country, the progress made   has been   very slow.   The ultimate objective should of course be to introduce adequate guidance services in all secondary schools, with a trained counsellor in charge of the programme.   Since, however, neither financial allocations nor training facilities for guidance will be available on such a large   scale, it is necessary that a short-range programme should be adopted for the next 20 years.   We, therefore, make the following recommendations :

(1)   A minimum guidance service should be made available to all secondary schools by having one Visiting School Counsellor for every ten schools located within a reasonable distance of one another, and by allocating the simpler guidance functions to the teachers.

(2)   At the same   time, in order to demonstrate what a really comprehensive guidance service is   like and what it can achieve, it would be desirable to set up comprehensive guidance services in a few carefully selected schools, preferably one in each district.

(3)   The necessary supervisory staff to inspect and offer consultation to the school workers should be appointed in the State Bureaux of Guidance.

We believe it is necessary that all secondary school teachers should be given some understanding of guidance concepts and simple guidance techniques as a part of the programme intended for every trainee. Special or advanced courses should be provided for those who wish to study the subject in depth. Every training college should have on its staff a person having at least the training considered essential for school counsellors. Provision should also exist for the in-service training of the training college staff in guidance and counselling.

Adequate arrangements should be made for the professional training of guidance workers. The training of career masters may be undertaken by the State Bureaux as well as the training colleges with the collaboration of the vocational guidance officers of the National Employment Service. Professional courses of longer duration should be offered by the universities. Until such courses are started, it may be necessary for the older State Bureaux which have been offering this programme to continue to do so. As the number of persons capable of conducting trainning programmes for guidance workers is extremely limited, higher level training programmes in guidance to prepare qualified guidance workers to undertake training and research should be initiated at the national level.

Other General Proposals. (1) Programmes for the development of guidance literature, occupational information materials, films and filmstrips, and psychological tests, need to be accelerated, care being given to avoid duplication of effort through increased communication among agencies working in these fields. Coordination of efforts should characterize all guidance programmes.

(2) Schools should be assisted in providing hobbies and recreational activities as well as part-time employment opportunities for their students. These should be organized in such a manner as to provide meaningful experiences for the students, and enable them to explore and develop their interests and abilities.

(3)   In addition to the training and extension programmes in guidance mentioned earlier, emphas:s should be laid on research pertaining to guidance in the Indian situation.

Search for and Development of Talent

Significance. A dearth of competent and trained manpower is now felt in nearly every branch of national life, and is probably one of the biggest bottlenecks to progress. Poor as we are financially, the poverty of trained intellect is still greater. We might do well to remember Whitehead's warning: 'In the modern would the rule is absolute—any race which does not value trained intelligence is doomed'.

Present Position. Native intelligence is generally distributed equitably throughout the population. If it is duly discovered and developed, our large population can be our most valuable asset. Unfortunately, very little of the available talent is now discovered and developed, due to several adverse factors :

—In a large majority of the homes, the environment is deprivatory on account of the illiteracy of the parents and poverty, and does not allow the available native talent to develop itself fully.

—A good deal of potential talent never enters school. At the primary stage, the proportion of children not enrolled varies from 10 to 60 per cent in different areas. Even among those who enter, about 40 per cent are eliminated in class I itself and only about 25 per cent belonging to about the top 20 per cent of families in the society, complete primary education. Secondary education is largely a privilege of the top 10 per cent of the families and higher education of the 5 per cent.

—Even the talent that enters school and succeeds in climbing the educational ladder does not flower fully because it is not discovered sufficiently early and is often studying in poor schools. For obtaining the best results in quality, talent has to be located early and allowed to grow in the best atmosphere and under the best teachers.

We still try to determine talent by considering total marks obtained in an examination. This is a very ineffective method. The highly gifted students are far too creative to be confined within the perimeters of classroom instruction, textbooks and examinations. The genius in one field is generally poor in several others and, in our examination system, a genius is more likely to fail or put up only a mediocre 'total' of marks than to come out at the top: Ramanujam and Tagore could not even pass the routine examinations where mediocrities shone. We should, therefore, search separately for each especial talent, whether in mathematics, science, literature, fine arts, sports or technology.

It is not an easy thing to identify gifted students, except perhaps in mathematics and, to some extent, in science. Sustained and energetic research is needed. But as talent is the most valuable asset a country can have, the returns will be immense. Moreover, the search for talent must be a continuous process and has to be taken up at all stages. The secondary stage, however, is the most crucial; and a reference has already been made to the manner in which universities can help in the identification of gifted students at this stage and help them to develop.

Recommendations. Elsewhere, we have made several proposals which will assist in this programme for the discovery and development of talent. The provision of five years of good and effective primary education to every child will enable the country to cast its net for talent to the widest extent possible. The large programme of scholarships proposed at all stages will ensure that all gifted students, or at least the top 5 to 15 per cent of the relevant age-group, will be enabled to receive the highest education possible. The placement programme which we suggest will also make it possible for them to study in the best institutions available at each stage.

In addition to these programmes, it is also necessary to introduce enrichment programmes for the brighter students in as many schools as possible and ultimately in every school. The performance of talented students in the enrichment programmes should be recorded in special certificates which will indicate to the colleges or other institutions of higher education their special abilities and attainments. Care should be taken to ensure that the enrichment programmes do not degenerate into coaching for passing examinations with higher marks. The flexibility in the school curriculum that we have proposed in the preceding chapter would enable the schools to provide enriched or advanced courses for the talented and help them to progress at their own speed. This will also release time for teachers to help the average and backward students.

A variety of extra-mural programmes can also be organized for the talented students, either separately by each school or by schools acting in cooperation or by the Education Departments. For instance :

(1) A five to six-week summer vacation programme can be arranged for a group of academically talented children from different schools, brought together to an educational centre having special facilities of staff, library, laboratory and equipment. The programme may be renewed for the particular group from year to year, so that the students get an opportunity to develop their special talent over a number of years.

(2) Well-planned visits may be arranged to laboratories, museums, and other places.

(3) Talented students may be brought into contact with persons engaged in the types of work for which the students show special ability or interest. These persons may be able to provide occasional opportunities for the students to work in their special fields.

(4) Hostels or Day Centres may be made available for those students whose home environment is not conducive to proper study.

In planning for the development of the talented student, it should be remembered that it is not only his intellectual competence or special ability that needs to be developed. The development of the emotional and social aspects of his personality, and of socially desirable attitudes, is also very important.

The Role of the Counsellor. The role of the counsellor in the promotion of talent can be very important. The counsellor with his detailed knowledge of each talented student is in a unique position to formulate a programme of enrichment for him and to suggest the necessary modifications in the curricular and extra-curricular requirements. Where special counsellors are not available, this task will fall on the teachers. It will, therefore, be necessary to train teachers for this responsibility through in-service seminars and special courses. It should be impressed on them that the classroom atmosphere and the attitudes of teachers is of considerable importance. In a social and educational set-up like ours where the relationship between the teacher and the taught is still largely authoritarian, the general tendency is to suppress any urges and interests that deviate from the class room. The first requirement for the promotion of talent, therefore, is for the teachers to create an atmosphere of free expression in the classroom and to provide opportunities for creative work.

Education of the Backward Child

With the rapid expansion of educational facilities, the number of backward children in schools is also increasing. Many of them drop out of schools at one stage or another, either because of their inability to satisfy the academic standards or the boredom and frustration they feel in the pursuit of an academic programme which is largely unrelated to their needs and interests. Though quite a few of these children manage

to enter high school or even college, their performance continues to be very poor.

Kinds of Backwardness. Backwardness is largely due to
one of two reasons which sometimes overlap : (1) mental
handicap or low intelligence, arising from hereditary or con-
genital factors or disease or injury; (2) under-achievement or
inability to perform up to the level of one's intelligence,
especially in persons intellectually well endowed, frequently
due to emotional conflict, lack of motivation, poor study
habits, cultural deprivation and economic handicaps. On the
basis of studies made in educationally advanced countries, it is
estimated that seventy-five per cent of the backward children
belong to the first category, usually referred to as the mentally
handicapped, and the remaining twenty-five per cent belong to
the second category, usually designated as the under-achievers.
In our case, the latter category would be obviously much
greater. Both these categories of pupils, for different reasons,
are unable to profit from normal education. The result is a
westage of educational facilities and of human resources,
neither of which a developing country can afford.

Meeting the Needs of Slow Learners. The mentally handicapped are generally classified into four groups: the idiots; the
imbeciles; the educable mentally handicapped morons; and the
dull or slow-learners. The first three groups of backward
children, who have an intelligence quotient below 75, cannot
benefit from formal education in ordinary classes. Suitable
provision should, however, be made for the education of the
dull, who on account of their slower rate of mental development, cannot learn at the ordinary pace of normal children.
In the ordinary classes, where instruction is traditionally
geared to the needs of the average child, the dull have to work
under a great hardship. They need individual attention, special
remedial help and probably also a modified curriculum to suit
their rate of learning. In big cities, it may be possible to
establish special schools for them as has been done in some
educationally advanced countries, but in most cases, special
classes in the ordinary schools and individual tuition to the

extent possible are the only general remedy. Such a treatment is likely to be better for their proper emotional and social development also.

Problem of the Under-achievers. The group of under-achievers consists of children who are not intellectually dull, but are at least of average and may even be of superior ability. The failure of such children should be of great concern to a developing country like ours, which cannot remain indifferent to this loss of potential manpower within the higher ability range. Several factors—physical, intellectual, emotional and environmental—contribute to the failure of the under-achiever to come up to the level of his latent abilities. The first step is to diagnose the causes of this failure by observation, interrogation and the application of psychological tests, if possible. Such a collation of data will make it possible to have a total appraisal of the situation and indicate lines of remedial treatment.

Once the child's errors and difficulties are located, a remedial programme should be formulated and carried out. The remedial programme should aim at correcting the basic errors, raising his attainment level in the subject or subjects, re-establishing his confidence in himself and in his ability to succeed, and creating for him new interest and motivation in his studies. The remedial measures should involve the student himself as much as possible and should be organized individually or in small groups. The assessment of the student's progress should be made not against any external standards but with reference to his own previous performance. Remedial programmes are particularly needed in reading, spelling and number work in the earlier stages, and in language and computational skills in the later stages.

Since these educationally retarded children are not under-achieving because of innate low mental capacity, their needs can be met by remedial arrangements within the school system. What the student requires is help for a limited period and within a limited area of study. This may be done by assigning the responsibility to one or two interested teachers during specific periods in the week. Where child guidance clinics exist —and this is a very limited facility at present—the help of highly trained personnel will be available for a group of schools at regular intervals. Remedial groups could also be set up after school hours, two or three days in the week, with subject specialists in charge of each group.

Guidance and counselling services have an important role to play in the education of the backward, especially with regard to identification of the group, diagnosis of their special defects and planning for their education and future occupation. But these services have not been developed and the programme has to be carried on with whatever help and guidance can be given by teachers in the school. The essential factor for success of the programme is the coordinated approach that the entire school faculty should make to the problem of these children with a degree of sympathy and understanding and with an insight into child psychology born out of long experience. The teacher should ordinarily be able to give some help to the under-achievers. Parent-teacher associations should be mobilized for enlisting the cooperation of parents in dealing with special cases. It is necessary, however, that there should be at least one child guidance clinic in each major town, and it should be adequately staffed. Serious cases of backwardness should be referred to these clinics for diagnosis and remedial help.

The New Programme of Evaluation

The evils of the examination system in India are well known to everybody. The baneful effects of the system on education in general, and secondary education in particular, have been discussed in the reports of several committees and commissions. The Secondary Education Commission after reviewing these defects at the secondary education stage, recommended a new approach to school evaluation and made a number of concrete proposals for the improvement of the external examination and the methods of internal assessment.

As a result of these proposals, a movement was started for examination reform, which gathered momentum with the establishment of the Central Examination Unit of trained evaluation officers by the Government of India in 1958. The outstanding feature of the new reform movement is the emphasis laid on the modern concept of evaluation which has found increasing acceptance in educational circles in India in recent years.

The New Concept of Evaluation. It is now agreed that evaluation is a continuous process, forms an integral part of the total system of education, and is intimately related to educational objectives. It exercises a great influence on the pupil's study habits and the teacher's methods of instruction and thus helps not only to measure educational achievement but also to improve it. The techniques of evaluation are means of collecting evidence about the student's development in desirable directions. These techiques should, therefore, be valid, reliable, objective and practicable. As the common method (and often the only method) of evaluation used at present in India is the written examination, a natural corollary of the acceptance of the new approach will be to improve the written examination in such a way that it becomes a valid and reliable measure of educational achievement. There are, however, several important aspects of the student's growth that cannot be measured by written examinations, and other methods such as observation techniques, oral tests and practical examinations, have to be devised for collecting evidence for the purpose. These methods need to be improved and made reliable instruments for assessing the student's performance and educational development.

Progress of the Movement for Reform. During the seven years of its existence the Central Examination Unit has made a multipronged attack for the popularization of new concept and techniques of evaluation. It has worked with thousands of secondary school teachers in seminars and workshops, introduced hundreds of training college lecturers to the new techniques, established a very large pool of test items, trained paper-setters attached to different Boards of Secondary Education, published a good deal of literature on evaluation and carried out or sponsored several studies and investigations on various practical problems in examinations. As the work of the Unit expanded, the Government of India approved of the establishment of Evaluation Units in different States during the Third Plan period. So far, State Evaluation Units have started functioning in 12 States and one Union Territory.

But the task is a stupendous one, and it will take considerable time for the new measures to make their impact on objectives, learning experiences and evaluation procedures in school education. The improvements already made in the external examination by the different Boards have not removed all its major defects. The objectives have not yet been enlarged to include the testing of application and problem-solving abilities. The character of the school examinations, at least in the senior classes, is determined largely by that of the external examination, and the new techniques of evaluation are not readily adopted in these internal examinations. Moreover, all the efforts in the direction of reform have been confined to the field of secondary education. No attention has been paid to the improvement of examinations at the primary stage, and hardly any to the problems in this area at the university stage.

Evaluation at the Lower Primary Stage. One of the main purposes of evaluation at the primary stage is to help the pupils to improve their achievement in the basic skills and to develop the right habits and attitudes with reference to the objectives of primary education. These objectives and their implications for evaluation should be made clear to the teachers. As has been suggested in an earlier chapter, it would be desirable to treat the lower primary stage covering classes I to IV as an ungraded unit, because this would help the children coming from different backgrounds to advance at their own pace. At the conditions in most primary schools, however, are not favourable to the general adoption of this procedure, we have recommended that the experiment should be tried out in the beginning in classes I and II, which should be regarded as a single ungraded unit. This will put an end to the existing practice of detentions in class I and the drop-outs and wastage resulting therefrom, and will also provide for continuity and flexibility in the educational programme of the first two classes. The two-year block may be divided into two groups, one for slow-learners and the other for fast-learners to enable different pupils to proceed at the level of their ability and move from one unit to another. Such a division, however, will be practicable only in a large-size school with more than one section in each class. If the experiment regarding the ungraded unit succeeds in classes I and II, it may be extended to the remaining classes of the lower primary stage.

Teachers should be prepared for the ungraded system through the regular training courses and orientation programmes and should be helped with a supply of diagnostic tests and remedial material. The orientation may be given by the State Institutes of Education. Observation techniques, which are more reliable for assessing the pupil's growth at this stage than mere formal techniques, of evaluation, should be used by teachers in a planned and systematic manner.

Evaluation at the High Primary State. At present evaluation in these classes is carried out largely by means of written examinations. We believe that due importance should be given here also to oral tests, which should form a part of the internal assessment. The teacher should be helped in such assessment with a rich supply of evaluation materials prepared by the State Evaluation Organizations, including standardized achievement tests. Diagnostic testing is necessary here and indeed throughout the school stage. In most cases, such testing will be through simple teacher-made diagnostic tests. Cumulative record cards play a vital role in indicating the growth and development of the pupil at each stage, his academic and emotional problems, and his difficulties of adjustment, if any, and the directions in which remedial action is to be taken to solve his problems or difficulties. We are of the opinion that cumulative record cards intended for the primary classes should be very simple, so that primary teachers can use them with just a little training. In the first instance, the cards should be introduced from class IV onwards in about 10 per cent of selected schools as an experimental measure; but once the majority of teachers are trained in evaluating certain important aspects of the child's personality and the proper maintenance of the records, the use of the cards may be gradually extended to all the higher primary and, as a next step, even to lower primary schools.

Is a Primary External Examination Necessary? An external examination at the end of the primary stage (class VII or VIII) to be taken compulsorily by all pupils was strongly recommended by some witnesses who appeared before the Commission. We were informed that some of the States which had abolished the external examination at the end of this stage had either re-introduced it or proposed re-introducing it in the near future. It was pointed out that an external examination was necessary for (1) maintaining certain uniform standards at the end of the stage; (2) providing a basis for choice of courses at the secondary stage; and (3) creating incentives for better teaching and learning. But all these arguments do not establish a case for an external examination of the formal type to be compulsorily taken by all the pupils in class VII or VIII. Though we have recommended elsewhere that the first national standard of attainment should be defined at the end of the primary stage, we do not think it necessary or desirable to prescribe a rigidly uniform level of attainment for all the primary school pupils in a State or even in a district, through an external examination. Moreover, instead of creating incentives for better teaching, the external examination intended for all will saddle teachers with standardized programmes and encourage the process of rote memorization, which is the besetting evil of teaching and learning methods in our schools today. Again, since full-time education at the lower secondary stage will provide, by and large, general education without any streaming, the argument regarding the choice does not hold good; and for the diversion of pupils to full-time vocational courses to be made available at the stage, an examination which will merely test intellectual ability and academic attainment will not be of much help. We, therefore, recommend that no compulsory external examination should be held at the end of the primary school stage.

While we are not in favour of a compulsory external examination, we believe that for the proper maintenance of standards, periodic surveys of the level of achievement of primary schools is necessary. We recommend that such surveys should be conducted by the district educational authorities to assess the standard of performance of the schools in a given area by means of standardized or highly refined tests prepared by specialists in the State Evaluation Organizations. This procedure will enable the education officers to pick out the weaker schools and help them to improve their performance. It will also assist the schools in finding out the weakness of their pupils for purposes of remedial work.

A Common Internal Examination for Inter-School Comparability. By making use of the standardized or refined test material referred to above, the district educational authorities may, if they so desire, arrange for a common examination to be taken by the pupils of all the schools in a district at the end of the primary stage. This common school leaving examination will be different from the school certificate examination now held in many States, because though the question papers will be set by the district educational authorities or by special paper-setters appointed by the State Evaluation Organization, the performance of the pupils of each participating school will be assessed by the teachers of the school themselves, and not by external examiners. The advantages of such a common final examination for the primary schools are obvious. As the question papers will contain standardized tests and highly refined and professional test items, the evaluation will be more valid and reliable than what is possible through the kind of annual and final examinations conducted in the ordinary primary school. Moreover, through such common tests inter-school comparability with regard to levels of performance in the district can be obtained, and this would be helpful, as shown above, both to the education officers and to the schools.

We would like to emphasize that the question papers in the different subjects at this common examination should be of short duration, each of not more than one hour or one hour and a half, so that the entire examination should be completed in two or three days.

The whole purpose of the proposal is to reform the existing examination by making it less formal, reducing its burden on the pupils' minds, and increasing its validity as a measure of educational attainment. The school at the primary stage plays the determining role in the total assessment of such attainment. The certificate regarding the completion of the course should be given by the school and not by the external agency, and this certificate should be accompanied by a statement showing the results of the common final examination, if any, together with the results of the internal assessment made by the school of the pupils' performance throughout the year, as shown in his cumulative records.

In addition to the common examination, special tests may be held at the end of the primary course for the award of scholarships or certificates of merit or for the purpose of identifying talent and pupils may appear for these tests on a voluntary basis. The evaluation of the pupil's performance in these tests will be done by external examiners.

Improvement in External Examination. At present the external examination in the case of the higher secondary class or the intermediate classes located in the school, the external examination is held by the State Board of Secondary (or Higher Secondary) Education and in the case of pre-university class, by the university concerned. We have recommended that the pre-university classes now located in affiliated colleges should be transferred to schools as higher secondary classes in a phased programme spread over ten years, and that the duration of the higher secondary course should be extended to two years everywhere by 1986. When these classes are located exclusively in the schools, the Board of School Education will conduct the external examination at the end of class XI (or class XII) as well as that at the end of class X. In the transitional period the present dual control will continue. What we state below applies to all external examinations at the school stage, whether they are at present conducted by the Boards or by the universities.

(1) Most of the weaknesses in the present system of external examinations are due to defects in the questions and the question papers set for the examination. The paper-setters are, by and large, appointed on the basis of seniority, subject competence, and experience in teaching. Very few of them possess the necessary knowledge and skill in the construction of valid and reliable tests. We are of the opinion that no major break-through towards the improvement of external examinations is possible unless (a) the technical competence of paper-setters is raised through an intensive training programme sponsored by the State Boards; (b) the question papers are oriented to testing not merely the acquisition of knowledge but the ability to apply knowledge and the development of problem-solving abilities; and (c) the nature of the questions asked is improved.

(2) Apart from the improvement of questions and question papers, many other procedures of the external examinations need to be made more systematic and scientific. For example, the marks of different subjects are added without being standardized. The determination of cut-off points, the award of grace marks and other similar methods are also not based on any sound rationale. All these factors tend to make the examinations scores less and less reliable. It is essential that scientific scoring procedures should be devised so that there may be optimum reliability in the assessment of the candidate's performance.

(3) With the ever-increasing number of students appearing for the Board examinations, the task of getting the answer scripts properly valued and of processing the results efficiently within a given time is becoming more and more difficult. It is

necessary that this process should be mechanized so as to make it more accurate and expeditious.

Large Incidence of Failures. The matter about which the public at large is most deeply concerned is not the irrationality of the scoring procedures or the inefficiency of the administrative processes, but the large incidence of failures in the external examination at the end of the school stage. An analysis of the results of the different Board examinations for the last five years show that about 55 per cent of the candidates appearing for the high school examination and about 40 per cent of those appearing for the higher secondary school examination fail regularly every year. In the case of the private candidates the percentage soars up to 70 or even more. Failure often has a demoralizing effect on the unsuccessful candidate. The failure of such large numbers of students, particularly after they have been screened year after year by means of annual and other school examinations, is a sad reflection on our methods of education as well as on our system of examination.

There is no doubt that if the measures suggested above for the reform of the external examination are properly implemented, the situation will gradually change in the years to come. We also believe, that with the proposed improvement in the curriculum, instructional materials and methods of teaching and the reorientation in the training of teachers, the incidence of examination failures will be reduced. But we do not think that a student should be branded as a total failure, if he passes in certain subjects but is unable to make the grade in others. There is no reason why he should carry with him the stigma of being declared an unsuccessful candidate if he has partially succeeded in his educational effort.

Certificates Given by the Board and the School. We recommend that the certificate issued by the Board on the basis of the results of the external examination at the end of the lower or higher secondary stage, should give the candidate's performance only in those subjects in which he has passed, but there should be no remark to the effect that he has passed or failed in the whole examination. The Board, however, should issue a statement along with the certificate showing his marks or grades in all the subjects. We further recommend that the candidate should be permitted to appear again, if he so desires, for the entire examination or for separate subjects in order to improve his performance.

On the completion of the course, at the end of the lower or higher secondary stage, the student should receive a certificate from the school also giving the record of his internal assessment as contained in his cumulative record card. This certificate may be attached to that given by the Board in connection with the external examination. We are however of the opinion that the external examination need not be compulsory for all the students of class X or class XI/XII. A student may choose to leave the school with the school certificate only without appearing for the external examination, and seek a job or even an entry into some vocational course on the basis of the certificate and the school records. It must be recognized, however that since admission to institutions of higher secondary education as well as of higher education will be selective, the authorities controlling such institutions will lay down their own rules of eligibility for admission. A student seeing entry into these institutions may have not only to pass the external examination in the subjects laid down and secure the prescribed grades but also submit himself if necessary to certain admission tests required by the institutions.

Establishment of Experimental Schools. We have suggested certain measures above for reducing the domination which the external examination exercises over school education. In order to lessen its importance still further, we recommend that a few selected schools should be given the right of assessing their students themselves and holding their own final examination at the end of class X, which will be regarded at equivalent to the external examination of the State Board of School Education. The State Board will issue the certificates to the successful candidates of these schools on the recommendation of the schools. A committee set up by the State Board of School Education should develop carefully worked-out criteria for the selection of such schools. The schools should not only be freed from the requirements of an external examination but should be permitted to frame their own curricula, prescribe their own textbooks, and conduct their educational activities without departmental restrictions.

This is a bold step in the direction of freedom and of educational experimentation. But the right given to the experimental schools should be reviewed periodically as institutions invested with such powers should continuously earn their privilege. We hope, however, that after the experiment is tried out successfully in a few shools, more and more schools will be released from the restrictive influence of the external examination and given the freedom to work out their own ideas in education.

Methods of Internal Assessment. We shall now pass on to the question of internal assessment to which a reference was made earlier in this section. This internal assessment or evaluation conducted by individual schools is of great significance and should be given increasing importance. It should be comprehensive, evaluating all those aspects of the student's growth that are measured by the external examination and also those personality traits, interests and attitudes which cannot be assessed by it. Internal assessment should be built into the total educational programme of the school and should be used for improvement rather than for certifying the level of achievement of the student. It must be pointed out that all items of internal assessment need not follow qualified scoring procedures. Some of them may be assessed in descriptive terms. The results should be kept separately and not be combined artificially with other results to form aggregate scores.

The written examinations conducted in schools should be improved on the same lines as the external examination. The use of standardized achievement tests, wherever available, is strongly recommended. There is need for developing other types of evaluation tools for improving internal assessment such as interest inventories, aptitude tests and rating scales. They should be prepared by specialists and made available to schools, and the teachers should be trained to use them through a network of in-service programmes. Teachers should also be trained to make simple tests of their own on the models supplied and use them for the assessment of the performance of their pupils.

We are aware that the experience of introducing internal assessment has not been very happy so far and that there has been persistent over-assessment by the weaker schools. This has led some critics to suggest that the system should be abandoned altogether. We cannot agree with this view. Internal assessment has to continue and its importance will have to be increasingly emphasized. To overcome the shortcomings discovered, we make the following recommendations:

(1) The results of the internal assessment and external examination should not be combined because the purposes and techniques of the two evaluations are different and because the results of the internal assessment of the different institutions are not strictly comparable. The results of the external and internal assessment should, therefore, be shown separately in the certificate(s) given at the end of the course.

(2) It should be an important point in the inspections of schools to review the internal assessment made and to examine the correlation between the internal and external assessments. Persistence in over-assessment should be regarded as a weakness in the school programmes. It should be taken due note of while classifying the schools and should also be related to grants-in-aid so that institutions which tend to over-assess their students persistently would stand to lose in status and finance. The grant-in-aid rules should also

authorize the Education Department to withdraw recognition for persistent irresponsible assessment.

Higher Secondary Examination during Transition. We have recommended above that the first external examination should be held at the end of class X or the first stage of schools education, and the second examination should come after class XII which will be the end of the higher secondary stage. At present, the higher secondary stage in all the State except Uttar Pradesh and Kerala ends with class XI after which there is the higher secondary school examination. This will continue to be the position till the duration of the course is extended to two years. During the transitional period, therefore, most students in the higher secondary school will have to appear for two successive external examinations, at the end of class X and class XI, within the period of a year. This is undesirable but cannot be avoided, particularly where the course of class IX, X and XI is not integrated. When the P.U.C. class gets transferred from the affiliated colleges to the high schools, the course will be a non-integrated one.

As a number of existing higher secondary schools with integrated courses are already in existence in some of the States, we do not insist that this integration should be broken up and the students of the schools should be made to appear for two public examinations within a year. There may be only one public examination for such students—the higher secondary school examination at the end of class XI. However, we would like to invite attention in this connection to the procedure that is followed in some areas, where the higher secondary school examination is staggered over a period of two years, the core subjects being offered for examination at the end of class X and the electives at the end of class XI. This procedure may be adopted with suitable modifications in other places. It must be remembered that the problem is a temporary one and will disappear when schools are organized on the 10 plus 2 pattern.

The comprehensive programme of evaluation that we have

described in the preceding paragraphs requires for its implementation a well-organized machinery both at the State and the Central levels. The Secondary Boards of School Education that now conduct external examinations at the secondary stage will be converted into State Boards of School Education with enhanced powers and functions. At the Centre, there will be a National Board of School Education that will be responsible for evaluation programmes at the national level. The composition, the powers and the functions at these Boards will be considered in the next chapter.

SUMMARY

1. *Teaching Methods: Discovery and Diffusion.* The continual deepening of the curricula should be accomplished by an equally vigorous improvement in the method of teaching and evaluation. The main factors responsible for the dull and uninspiring school teaching today are the rigidity of the educational system and the failure of the administrative machinery to diffuse new educational practices to schools. These weeknesses should be overcome.

(1) *Elasticity and Dynamism.* A good educational system should be dynamic, flexible and discriminating enough to help institutions and teachers to proceed along different levels of development—the good schools be free to go ahead on creative and experimental lines while the weaker ones should be supported to gain a sense of security.

(2) Such elasticity and dynamism are possible if the experimenting teacher is supported by the administrative authority, a general atmoshere of reform, the encouragement of the head of the institution, a mastery of subject-matter, leadership provided by training institutions, and the availability of teaching materials.

(3) Elasticity in a school system will have little value if new practices developed are not diffused to schools and

teachers given skilled help in trying out innovations. The educational administration can encourage and hasten the diffusion of new teaching methods by:

—combining permissiveness with persuasion;

—approaching the new methods in stages according to the ability of schools;

—giving necessary in-service training to teachers;

—providing adequate guide materials which should be constantly revised and improved.

At the same time the administrator has to guard himself against letting any 'progressive' measure settling down into another orthodoxy.

2. *Textbooks, Teachers' Guides and Meterials*

(1) Provision of quality textbooks and other teaching-learning materials is a key programme for raising standards at comparatively low cost.

(2) A comprehensive programme of textbook production at the national level should be implemented by mobilizing the best talent in the country on the lines already being attempted by NCERT. Such books will facilitate the definition and practical indication of expected standards. They will also help in national integration.

(3) The Ministry of Education should take steps to establish in the public sector an autonomous organization, functioning on commercial lines for the production of textbooks at the national level, especially scientific and technical books. A small committee may be set up to work out the details of the project.

(4) The effort at the national level should be supported

and augmented by each State setting up an expert section for the production of textbooks.

(5) The preparation, try-out and evaluation of textbooks should be the responsibility of the State Education Departments. The production aspect of the textbooks may preferably be done by the State Education Departments, wherever possible, through their own textbook presses. The sale and distribution of textbooks are better left to the student cooperatives and not be assumed directly by the Departments.

(6) The production of textbooks and teaching aids at the State level should preferably be entrusted to an autonomous agency functioning in close liaison with the Education Department.

(7) The machinery set up should be such that the textbooks are subjected to continuous revision and improvement.

(8) At least 3 or 4 books should be provided in each subject to provide a multiple choice of books for the schools.

(9) Liberal policies should be adopted for remunerating authors.

(10) The entire organization of State production of textbooks should be run on a no-profit-no-loss basis.

(11) Manuscripts should be invited from a variety of sources including teachers, and a high-level committee of professional persons should select and approve manuscripts.

(12) Teachers' guides and other instructional material should supplement textbooks.

(13) Lists of minimum teaching aids and equipment needed

by each category of schools should be prepared and steps taken to provide the equipment to every school on a high priority basis.

(14) .Education Departments should work with the All-India Radio for the use of radio lessons, supplemented by printed guide materials for teachers and pupils. Broadcasting of special radio talks specially designed for teachers in the mornings and evenings will help teachers in lesson preparation. Sophisticated forms of newer techniques would not be suitable at present in the general run of schools but may be tried out experimentally in teacher-training institutions.

(15) Teachers should be helped and trained to rely on inexpensive and locally available or improvised teaching aids. Costly equipment should be shared by schools in a neighbourhood.

(3) *Class Size.* (1) Classes of somewhat larger size than what is strictly considered as desirable cannot be avoided in our country for a long time. However, it is necessary to restrict the number of pupils admitted to each class to a maximum of 50 in the lower primary, 45 in the higher primary and lower secondary, and 40 in higher secondary classes.

(2) *Multiple-class Teaching.* Research should be undertaken in the problems and techniques of multiple-class teaching. Training institutions should orient teachers to these techniques.

4. *School Buildings.* (1) In view of the present unsatisfactory position regarding school buildings, it is necessary to take steps to clear the backlog of unconstructed school buildings as well as to provide additional buildings for new enrolment.

(2) Allocations for construction of school buildings should be increased in the Central and State budgets, and community resources mobilized on the basis of equalization. Loans and

grants-in-aid should be given on a liberal basis to private schools for the construction of buildings.

(3) *Reduction of Costs.* The norms and guidance already available for spacing and planning of school buildings should be put into practice.

(4) In view of the shortage of traditional building material and the cost involved, well-designed and constructed *kacha* structures should be accepted as part of the school system.

(5) *Buildings in Rural Areas.* In rural areas, efforts should be made to encourage local initiative and contribution in putting up school buildings. The 'nucleus' approach suggested by the Ministry of Education is recommended for general adoption.

(6) *Buildings in Urban Areas.* Economy in these buildings should be effected by using locally available materials, omission of certain finishes, and acceptance of a lower standard of construction. Temporary structures may be used, wherever possible, and improved techniques of construction may be adopted in putting up pucka buildings.

(7) *Expeditious Construction.* In order to accelerate provision of school buildings, construction in rural areas may be entrusted to local communities or village panchayats, and in urban areas, municipalities and corporations may be utilized for the purpose.

(8) In order to supervise and guide the programme of construction of school buildings and introduce improved techniques, an Educational Building Development Group should be set up in each State within the Public Works Department and working in close association with the Education Department. These groups will standardize details of construction in the region so as to make possible the mass production of the components on a factory scale. A similar Building Develop-

ment Group should be set up at the Centre to coordinate the work of the State groups.

(9) To avoid delays in the construction of government buildings, a separate unit of the PWD should be set up for the execution of education building programmes. At a later stage an Education Building Consortia may be set up to exploit the advantages of industrialized buildings.

(10) The economy measures worked out by the Educational Building Development Group should be made known to private institutions and grants-in-aid given on the basis of upper cost limits.

5. *Guidance and Counselling.* Guidance and counselling should be regarded as an integral part of education, meant for all students and aimed at assisting the individual to make decisions and adjustments from time to time.

(1) *Guidance at the Primary Stage.* Guidance should begin from the lowest class in the primary school and in view of the large numbers of schools involved, the programme may be introduced through simple measures such as (a) familiarising teachers under training with diagnostic testing and the problem of individual differences; (b) organizing in-service courses for primary teachers; (c) producing occupational literature ; and (d) helping pupils and parents in choice of further education.

(2) *Guidance at the Secondary Stage.* Guidance at the secondary stage should, among other things, help in the identification and development of the abilities and interests of adolescent pupils. The ultimate objective should be to introduce adequate guidance services in *all* secondary schools with a trained counsellor in charge of the programme. But in view of the limited financial and personnel resources, a short-range programme should be adopted for the next 20 years consisting of—

(a) a minimum guidance programme for all secondary

schools through a visiting school counsellor for a group of ten schools, assisted by the school teachers in the simpler guidance functions;

(b) comprehensive guidance programme in selected schools, one in each district, to serve as models; and

(c) provision of necessary supervisory staff in the State Bureaux of Guidance.

(3) All secondary school teachers should be introduced to guidance concepts through pre-or in-service training. The training colleges should be suitably staffed for the purpose.

(4) *General.* Arrangements should be made for the professional training of guidance workers by the State Bureaux of Guidance and training colleges. Advanced training should be organized at the national level.

(5) Ancillary programmes should include the production of guidance literature and materials and research into problems of guidance in the Indian situation.

6. *Search for and Development of Talent.* (1) The search for talent must be a continuous process, pursued at all stages, but the secondary stage is the most crucial.

(2) In addition to programmes of enrichment and advanced curricula, a variety of extra-mural programmes should be organized for the talented such as summer schools, visits to places of educational interest and provision of hostels and day-centres for those whose home environment is not conducive to study.

(3) Teachers should be oriented to the special techniques of dealing with the talented children, especially to the need for providing an atmosphere for free expression and creative work.

7. *The Backward Child.* Neglect of backward children leads to wastage of educational facilities and human resources and it is necessary for a developing country to reduce this wastage to the minimum. In particular, attention has to be given to the under-achievers who represent a loss of potential manpower often of high ability. Steps should, therefore, be taken to diagnose the causes of under-achievement and to formulate and implement remedial programmes within the school system, with the help of interested teachers and child guidance clinics, where available, and parent-teacher associations.

8. *Evaluation.* Evaluation is a continuous process, forms an integral part of the total system of education and is intimately related to educational objectives. It exercises a great influence on the pupil's study habits and the teacher's methods of instruction and thus helps not only to measure educational achievement but also to improve it.

(1) The new approach to evaluation will attempt to improve the written examination so that it becomes a valid and reliable measure of educational achievement and to devise techniques for measuring those important aspects of the student's growth that cannot be measured by written examinations.

(2) *Evaluation at the Lower Primary Stage.* Evaluation at this stage should help pupils to improve their achievement in the basic skills and development of right habits and attitudes.

(3) It would be desirable to treat classes I to IV as an ungraded unit to enable children to advance at their own pace. Where this is not feasible, classes I and II may be treated as one block divided into two groups—one for slow and the other for fast learners. Teachers should be appropriately trained for the ungraded system.

(4) *Evaluation at the Higher Primary Stage.* In addition to written examinations, weightage should be given at this.

stage to oral tests as a part of internal assessment. Diagnostic testing should be through simple teacher-made tests. Cumulative record cards are important in indicating pupils' growth and development but should be very simple and should be introduced in a phased manner.

(5) *External Examination at the End of the Primary Stage.* Although the first national standard of attainment is to be set at the end of the primary stage, it is not considered necessary or desirable to prescribe a rigid and uniform level of attainment through a compulsory external examination. However, for the proper maintenance of standards, periodic surveys of the level of achievement of primary schools should be conducted by district school authorities through refined tests prepared by State Evaluation Organizations.

(6) *A Common External Examination for Inter-School Comparability.* The district educational authority may arrange for a common examination at the end of the primary stage for schools in the district, using standardized and refined tests. This examination will have greater validity and reliability than the school examination and will provide inter-school comparability of levels of performance.

(7) The certificate at the end of the primary course should be given by the school and should be accompanied by the cumulative record card and the statement of results of the common examination, if any.

(8) In addition to the common examinations, special tests may be held at the end of the primary course for the award of scholarships or certificates of merit and for the purpose of identifying talent.

(9) *Improvement in External Examinations.* External examinations should be improved by raising the technical competence of papersetters, orienting question papers to objectives other than to acquisition of knowledge, improving the nature of questions, adopting scientific scoring procedures, and

mechanizing the scoring of scripts and the processing of results.

(10) *Certificate given by the Board and School.* The certificate issued by the State Board of School Education on the basis of the results of the external examination should give the candidate's performance in different subjects for which he has appeared and there should be no remark to the effect that he has passed or failed in the whole examination. The candidate should be permitted to appear again, if he so desires, for the entire examination or for separate subjects in order to improve his performance.

(11) The student should receive a certificate also from the school, giving the record of his internal assessment as contained in his cumulative record card and this should be attached to that given by the Board.

(12) *Establishment of Experimental Schools.* A few selected schools should be given the right of assessing their students themselves and holding their own final examination at the end of class X, which will be regarded as equivalent to the external examination of the State Board of School Education. The State Board of School Education will issue the certificates to the successful candidates of these schools on the re-commendation of the schools. A committee set up by the State Board of School Education should develop carefully worked-out criteria for the selection of such schools. The schools should be permitted to frame their own curricula, prescribe their own textbooks, and conduct their educational activities without external restrictions.

(13) *Methods of Internal Assessment.* Internal assessment by schools should be comprehensive and evaluate all aspects of student growth including those not measured by the external examination. It should be descriptive as well as quantified. Written examinations conducted by schools should be improved and teachers trained appropriately. The internal

assessment should be shown separately from the external examination marks.

(14) *Higher Secondary Examination.* During the transition period, higher secondary students will have to appear for two successive external examinations—at the end of classes X and XI, within one year. Where, however, the courses in classes IX to XI are integrated, the examination at the end of class X need not be insisted upon.

9

Educational Technology

Introduction

It has not been possible in India so far to develop a theoretical model to define the concept and practices in the field of educational technology. Efforts have been made at the All India level to publish some material in the form of the year book of educational technology and bring out a journal by the association of educational technology. But they are mainly a conglomeration of stray thoughts by individuals and have no connection to research or experimentation in the field of educational technology. The concepts have only been borrowed and have been prevented without clear perception on the subject.

The fact however, remains that in a country like India where 64% people are illiterate, never methods of teaching are needed to convey the messages easily and rapidly to the educations. Local research is needed in the field. So far only American concepts are being blindly followed by the Pundits of Indian education both in the bureaucracy and in the schools and colleges.

This chapter is mainly based on essays written by American educators to help the reader to frame his own conclusions on the subject. This has been deliberately done to avoid confusion and misunderstanding.

EDUCATIONAL USES OF INFORMATION TECHNOLOGY

Since the development of the radio, people have proposed that communications technology provide major improvements in the delivery of education. Research on "teaching machines" dates back to the 1940's, before the general introduction of computers into the marketplace. Since that time, there has been continual research, development, and implementation of techniques for using information technology in various aspects of education.

OTA investigated what is known and what has been proposed about possible applications of information technology to education.

FINDINGS

Information technology is capable of becoming a major resource for the delivery of educational services over the next decade :

— It can be an effective delivery mechanism for most existing forms of education.

— It provides capabilities for responding to new demands that traditional schoolroom education cannot meet adequately.

— The cost of information products and services for educational applications will continue to drop with respect to other items in the educational budget.

The principal benefits will be realized from combinations of new technologies rather than from any single device.

Most educational applications will be based on hardware technology that is originally developed for a broader consumer market. The only exceptions will be devices designed for specialized industrial uses—e.g., flight training for airline pilots—or education and training for the handicapped.

It is impossible to predict with certainty the technological base that will exist for educational use. Some of the products and services now projected for the next decade, and described in chapter 4, may not survive the competition for the consumer's money. This uncertainty may inhibit the rapid development of software and services particularly oriented to the education market.

The provision of high-quality, reasonably priced educational software is the principal technological challange. Low-cost hardware will be widely available to most homes, officers, and schools.

FUNCTIONS OF EDUCATIONAL TECHNOLOGY

There are a variety of ways in which computers and communications technology can provide educational services. In some cases, different types of applications will require different technologies; in other cases, the same type of technology can be used to provide different types of services.

Passive Instruction

The oldest instructional use of information technology is simply to present information. The textbook is the traditional passive instructional system. Projection media—slides, filmstrips, overhead transparencies, and pictures—are more modern forms. Educational radio and television have experienced quiet but steady growth since the late 1950's and early 1960's. Video cassettes and video disks will provide even more flexible tools for presenting video-based instructional material.

The best known recent examples of passive instructional programming are the "Sesame Street" and "Electric Company" programs produced by the Children's Television Workshop with partial Federal support. These programs were intended to supplement, not replace, normal schooling.

Sesame Street is intended to teach preschool children some basic concepts and learning attitudes. Electric Company is principally aimed at supplementing reading instruction at the grammar school level.

At the other extreme, a full alternative to traditional education is the "Open University" in Britain, which has conducted a full college degree program for over 11 years, based principally on passive instruction using the broadcast networks. In the United States, the Corporation for Public Broadcasting is developing an educational program along similar lines in cooperation with universities across the country.

New technology for video production is also having an impact on educational uses. *Computer animation* systems have become considerably less expensive than older, hand animation techniques. *Video processing* uses computers to perform elaborate modification of video images. Both of these technologies are widely used in commercial television and motion pictures, but they are also particularly attractive for instructional application in which concepts and processes that are subtle and difficult to visualize need to be illustrated. Complex physical processes, such as fluid flow or load stresses on structures such as bridges, can be simultated on a computer and displayed as dynamic graphic images. In addition, video cassette recorders (VCRs) and video disks promise to relieve students from the dictates of schedule. The VCR, in particular, allows—copyright law permitting—instructors, and students to copy instructional programs off the air and play them back at some later time. Video cassettes and video disks will provide alternate mode of broadcasting for the distribution of instructional material.

Passive instruction systems have the following characteristics :

— All educational decisions are in the hands of the providers; what information is to be presented, for how long, in what sequence, and even—in the case of such current instructional broadcasting—the schedule— when it is shown.

— The boundaries between entertainment, public information, and educational services can become blurred. A shakespeare play, a concert, or an informational series such as the successful Cosmos series carried by the Public Broadcasting System, may all the considered important instructional resources as well as entertainment.

Interactive Instruction

This technology is used to teach a specific subject or skill directly to a sudent, guiding the learner through a sequence of steps involving the presentation of information, drills and exercises designed by an instructor. Interactive instructional systems require the student to communicate with the device, allowing the system to vary the pace of instruction, select among alternate sequences of presentation, test for understanding, and alter the content according to the specific needs of the individual.

Computer-assisted instruction is the best known interactive technology. A student sitting at a computer terminal works through a series of "frames" that teach and test understanding. If the student is progressing slowly, the computer branches to an alternate style of presentation or a remedial section. If the student has mastered that section the computer jumps ahead to more advanced material.

The Plato system was one of the better known experiments. It was developed by researchers at the University of Illinois and Control Data Crop. With principal funding from the Federal Government, the system originally combined a new type of interactive graphics terminal with a large multiterminal computer system and an elaborate language specifically designed to create instructional programs. While Plato was originally a very expensive experimental system, most of its underlying concepts survive in commercial instructional systems now marketed by Control Data.

Four factors have more recently revived interest in interactive instruction :

(1) the rapidly declining costs of computers and the advent of the desktop computer,

(2) the escalating labor-intensive costs of traditional schooling,

(3) an improved understanding of how to create instructional packages, and

(4) the development of alternative delivery mechanisms that link the computer with other technologies, such as video disk and interactive cable.

The video disk is good example of how new technologies can be combined to form instructional systems. The video disk contains an extensive data base of text, still images, and film. The computer controls the sequence of presentation and, using an educational program contained on its floppy disk and information stored in the remote data base, interacts with the student.

The video disk, for example, might contain several thousand images of microscope slides. The data base would have full descriptive information on the subjects illustrated by the slides, indexed in various ways. Educational software on the computer would take a student through sequences of slides and text presentation, providing information and administering tests. While the computer program would be designed to achieve a specific instructional purpose, the slide catalog and data base would be intended to be more widely applicable for research and education.

Several experiments are under way to develop instructional

packages using combinations of video disks and personal computers. The Minnesota Educational Computing Consortium is developing a series of video disks in basic economics. The first disk of a planned 6-disk series has been produced and tried in the classroom with favourable results. Other companies are developing products aimed at the industrial training market; and a few firms, such as IBM, are already using interactive video disks for employee training.

Interactive instructional technology has the following characteristics :

— It allows the system to customize teaching to the particular level of understanding, learning style, and ability of each individual student.

— The system can be designed so that students can pace themselves.

— Because individualization and self-pacing may not fit well with traditional schooling, large-scale implementation of inter-active instructional technology in the schools may engender substantial institutional resistance.

— Instructional software is often divided into discrete packages, each designed to teach a specific skill or item of information. An instructional curriculum (say, a fifth grade mathematics course) is a collection of these packages, which, for a full course, may number into the hundreds.

— Extensive design effort is needed to create each module. The material to be taught must be broken down into framesized pieces. Tests of understanding must be devised, and the paths that students are most likely to take in going through the material must be anticipated.

— Because they are so carefully tailored, interactive

curricular packages are inflexible. They are not generally useful for any purpose, clientele, or environment other than the specific one for which they were designed.

— The skills required both to produce software and to assist students with its use are substantially different from traditional teaching skills.

— Some experts suggest that smaller instructional modules can be designed to fit into the regular course of instruction, permitting a gradual introduction of educational technology. Others maintain that the principal educational benefits of technology are lost with such an incremental approach.

Learning Environments

The interactive instruction technology described above can be used to create a special environment—a language, simulation, or data base—that can be manipulated by the student.

For example, special computer languages, such as LOGO, can help learners gain particular problem-solving skills. Languages such as VISICALC, a system designed for business users of small computers, can be a powerful tool in teaching accounting principles and financial planning techniques.

Another form of learning environment is the simulation. A simulation of a laboratory experiment for a physics course, for instance, might present on a television screen a variety of weights and springs. The student would be allowed to "connect" them in various configurations, to apply forces of prescribed amounts at different points in the arrangement, and to measure and record the results. Working with this system for only a few days, a student would learn some basic principles of mechanics. As another example, large-scale simulations can be made of physical processes or of equipment that might be too expansive or dangerous to use in person. Simulated nuclear powerplants provide vehicles for training new operators; simulated aircraft are used for pilot training.

For medical education, computer-controlled robots can be used to simulate injured or ill human beings. A small computer presents the student with an instructional sequence where proper techniques are illustrated using a computer-controlled video disk. The student then practices on a dummy equipped with sensors monitored by the computer, which in turn, presents the results to the student.

Simulations of economic and social systems are used to teach political science, economics, and management. Business management games are one of the earliest educational applications of computers, and they have been deeply integrated into the curricula of many business schools. Other educational applications range from simple economic simulations on small computers to elaborate simulations of city management and international politics that require very large computer systems. The Defence Department makes extensive use of computer-based simulations to train senior decision makers in crisis management.

Using information technology to provide a learning environment has several implications :

— An instructional program can be applicable over longer course periods and for a greater variety of educational uses than can an interactive module that concentrates on a single teaching unit.

Since the interaction is so flexible and is directed in large part by the students, instructors and student need documentation and supplemental curriculum materials appropriate for using the system to meet their particular educational objectives. Except for large simulations (such as flight trainers) that may require special hardware, the principal cost of "learning environment" applications will be in developing these supplemental curricular materials. Developmental costs for the programs will, in general, be written off against a much larger customer base.

— Because it fundamentally changes both content and the way material is presented, use of an automated learning environment may require extensive changes in course content or even a broader redesign of an entire curriculum.

Information Resource

General information literacy is needed for all individuals to work and to participate fully in an information society. In addition, for most professions, specialized computer and communication-based systems are rapidly becoming indispensable tools of the trade. Students must learn how to use these services as part of their early training.

For these reasons, in addition to being an instructional tool, the computer in education is viewed as an intellectual and problem-solving resource, akin to the library or laboratory. Information services will need to be both broad enough to support general education and specialized enough for particular subject matter. Examples of specialized systems include computer-aided design systems for industrial engineering students, on-line legal or medical information retrieval systems for use by law students or doctors, and automated accounting and financial analysis systems for business students.

In addition to these specialized resources, students in all fields will need constant access to information services and computer facilities for their work. One engineering school is experimenting with providing a desktop computer to some of its entering freshmen, with a view toward giving computers to all students in the future. A graduate school of business has already adopted a similar policy for its entering students. The leader of the movement to provide all undergraduate students with computer access has been Dartmouth College, which, for well over a decade, has operated with a policy of universal computer literacy and free student access to computer terminals.

/ The role of the computer as an educational resource on campus is blending with the view of libraries as automated information centres. Many college and university libraries have been among the leaders in this movement—first in automating their management, then in providing users access to computerized bibliographic services. Their ultimate goal is to provide full text, on line retrieval. As these trends continue, the computer center and the library will actually merge into a single, automated information utility.

Regional and national networks will provide scholars with access to information and computational resources anywhere in the country EDUCOM, a nation wide consortium of universities and colleges, has been developing this concept for several years and now offers its members access to EDUNET, a nation-wide resource-sharing data communication network.

Administration and Instructional Management

Information technology can be used by the teacher to help plan coursework and manage the classroom. Computers not only assist with mundane daily tasks such as grading and recordkeeping but can also help keep closer track of the daily accomplishments and problems of individual students. Teacher attention can, thus, be more focussed on individual student needs. Teleconferencing via radio, television, or computer allows teachers to exchange experiences, develop curricula, and coordinate educational programs among a number of schools in a district.

Distribute Education

The distribution of services to those who need them has

always been a difficult problem, for the educational system. for as long as education has been provided by schools, the distribution problem has been responsible for institutional constraints of both time and location on the student. That schooling takes place on a physical campus, attended principally by young people, may be more reflective of the limitations of the traditional schooling system than it is of the current needs of society for education. Chapter 6, which examines the state of the educational system, concludes that a significant gap may exist between the forms of educational needs of a modern information society and the traditional institutional forms of educating.

Information technology is a tool that can address these to distributional problems—distance and time. In the past, television and radio have been used for this purpose, often to good effect. However, their applicability has been limited both by the need to use expensive and scarce broadcast facilities to serve a relatively small clientele and by the inhability to provide interactive services.

Modern technology removes these barriers. Communication facilities such as cable, direct broadcast sattellite, low-power television, and video cassette and video disk will greatly increase the number of information channels coming into the home and office. Two-way cable, remote conferencing facilities, and optical video disk microcomputer systems provide the capability for interactive education.

Among the particular applications of information technology for distribution are the following :

— *General educational services to dispersed populations* : Some geographical regions need to provide schooling to a sparse population spread over a large area. Communications technology such as direct broadcast sattellite or low power television allows educational programing to be broadcast at low cost to small rural communities and even to individual residences.

Video cassettes, video disks, and personal computer programs can be distributed physically by mail.

— *Specialized educational services to small populations* : Some groups in society that have very specialized needs for educational services are not concentrated geographically. Only by providing courses regionally or nationally can a critical mass of students be assembled to justify the expense of the course. Information systems provide that wider market. For example :

  — Advanced professional training, especially continuing education in such fields as medicine, law, and engineering, in which knowledge advances at a rapid rate.

  — Unusual educational needs, such as accelerated science programs for the gifted or courses conducted in a foreign language.

  — Instruction in subjects for which experienced teachers are scarce or courses conducted by outstanding scholars and leaders in a field.

— *Education for the homebound* : For a number of reasons—e.g., illness physical handicap, or age—many individuals in society cannot travel physically to attend a class. Information technology can provide educational services directly to the home, hospital, or workplace.

— *job-related education and training in the workplace* : There are a number of barriers to workers who wish to take job-related instruction. Attending regular classes is difficult due to competing demands on their time, travel to a campus may be burdensome, and there is reluctance on the part of some order individuals to sit in a classroom and compete with younger students. Information technology, by bringing the course to the workplace, can remove some of these constraints.

Testing and Diagnosis

Computers have been used for some time to grade and analyze the results of college admission exams, intelligence tests, and a variety of psychometric examinations designed to explore the values, attitudes, and thinking patterns of individuals. Educational testing can be thought of as having four basic roles :

— *Strategic* : Testing helps assess a student's general levels of understanding and learning strategies. It is used to determine what classes and courses of study a student should pursue, and what instructional approaches would be most effective for him. After a course, testing measures the skills and knowledge that the student.

— *Tactical* : Testing also takes place during instructional sequences to determine how the student is progressing through the course and to detect and diagnose difficulties the student might be having.

— *Gatekeeping* : Testing plays an increasingly important role in supporting decisions to institutions and to programs of study. It is a basis for allocating scarce resurces (e.g. admission to a prestigious college or university) and for the granting of licenses to practice professions.

— *Certification* : Testing plays an important role in certifying the knowledge and skill of individuals, qualifying them to pursue professions such as medicine or law, or attesting that they have progressed along certain educational or training peths.

Modern information technology will likely have several effects on testing :

— Continual testing of students' progress and levels of understanding is an important pedagogical tool, even in a nonautomated teaching environment. However it is very demanding of a teacher's time. Automated systems will allow much closer monitoring of student and class progress in a normal classroom environment.

— Automated teaching systems depend on continual testing and evaluation to direct the presentation of material.

— Automated instruction may lead to a decoupling of instruction from institutions—in the sense that a student moves freely between home, job, and school for coursework. This trend will create greater need for strategic testing to determine appropriate instructional programs for students.

— Institutional decoupling will also require more testing for purposes of certification. Traditionally, an engineering degree was obtained by following a course of study at one department. Certification was the degree earned by successfully completing the program.

— The accelerating growth of knowledge is pressuring professions such as medicine, law, and engineering to require retraining and periodic renewal of certifications.

— If traditional forms of education become increasingly extensive and, hence, scarce, gatekeeping requirements will inevitably continue to grow in importance. The current competition for entry into medical school illustrates this trend.

— On the other hand, automated learning systems may make certain types of education and training far more accessible and affordable. If that occurs, gatekeeping may take place not on entry to the education program, but in licensing to practice.

CAPABILITIES OF EDUCATIONAL TECHNOLOGY

None of the technologies and services described in the chapter 4 overview has the capabilities required to support all of the applications listed above. Hence, the growth of an extensive automated education network will depend on the integration of information technologies.

Each particular technology—cable, personal computers, etc.—has some but not all of the capabilites necessary to provide effective education. Thus, the basic message is that different information technologies will need to be linked in order to provide all of the capabilities needed for extensive automated learning systems to be developed. As shown in chapter 4, such integration is already taking place for other applications.

COST AND EFFECTIVENESS

For many years, the cost and effectiveness of educational technology has served to circumscribe the debate about whether and how it should be used. OTA found that :

> There is a substantial amount of agreement that, for many educational applications, information technology can be an effective and economical tool for instruction.

This conclusion is based on a number of observations :

— Research exists, some of it dating back years, to suggest that students do learn as well or better from educational technology than from convential means. Little evidence exists to the contrary. Much of the past debate centered around whether technology was *more* effective than conventional means and hence warranted substitution for traditional classroom instruction.

— Costs for labor-intensive education and training methods continue to climb faster than the inflation rate, while costs for information technology continue to drop precipitously. These trends will result in a steadily growing number of applications in which technology-based instruction is clearly the most-effective method.

— For many educational and training needs—e.g., educational services to the homebound, to geographically isolated regions, or to the workplace—there are few viable alternatives to the use of technology, provided that it works adequately. In a growing number of instances, teachers qualified to teach in certain fields—Such as science, mathematics, or blingual education—are difficult to find. In these cases, technology may be the only means by which such education can be provided.

This is not to say that there are no potential limitations or dangers in the uncritical use of educational technology nor that there is no need for additional research in the field. In fact, in the eyes of some critics, a number of questions remain unanswered.

— Will access to computers reduce the ability to practice and learn basic skills? Some parents and teachers are concerned that student use of hand calculators may lead to the atrophy of simple computational skills. Some modern word processors incorporate spelling correction facilities, and future systems will probably incorporate simple grammatical analysis and correction. Will use of such technology decrease a student's grasp of writing mechanisms?

— Does the medium have characteristics that, when exploited, distort the educational message or produce subtle side effects ? Some observers, for example, have suggested that television educational programs such as Sesame Street may reinforce short attention spans. A similar example is the finding of some developers of interactive computer based reading programs that, in order to maintain student attention, shorter passages must be used on video screens than would be needed to maintain student attention for reading exercises on paper.

— Most research on technology-based education has focused on the development of well defined skills, such as arithmetic computation or foreign-language vocabulary. While proponents argue that computers can encourage the development of new problem-solving skills, critics suggest that education of the more general conceptual skills could suffer.

— If, over the long term, education is provided principally by technology, what are the unintended long-term impacts on social, cognitive, and psychological development ? Very few answers to this important question are known. However, since it would take several years before technological and institutional changes could create such a possibility on a massive scale, there seems to be adequate time to study it.

— Do particular characteristics of information technology subtle favor some types of students psychologically or cognitively ? Do differences exist that tend to favor performance by sex, age, social class, or values ? These questions are important when dealing with issues of social equity.

THE TECHNOLOGY OF LEARNING RESOURCES SERVICES IN HIGHER EDUCATION

John G. Berling

Saint Cloud State University

People knowledgeable in the field of technology, whether they work in education or not, would probably agree that the use of technology in the profession of teaching and learning has not reached its true potential. While external reasons for this apparent non achievement of potential are numerous, few organizations have looked at internal adjustments as avenues for achieving a higher level performance. A point of view on this subject that is seldom articulated or addressed suggests that each time a new technological breakthrough occurs, it is too often viewed as a separate and isolated entity and offered as a cure for all the existing educational ills. For this reason the positive impact of combining and integrating educational support technologies has seldom, if ever, been realized.

Library, audiovisual, television, instructional, development, message design, telecommunications, interactive video, computer-assisted instruction—all these terms are familiar to everyone working in higher education. Standing alone, each is built on a substantial body of knowledge; each creates its own set of utilization and administrative problems. Generally speaking, current higher education practice finds that each of these technologies is utilized with only a remote awareness of the possibilities for positive interaction with the others. This interaction is the thrust of the learning resources organization an organization that merits further investigation and analysis by higher education.

The learning resources services (LRS) model makes it possible to combine the strengths of the appropriate technologies to be applied to the solution of teaching and learning problems. This paper examine how one university has, during the last twenty-five years, attempted to implement the definition of instructional technology that was reported in the 1970 statement of the Commission on Instructional Technology :

> instructional technology goes beyond any particular medium or device. In this sense, instructional technology is more than the sum of its parts. It is a systematic way of designing, carrying out, and evaluating the total process of learning and teaching in terms of specific objectives, based on research in human learning and communication and employing a combination of human and nonhuman resoucres to bring about more effective instruction. The widespread acceptance and application of this broad definition belongs to the future. Though only a limited number of institutions have attempted to design instruction using such a systematic comprehensive approach, there is reason to believe that this approach holds the key to the contribution technology can make to the advancement of education (p. 19)

The LRS model has five program elements that will be analized :

(1) human resources,

(2) instructional materials,

(3) instructional equipment,

(4) preparation of the Information Specialist, and

(5) program costs.

Human Resources

The human resources element in any organization creates many complex problems and challenges. So it follows that the most important tasks within the human resources element of the LRS model are hiring, assignment or placement of personnel, and development of personnel. Faculty entering the organization must possess a broad background. Academic preparation in library science, audiovisual education, and instructional development is required. The degree may be in any one of the disciplines, but preparation in several others will be required before tenure is granted. For example, a person entering the organization with a master's degree in library science must have in addition a required number of credits in instructional technology. All of the professional personnel are academically prepared to address service questions from the broadcast possible perspective, for the learning resources concept does not establish a hierarchy among the media. Higher education with its traditional print orientation has been challenged to face information and communication problems without the prejudice that one medium has greater validity than another. It is the responsibility of LRS personnel to provide direction to this important information age challenge.

The most successful persons will be specialists able to adapt to changing situations, and they will flexible and constantly motivated and challenged by the service needs of the user. New candidates must be carefully screened so that the emerging needs are addressed. The change in the discipline and practice covered within LRS concept requires retraining, since LRS faculty and staff turnover is not as rapid as the change occuring within the associated technologies. Professional development programs clearly be related to current trends. Given the need for objective measurement, academic evaluation, and professional development, the personal characteristics of the media professional should not be overlooked.

The growth of information combined with changes in communication systems comples LRS faculty and staff to be adaptable, creative, and flexible in their approach to service. The art of combining a portion of the two most rapidly growing industries in the United States (Porat, 1977)—information and service—and sharing these advances with university faculty and students is indeed a challenge. Today most institutions of higher education have some people using the newer technologies in isolated situations, but few have a group of dedicated persons organized for the sole purpose of providing resources for learning based on the broadcast perspective. LRS faculty and staff can provide a university with some assurance that all the resources and technology available within the budget constraints of that institution will be utilized to the fullest potential.

Any description of the human aspects is not complete without some discussion of the interchange necessary among faculty, staff, and users. The utilization of technology necessitates the development of "user friendly" equipment and procedures or routines. Staff assignments within learning resources are shifting away from backroom cataloging and similar support activities to a higher level of interaction with users. Consequently, job descriptions and recruiting emphases must reflect the changing service responsibilities.

Instructional Materials

University library budgets have been developed under stress for several years. Traditional formulas have been used to evaluate the adequacy and quality of collections, but the newer technologies have not been incorporated in the assessment. The most often used measure of the quality of a collection is still quantity, that is of counting volumes or things. This method certainly has some value, especially in the research library, as most information today continues to be stored and retrieved via the book. Its pervasive application, however, in higher education settings provides a cause for concern. Efforts should be made to use technology-based systems to assess how well the users needs are being fulfilled. This will allow for the development of libraries on the basis of need rather than current quantitative standards.

The periodical collection offers unique opportunities for cast-effective change without a deterioration in service. Communication systems assure availability of articles from a periodicals that may then be dropped from a collection as a paper subscription. The displacement of a paper subscription (near and dear to the heart of some professors, who feel that no self-respecting library would be without one), even if it is unused, creates frustration and tension. This tension can be eased by the assurance that resource needs will be met; the confidence can be developed when appropriate services are provided in a timely manner by alternative methods.

Another important consideration in bringing information to persons in a cost-effective manner concerns departmental ownership. Sometimes services should and must be duplicated; but in such instances, clearly defined, functional needs should be articulated. The right of a faculty member in a department to have his or her learning resources needs met is paramount; however, the manner in which such needs are met should not be his or her decision alone. Competing and equally important needs in departments and agencies within the university must also be considered. For example, certain materials and equipment are useful only to certain departments, but a great many are seldom used and can be shared. How this sharing can be effectively and efficiently accomplished is the continuing challenge of LRS.

A goal of all aducational institutions is the improvement of instruction so that learning by students will always be at the optimal level. To reach this goal, most universities will provide some level of instructional development. The LRS model provides a preferred location for developers to reside administratively, since books, films, videotapes, and so forth generally provide some of the needed background information. The model facilitates the interactions of the developer with the appropriate university faculty and the materials collections. It promotes instructional development as a continuous process with the goal of improving teaching through systematic planning and communication. A university faculty person entering any part of the system will be referred to the level of service and support most likely to fulfil his or her needs.

Requests that can be effectively and efficiently accommodated by the LRS model are those involving the production of instructional materials. Materials relating to content are easily retrieved from any one of the university owned collections. Further, the person managing such a collection may become a member of the production team. Collection development is also enhanced because weakness in the collections are often identified during the production process.

Instructional Equipment

A key element of the LRS model is the acquisition and distribution of the instructional equipment. An online inventory provides current status information on all university owned instructional equipment. A computer-based maintenance, scheduling, and monitoring package assists in keeping the equipment serviceable and also provides information for future use. Practical cost-effective equipment is acquired, because useful background information is available for decision making. All the components mentioned above must be present to make a centralized distribution system successful, but the system will still fail without the services of a LRS professional to negotiate and identify the functions that the equipment is expected to fulfil. Faculty and student needs must be served in a perceptive, nonjudgemental manner. The ability to say no to a request for a certain brand of equipment but at the same time show how the needed functions can be addressed is essential to the success of the program.

Preparation of Information Specialists

An instructional program that prepares persons to become information specialists is readily accommodated by the LRS model. Graduates from this program enter careers in schools, government, public libraries, business, and industry. The teaching unit supports its own faculty based on full-time equivalent (FTE) production. These FTE positions are utilized in such a manner that the expertise of the entire LRS professianal staff is available as needed. This ensures that students will be able to acquire both breadth and depth of content and experience in completion of their studies. A practicing cataloger teaches cataloging, a television producer teaches the television production class, and so on. In addition to the availability of quality faculty, accessibility to the university's information, prodution, and communications equipment is also assured. The students are able to interact with the types of systems they are studying in the classroom. Professional production capabilities, along with the latest technologies are available for exploration and instruction.

Program Costs

Empirical evidence seems to indicate that expenditures for staff, equipment, and materials compare favorably with other models in institutions of similar size and scope. Comparisons of book, equipment, periodical, and personnel budgets over the past five years show that monetary outlays fall below that of comparable universities. On the other hand, service is rated high by the users as well as by outside evaluators. It is fair to generalize that the various services addressed in this paper bear similar costs to those located in different settings. Therefore, the sharing factor in the areas of faculty, equipment, and facilities seems to be providing a significant bonus to the campus community.

Summary

Professional associations and organizations, along with educational institutions, have acclaimed the wonders of the of the new technology only to find that their early hopes for it were probably too optimistic. A statement attributed to Benjamin Franklin rings true. He said, "Human happiness is produced not so much by great pieces of good fortune that seldom happen, as by little advantages that occur every day." LRS faculty and staff can provide superior service through the identification and use of those "little advantages." The fact that this learning resources model provides a larger base from which creative projects can be launched is such an advantage. The model also provides for physical and organizational proximity, which should provide for better communication and as, a result, better service. In addition, partnership with other institutions in the community and with business and industry are enhanced. An organization designed to acquire and share learning resources for a campus is well equipped to develop partnerships beyond the confines of the university.

This type of service, however, requires some centralization of budget, which of course is anathema to some. Centralization should and indeed must occur until the ability to serve is reduced because of it. The establishment of this five line between centralization and decentralization may well be the most critical undertaking in the establishment and operation of a LRS model. The entire faculty and staff must be involved in the drawing of that line; even while it is being drawn, forces are at work that may well affect the scope and breadth of that line. This is the nature of service.

Information specialists should be challenged by the changing needs of the users and try to meet them on a continuing basis. They must avoid the human urge to protect the more comfortable ways of the past when they obstruct the path of the present or the future. This should not be misconstrued as an attempt to show disrespect for past efforts; instead, it is an attempt to address the future in a positive manner. Not all universities can or should do exactly what this university has done. Each institution must address its resource problems in light of its own mission, but it is hoped that the idea of sharing the unused, the unknown, and the unidentified resources can be addressed in some way on every university campus. LRS is not a place; it is a program composed of people and equipment and collections. All of the components of this program exist on every campus. It is the responsibility of the administration at each campus to blend them in the most productive manner.

REFERENCES

Commission on Instructional Technology, (1970). *To Improve Learning, A Report to the President and the Congress of the United States* (Syst. of Docs. Y4. ED 8/1 : L47). Washington, DC : U.S. Government Printing Office.

Porat, M. (1977). *The information economy : Definition and Measurement* (Office of Telecommunications Special Publication 77-12 [1]). Washington, DC : U.S. Government Printing Office.

APPENDIX

ABOUT THE COURSE

Introduction

The course was intended for teacher educators working in the field of Educational Technology in universities, training colleges as well as key level persons in audio-visual departments of States SCERT. There were about 20 seats for this course. Out of 41 applicants, 20 participants were selected for this course. Finally 14 participants from various states— Gujarat, Madhya Pradesh, Maharashtra, Rajasthan, Jammu and Kashmir, Uttar Pradesh and Union Territory Delhi participated (list enclosed in appendix).

The main purpose of the course was to orient participants towards educational technology and its various dimensions (theoretical and practical) so that they in turn could train teachers in their respective institutions. To meet this purpose, a lot of preparatory work was done for formulating the course-objectives and course-contents. Firstly draft course content along with objectives was prepared. This was finalised in five successive meetings with all Heads of Divisions of CIET under the Chairmanship of Joint-Director, Besides this, time plan for each lecture/demonstration/practicum was also planned. In order to provide background of the course to participants in advance, briefs of each lecture practicum was also prepared in consultation with resource persons from faculty of C.I.E.T. Training booklet consisting of course content, objectives, Time plan, briefs of lectures and resource persons along with reading list of important books was also prepared.

Objectives

The specific objectives of the course were as follows:

To familiarise participants with the

i) theoretical frame work viz concept, sub-system and scope of educational technology (ET).

ii) characteristics and potential of different types of Graphics aids and media (small format and Mass)

iii) process of development of different types of Graphics aids, Audio/Radio and ETV programmes.

iv) hardware (equipment) used in the production of tape slide/Radio-audio, ETV programmes.

v) practical experiences in preparation of instructional materials/scripts used for different types of Graphic aids/media.

vi) the utilisation, evaluation and dissemination of various types of broadcasting & non-broadcasting programmes.

Course Content

On the basis of above mentioned objectives, the modular form of course content was formulated. The course was devided into five modules and project work.

Module I—Theoretical frame work of Educational Technology

Module II—Graphics.

Module III—Aduio/Radio Programmes

Maduie IV—ETV Programmes

Module V—Information & Dissemination

Module VI—Project work for production of tapeslides,

audio/video programmes using principles of educational Technology.

(Detailed course content is enclosed in appendix)

Design

The course was designed in sush a way so that balance between theoretical and practical dimension of Educational Technology could be maintained. The first half of the course was devoted towards theoretical aspects of E.T. which included lecture demonstration and preview of tapeslide, Radio/audio and ETV programmes. Educational tour was also arranged. The second half of the course was utilised for practical work which consisted of script writing and production of tapeslide, audio and video programmes. Audio programme could not be produced due to some other courses in educational Radio Division of the institute during that period. The last day was planned for evaluation of the course and summing up session.

(Day to Day Programme may be seen in appendix).

PROCEEDINGS OF THE COURSE

Summary Reports of Day to Day Activities

31st January 1989

The course commenced with a welcome and introduction of the participants as well as the resource persons.

Dr. M.C. Sharma Coordinator of the Course . . . highlighted the objectives of the course. He stressed that the course is intended to Orient the teacher educators towards the theoretical dimensions of educational technology. Accordingly the participants would be exposed to the hardware as well as preparation of soft-ware & programme production in educational technology.

Prof. J.S. Rajput, Head, Eductional Script Training & SIET Coordination, CIET, in his keynote address spoke about the need of educational technology in our educational system in the context of New Education policy. He said that the actual success of this course would depend on the follow-up activities to be taken up by the participants in their respective areas/institutions.

Prof. C.H.K. Misra . . . further clarified the concept of educational technology and how it stands today. According to him the concept needs a lot of clarity as well as optimistic approach. There was sharing of expectations among the resource persons and the participants. The participants individually gave some ideals about their experience in educational technology and what they expected from this course. The faculty members also desired a "total involvement" of the participants.

MODULE I

Prof. Mishra initiated certain basic questions about the teaching learning process like why (purpose) and what (content) to teach, how (method) to teach which incorporates the method, media and techniques. The difference between the method and media marked out. The importance of sequencing and its relevance to the target audience was pointed out. From the broad purpose of instruction, the specific objectives are drawn. Based on these lines, educational technology is a structured and planned way of instruction. Still it is a flexible approach to incorporate self-evaluation and correction. Thus, it is a dynamic approach demanding a purposeful autilization of all resources available in a particular instructional situation.

Dr. Mullick introduced the 'Systems Approach' as a method of analysing, planning and evaluating a process as well as a problem solving approach. A system is viewed as an enterprise consisting of men and material to achieve certain purpose. A system is characterised by the parameters like (i) input (ii) process and (iii) output in its environmental functionalities and constraints. The objective of the systems approach is optimisation of all the components which are linked with each other. Systems approach helps to have a wholistic, rational way of solving problems by analysing the components or subsystems and their relations with each other. The examples of formal and nonformal system of education were given to signify the difference between the functionalities although the components are same.

Shri Chandra Bhushan conducted the first session after lunch on communication. The participants inductively arrived at the definition of the term. The process of communication was built up on the basis of questions like who says what, on what channel, to whom and with what results ? Delineating the various activities carried out by the teacher, the communication is ideal when the gulf between the teacher and the learner is minimised.

The participants were shown a short film produced by CIET. "Castles in the air". It was followed by the views of the participatnts regarding the message it conveyed, whether the situations to convey the message were appropriate and the target audience. According to the views expressed by the participants the film intended to create an awareness to the depleting natural resources and gradual deterioration of the environment.

1st February, 1989

The day commenced at 10 a.m. with a short summary of the previous day's proceedings.

Dr. Misra in his summing up emphasised on two major points—

(1) Communication is a people process.

(2) Intended message and the real message have a gap and ET aims to bridge this gap.

He later on outlined the Instructional Technology system (ITS). In this system the focal points were.

(1) Insistance on optimization of the different components of the system.

(2) Planning is done backwards while instruction proceeds forward.

(3) Optimization could be done only by empirical testing. No fixed formula or guidelines could be drawn on how to optimise.

In the next session Dr. M.C. Sharma dealt at length on Instructional Models and their applications in Instruction. At the outset he underlined the necessity for an Instructional Model—that is was a set of plans which could provide guidelines for designing instruction to achieve certain goals.

The different Instructional Models were:

(1) Social Interaction Model.

(2) Personal Model.

(3) Modification Interaction Model.

(4) Information Processing Model.

From the point of view of ET, Information Processing was the most important. Under this category, there are three models—

(a) Bruner's concept Attainment Model.

(b) Asubel's Advance Organiser Model.

(c) Taba's Enquiry Model.

Dr. Sharma outlined the various features of Bruner's and Asubel's Models. While Bruners emphasised *thinking STRATEGIES* in the attainment of a concept. In view of Asubel it was *meaningful learning* which was important, the best strategy according to Bruner was conservative focussing. The syntax of three of his models.

(1) Reception model.

(2) Selection Model.

(3) Unarranged Material.

Was presented. The syntax of Asubel's Advance Organiser Model was also shown. Both Bruner's and Asubel's Models were illustrated with examples. The Enquiry model was incorporated in both Bruner's and Asubel's models.

In third pre-lunch session, Dr. Mullick conducted a practicum session on the application of systems approach for solving Educational Problems.

The specific problem chosen was improving the performance of students of a rural school and with reference to this, the systems approach was applied to find out the Educational problems. Problems were envisaged by the participants in the areas of human resources, materials and learners. A number of problems in the three areas were put forth. Some of them were

(1) Motivation of teachers.

(2) Poor Coordination between the teachers, Headmasters and the other back-up agencies.

(3) Multiple-class teaching.

(4) Back of teacher-parent interaction.

(5) Less of community involvement.

(6) Lack of optimization of the use of existing materials available.

(7) Difficulty in the access to available material.

Dr. Mullick also dealt with other specific examples to clarify some aspects. At the end of the session, all the participants were given an assignment where the problem was to optimize the use of Audio-Visual Resources available in our institutes.

The first post-lunch session was devoted to a discussion on Research areas in ET. Dr. J. Singh highlighted some of the research areas. For this, he first divided the field of ET into two areas.

(1) Technology in Education

   —dealing with hardware

(2) Technology of Education

   —software—process and development systems approach.

In the *field of hardware* the following were possible research areas.

(1) A survey or census of agencies producing hardware, suppliers of hardware and availability of hardware.

(2) Present status with respect to
   —availability of materials.
   —supply agencies.
   —availability of training courses/agencies

(3) future projection
   —This area dealt with prediction of the hardware requirements for the future.

(4) Cost effective studies/Economics of different hardwares.

In the *field of process and development of software* the possible research areas are:

(1) Feed forward research.
   This included research in
   —diagnostic findings of needs by participant-observation.
   —audience profile.

(2) Formative research

—testing of the script before formalisation.

(3) Testing

—in ETV programmes.

—Content analysis

In the *field of systems analysis* possible research areas were:

(1) In summative evaluation of materials.

(2) Evaluation of the system itself.

This could be done by case study method or Experimental method.

The final session of the day was a practicum on the Evaluation of an ETV programme conducted by Dr. Kanade.

The participants were shown a "15 minute film" which was made by the C.I.E.T. as a part of the mass Orientation programme for the teachers.

After the film was shown the participants were given an exercise on evaluating the film. They were asked to comment on:

(1) Aim/message of the film.

(2) Comment on 12 aspects of the film.

(3) Comment on the same 12 aspects using a rating scale.

(4) Using the same proforma in groups.

Dr. Kanade explained the difficulties faced by the investigator in analysing such a large number of response and also showed by way of examples how the data could be collected and analysed in a simple and systematic manner and audience profiles made.

2nd February, 1989

The previous day's report was presented. After that Dr. C. H. K. Misra while talking on the production of Video films said that three main purpose of the film must be kept in mind:

(1) The film should properly convey the message.

(2) It should relate past experiences of the audience with the present and the future.

(3) It should entertain.

MODULE II

Dr. T.R. Bawa took the first part of his lecture on Graphics in Education. After briefly outlining the history of E.T. and its future prospects, he explained the importance of using Graphics particularly in a developing country like India with limited resources. The advantages of Graphic aids explained were:

—Their attractiveness

—Their inexpensiveness

—Ease of preparation

—Ease of use

—Portability

Guidelines on how to plan and prepare Graphic Instructional material were also given. Some of them were:

(1) Clarity of message.

(2) Try out of several approaches to presentation.

(3) Pictoral Thinking.

(4) Use of colour.

A number of examples were shown on how these principles could be applied.

A session on "Blackboard" was conducted by Dr. S.P. Mullick. The participants were given a book entitled "Operation blackboards—a project" and the types of black-boards illustrated in the book were discussed with reference to their advantages and disadvantages. Some suggestions on new types of blackboards which could be made, were made by some participants. Mr. K.K. Chainani was also present during this session and made some valuable suggestions.

A session on "Visual communication" was conducted by Shri K.K. Chainani. He outlined the salient features of visual communication and emphasised that a combination of different strokes make visual. Every feature was illustrated by a number of examples. All the features illustrated were again combined and shown on a visual entitled "A boy going to school". This was worked out on the black board and different combinations of strokes, mater in the visual and those were suggested by the participants in making an effective visual.

In the last session of the day Dr. Harmesh Lal discussed the "Low cost teaching aids". Giving a brief outline of the project taken up in 1977 by the Deptt. of teaching aids (NCERT) in Madhya Pradesh, he stressed on the need for use of these teaching aids especially in rural primary schools. Two films "Low cost teaching aids" were shown. While evaluating the films, some basic questions were raised:

(1) Are low-cost teaching aids really low cost ?

(2) Do some low cost aids distract the concept like the example of making geometrical figures ?

Based on this, a discussion led to the question on whether the philosophy behind the production of low cost teaching aids was right. Dr. M.C. Sharma then explained the basic philosophy behind low cost teaching aids.

3rd February 1989

After the presentation of the previous a day's report, Dr. Misra spoke briefly on the concept of Simulogy. Then Dr. Bawa, conducted on the second part of the lecture on Graphic Aids where he elaborated on the use of charts. The following aspects were discussed.

(1) Purpose of Charts.

(2) Characteristics of Charts.

(3) Types of Charts.
   —Flow Chart.
   —Tree Chart.
   —Data Chart.
   —Flip Chart.
   —Strip Chart.

Each type of chart was discussed and illustrated with examples:

A session on "Tape-slide material in Education" was taken up by Shri K.K. Chainani. The blue-print of making a slide was discussed with all technical details. This was followed by the viewing of a filmstrip on "How to make a hand-made film-strip" and on "Silk screen printing".

In the afternoon, various tape slide programmes were screened for the participants which were then evaluated. The tape slide programmes were:

(1) 3 tape slide programmes of a five part series on Population Education.

(2) Covalent and Ionic bond.

While evaluating the Population Education Programme, some of the views expressed were:

(1) Visual were powerful with excellent photography.

(2) The message was accurately conveyed.

(3) Use of colours in showing different statistics was effective.

After the tape-slide programme on covalent and Ionic bond was viewed. The following observations were made:

(1) Too many concepts were covered.

(2) An understanding for the colours used in the visuals to denote difficult symbols was not shown.

To the observation that too many concepts were covered, Dr. M.C. Sharma pointed out that this programme of 40 slides could be broken up into smaller units and then covered in 3 or 4 parts.

6th February, 1989

After the presentation of report, Dr. Misra clarified some aspects of simulogy at a request from the participants. He defined simulogy as a science of signification. Simulogy's features were:

—Signs without language could communicate.

—"Places" signified different things.

—Men and material could be manipulate to signify something.

MODULE III

ETV in India

Dr. M.M. Chaudhri traced the History of ETV transmission in India. Referring to its development in the past 30 years. Since Delhi started the first school broadcast in 1959, Dr. Chaudhri said that ETV transmission had come a long way. At present the UGC programmes were 50% imported and 50% indigeneous but the ETV programmes for schools produced by CIET were 100% indigeneous. ETV in India could be divided into 4 different units :

(1) Training

(2) Production Facilities.

(3) Transmission

(4) Access

The major problems at present were in the field of training and in making ETV accessible to the viewers.

ETV had a major role to play in being able to provoke thinking, in making the viewers creative and in making them solve problems. A healthy coordination was necessary between the medium, content and audience.

ETV Curriculum—Need and Preparation

Dr. Misra in the session on ETV curriculum said that the Educational Philosophy on which the curriculum was based was most important. According to him curriculum is based largely on four philosophies.

(1) Porennialism

—Education is to convey the basic truths.

(2) Essentialism

—to bring out the prominent "essential" elements and all educational details to be put in terms of those elements.

(3) Purposivism

—emphasis on meaningfulness in real life.

(4) Constructivism.

—Education should teach the student to construct again, to challenge every basic truth, create problems. and solve them.

These philosophies were further elaborated in terms of the general goals, specific goals & objectives. Dr. Misra felt that an ETV programme has to teach students how to think reason and how to approach life and the ETV curriculum has to be thought of well in advance.

At the end of the session, the participants were divided into two groups and a subject "Dangers of Smoking" was given to each group. A curriculum outline for a 5 minute TV film was to be prepared by each group. The target audience for one group was students between 9 and 14 years and for the other group the audience was a group of teachers.

Communication by TV

In the afternoon session, Shri Chandra Bhushan while talking on Educational communication by TV, traced the history of TV communication in the world and in India. He then informed the participants on how communication satellites were developed. The strengths and weaknesses of TV were discussed at length. Shri Chandra Bhushan again emphasised the selection of the best media would depend on the content/subject. This was stressed on and then demonstrated with the help of an exercise. The participants were given a questionnaire "Media Selection Quiz". In that a list of subjects was given and the participants were asked to select the best media for that particular subject. The responses of all the participants were then analysed to arrive at the best media needed for that subject.

7th February, 1989

After the presentation of report, Dr. Jagdish Singh gave the detailed transmission network of Indian Television through INSAT-IB. While emphasising the need for more transmission time for ETV programmes, he informed the participants that with INSAT-IC having come into force as a stand by to INSAT-IB and with a series of INSAT-II satellites in the near future, ETV transmission would be given a complete separate channel.

The first formal session of the day was Shri G.D. Shukul's session on "Script Writing for ETV". In Developing a script from an idea the following problems could be faced:

(1) Difficulty in translating the idea into a script.

(2) Workability of ideas.

(3) Production effort—while writing a script, the following points should be kept in mind:

   (a) The script should be within the framework of the set objective.

   (b) It must be capable of attracting audience attention

   (c) It must inspire production.

   (d) The best format for script should be chosen.

   (e) Shri Shukul then outlined the various steps in script writing viz. :

      (a) Selection of Theme.

      (b) Outline of Script.

      (c) Final Script.

In his conclusion, Mr. Shukul felt that a script writer for ETV must be acquainted with the production processes so as to know the technical limitations of T.V.

Techniques and Formats-Script Writing

Dr. S.P. Banyal explained the various techniques and formats used in ETV script writing. The different formats which could be used were :

(1) Drama.

   —Play
   —Story telling
   —Musicals

—Dance

—Serial

—Series.

(2) Documentary.

   —Commuted

   —Sponsored

   —On nature; geography.

(3) Interview.

(4) Quiz.

(5) Newscast.

(6) Magazine.

(7) Commercials/advertisements.

Dr. Banyal elaborated on the various formats and explained that the choice of a format depended on the content. The salient features of the formats were explained with the help of two films which were screened.

The post lunch session on script writing was conducted by three resources persons—Shri G.D. Shukul, Ms. Madhu Pant and Dr. Manjula Mathur. The participants were divided into four groups and each group was asked to select a topic for script—writing and present an outline with reference to the following :

(1) Target Audience.

(2) Duration.

(3) Broad Objectives.

(4) Specific Objectives.

(5) Content.

(6) Format to be used.

The topics chosen by the four groups were :

(1) Water Pollution—Its causes and effects.

(2) Health-Education for you.

(3) Operation of set theory.

(4) What is Educational Technology.

9th February, 1989

Dr. Jagdish Singh & Dr. M.C. Sharma answered some querries on script-writing after the presentation of the report. Some of the points highlighted were :

—Audience interaction is essential before producing a script.

—There should be no factual errors.

—Ideas should be repeated in the script at regular intervals for reinforcement.

—Drastic jumps from one idea to another should not be incorporated in a script. At every stage, a relaxation period should be given.

Educational Communication by TV

The entire process of an ETV production was explained in detail by Shri Chandra Bhushan. Laying emphasis on the fact that TV production was a people's process, he said that the good coordination between the physical Infrastructure and the people would lead to a good production. The elements of a TV Production were elaborated as :

(1) Ideas.

(2) Resources which included :

Visual :

(a) Pictures/graphics/captions.

(b) Things.

(c) People.

(d) Film Excerpts.

(e) Places.

(f) Set and light.

Audio :

Sound/Music

(3) The Language of TV (Visual Language).

This included —Different Camera shots.

—Devices/transitions.

The different Camera shots were illustrated by Mr. Gupta, Cameraman with a camera and using the participants as subjects so that they would watch it on the monitor :

Hardware in TV

The second session of the morning was devoted to discussing the various hardware (equipments used in T.V.) by Mr. A.S. Tyagi. He explained that the main problem with too sophisticated equipments was that they became reduntant or outdated very soon, for example the format of a VTR changed every 4 years and that of a camera every 6 years. Due to this serting up a studio in an educational institution would be a problem because the heavy investment in hardware would become useless if the equipment becomes outdated.

He explained the various VTR's and cameras used in TV production today and explained the advantages and disadvantages of each. He also gave the price range of different equipments available in the Indian market and worked out the cost of setting up a small studio. Mr. Tyagi also gave some guidelines on purchasing VTR's and cameras.

The post-lunch session was again devoted to discuss the elements of ETV production. Mr. Chandra Bhushan elaborated on other aspects of TV language like the floor manager's signals. The floor manager, Mr. Sharma illustrated the use of various signals used in a studio during production. The process of converting the draft scipt into a camera script was explained using many examples by Mr. Chandra Bhushan. Other aspects of production like the use of camera cards, blocking of shots, recce, the producer's role in arranging for resources like—visual resources, talent, technical and financial resources were also discussed.

The above aspects were than highlighted with the help of three films shown to the participants. The films shown were "special effects in film", "Words and Pictures" and "the making of a live TV film".

9th February, 1989

Evaluation of ETV Programmes

After the presentation of report. Dr. Jagdish Singh discussed at length on evaluation of ETV programmes. He at the outset, differentiated between research and Evaluation. The following points were put forth:

(1) Purpose of evaluation is to improve and not to prove.

(2) All evaluation should be objective based.

(3) Evaluation is suggestive.

(4) Evaluative methods depend on the type of audience.

Dr. Kanade later explained the practical aspects of ETV evaluation. He pointed out a difference between traditional evaluation and evaluation in E.T. In traditional evaluation the teacher was evaluated whereas in E.T., the audience evaluates the teachers and methods. He further illustrated how difficult it was to evaluate any qualitative aspect while it was relatively easy to evaluate any aspect which was concrete. He then conducted an exercise to illustrate this point by asking the participants to judge the distance between two cities and then define the concept of violence. From the responses of the participants he demonstrated that though the distance between two cities could be judged with a certain degree of accuracy, a qualitative concept like "Violence" could not be defined very accurately as a certain element of subjectivity crept in.

The participants were given the opportunity to attend a demonstration of "Computer Graphics" by a team of experts from France. The experts said that Graphics could be used to great effect in education for Mathematics, Natural Science and Geography. Different animation techniques were shown like separation, manipulation, picture-by-picture animation, interpolation were shown some computer graphics of 3 Danimation were also viewed. The experts discussed with the large audience about the training period needed to master the technique and other details like cost per programme etc.

In the post-lunch session, Dr. Harmesh Lal talked on the various features of ETV transmission. He described the role of C.I.E.T. and S.I.E.T. is in the production, transmission and evaluation of ETV programmes. The programmes were sent in a capsule and a capsule consisted of the tape of programme of 45 minutes, a cue-sheet and a transmission schedule which was sent in advance to the teachers. Later on capsule prepared by C.I E.T. was shown to the participants.

The process of editing an ETV film was explained to the participants in the editing room by Sh. Taneja and Mrs. Pushpalata. The basic requirements in editing like two monitors a master tape, process of deleting portions, transferring of audio-video from one tape to the master tape was also demonstrated.

The theoretical aspects of editing were then discussed with Sh. Chandra Bhushan. He explained the process of editing which essentially meant joining the different shots in a meaningful sequence. This required extreme patience and was a time consuming process. Editing was done as per the requirement of the producer's script.   Editing could be done by the producer himself or by a professional editor.

10th February, 1989

Mr. Chandra Bhushan clarified some aspects of the techniques of animation in a question-answer session.   He pointed out that the characters and situations in animation are unreal.   He differentiated between the vartious types of animation like paper animation, cut out animation and film animation.

MODULE IV

Information and Dissemination

Prof. Verma in his lecture on "Information and Dissemination" at the outset, emphasised the need for information. He gave statistics of how print material like periodicals, newspapers and documents had more than doubled in ten years. He then listed the various sources of Information and how information could be stored. With regard to dissemination, Prof. Verma felt that a major hurdle was that there was no cultural change in the thinking of the present librarians and this was essential as there was to be a redical change in the process of dissemination.   He then elaborated on the various methods of disseminating information and showed various types of documents that could be prepared in disseminating Information.

The function, purpose and availability of material at the media resource centre was also discussed by Prof. Verma.

Dr. Kanade also concluded his lecture on evaluation and also gave examples of advanced Information technology in other countries.

The participants visited the Central Production Centre (CPC) and Media Communication Research Centre. Two senior personnel of the Centre, Mr. Thygarajan and Mr. Nag took the participants around. The CPC has two studios A and B with all the latest equipments available in the world in the field of T.V. production. Four sophisticated Cameras and light upto 500 kw (which can be electronically monitored, through a console) are there for every studio. Each studio has a production control room (PCR) where all special effects can be monitored, an audio room (with 24 channels), a paint box (for computerised graphics) and an advanced digital library system (DLS). The post production facilities available at the CPC were also shown to the participants. The CPC is used only for special programmes and it is not open to use for outsiders.

13th February, 1989

After the report presentation, Dr.C.H.K. Misra talked about the role of an educational technologist. He said that for a social change to occur a critical massage is necessary. The continuum of technology extends from minimal technology to ideal technology and there is a parallel continuum of minimal target to ideal target.

The scripts on "Dangers of Smoking" were then discussed and some revisions were suggested by Dr. Misra.

Dr. Rajput discussed the curriculum of ETV programme. He talked about the levels of curriculum viz. ideal, formal perceived, operational and experimental levels. Two approaches to curriculum development were discussed i.e. through environment and through relationships. Through the environmental approach, the real life situation could be investigated and in the relationship approaches—change, knowledge, values and aesthetics were the four dynamic elements.

Two video films—one on Friction and the other on Bernoulli's principles were screened and the formats of the two scripts were discussed.

In the afternoon, the participants were divided into four groups. Three groups opted to work on scripts for ETV programmes and the fourth group decided to work on a script for a tape slide programme. The groups then worked on formulating a content outline for the scripts on the basis of the subject/topic chosen by them.

14th February, 1989

After the previous day's report was read, Prof. Misra stressed the importance of educational technology as a process of instructional strategy. He emphasized that in our country education should have better access and better application through media. It should not be costly. To make educational technology serve our country (i) It should be a team work (ii) It should emphasize software over hardware and (iii) while choosing a topic, the main criteria should be that it should reach the poorest of poor students.

He also stressed that, since manpower is precious in educational technology, certain qualities have to be there in an educational technologist. An educational technologist should be a detailed minded person and he should be non-egoistic. He should have a scientific temper and he must be a participative and active member of the team. In an educational persuit, everything should be open to questions. He also said that parallel to instructional strategy is the social change. One has to act for a social change and not wait for it to happen. Only a critical mass of workers who are aware of this, can change the situation.

Dr. M.C. Sharma introduced Dr. L.G. Sumitra, Mrs. Swarna Gupta and Dr. Sarojini Pritam, a 3-member team of the Educational Radio Division. The session started in the form of team teaching.

Dr. Sumitra explained that broadcast of Radio/audio programmes for schools have been on the air for over forty years, but studies have shown that there is non-utilization of these programmes or there is a gap in using this media. This was attributed to limited transmission time, non suitability of listening time, non-linking of programme with the particular topics attitude of the teacher towards the programme as superfluous and ignoring the programmes. Besides it has to be a highly localized medium. The main blame for this has been on the educationists.

In order to overcome these difficulties, it was suggested that there should be a proper coordination among the AIR, CIET, SIET and ET Cells, it should be need based and there should be a uniform time-table to fit in the programmes.

The post-coffee session was conducted by Mr. S Gupta on process of production and techniques of radio programmes. The question raised . . . was "How can we make this media reach ?" Here she emphasized that the process of Radio Audio production should involve—

Firstly the *planning stage* where objectives of a concerned idea have to be formulated. The need assessment is also an important fact which includes audience research and curriculum awareness.

(2) The *development stages* consists of identification of areas development of brief. In this stage, attention span & other factors have to be kept in mind to make the programme successful. During development of a brief-objectives, target groups, subject areas etc. have to be kept in mind.

(3) The *scripting stage* : The brief was discussed thoroughly with the writer before writing the script. Mrs. Gupta emphasized that during scripting stage-language, sequence, presentation, clarity of ideas, music effects and several other aspects are to be remembered because the greatest advantage of sound lies in its direct appeal to the imagination.

(4) The *evaluation stage* : Finally the script has to be evaluated to see if it fulfils all the objectives. An audio programme on "Sangeet" made with Ustad A.A. Khan, which was produced to introduce the concept of ragas to 5+ age group was played. It was an unscripted programme and for

this, selection of a spontaneous person who can create an impact on the audience was important.

The afternoon session was on scripting and formats of radio/audio programmes by Dr. Sarojini Pritam. She discussed the different types of formats used in writing a radio script. She said that to make an eductional programme through broadcast a success, it should be done through proper devices. A format becomes necessary becuase of the need. It should be communicated properly in an interesting manner. And should not be a burden on the mind of the children.

Several audio programmes having different formats were played to enhance that

(1) Audio scripts should be authentic, full of information and interesting;

(2) Should not contain too many points;

(3) Should encourage children to be mentally involved in the progrəmmes; and

(4) Various techniques of script writing should be used effectively to repeat ideas in the programmes.

Audio programmes were played on nursery rhymes, Ekalavya' and on the concept of measurement (without music) and those which were produced by teachers and trainees.

15th February, 1989

The morning session started at 9.30 a.m. in the Mother School Wing. It was addressed by Prof. Mrs. Shukla who talked on "Evaluation of Audio Broadcasts". She stressed on the need for designing an audio programme skillfully and best suited for the learners. She pointed out that while the print media had the facility of a priority evaluation, the electronic media suffered from the limitation imposed on it by the media itself and therefore evaluation became an important factor. She suggested that the production activity should be detailed and no loose ends left before going into actual production. Language, modality of presentation, delivery and tape quality should be very closely monitored. Audio tapes were then played for the participants. The participants were asked to evaluate the programmes and different view points were put forth in the group discussion.

In afternoon session the participants were taken around the audio studio and the different hardware used were shown to them by Mr. Bhushan. Dr. Sumitra then gave detailed guide-lines on how the script for an audio programme should written. The participants were then asked to write a script for pupil teachers on "How to use audio programmes in the classroom". After the draft scripts were written, . . . they were analysed and discussed. Dr. Sumitra felt that in audio programmes simple words should be used so that communication would not be difficult.

16th February, 1989

After presentation of the reports of previous day activities by participant Dr. Misra asked each group to present two objectives of their programme on the black board. He then suggested that the objectives must contain specific action verbs and should not be ambiguous. The participants were asked to revise their objectives so as to make them more speci-fic. He then brought out the difference between learning and performance. While learning was an unseen process, perfor-mance could be seen, measured and repeated. In this light, he felt that the objectives must be able to satisfy a criterion test. For this, questions should be asked against each objective to see whether the objectives could answer the questions satis-factorily. A flow chart of the pre-production activities was then drawn on the board and each step in the chart was dis-cussed in detail.

Each group was ask to write script on the topics already been selected by them.

17th February, 1989 and 20th to 24th February, 1989

Group A: ETV programme on the fuse wire and its use.

Team Members: Harsha Merchant

Sukhdeo Prakash Mathur

Vasudha Kamat.

On the 20th of February, 1989, the group finalised the script . . . consultations with the media experts. The talents needed for the film were finalised and the location for the video film was also chosen.

On the 21st, the final touches to the script were given after discussion with the producer, Mr. Balakrishnan and rehersals were carried out with the talents. In the afternoon, the film was shot.

On the 22nd, the continuity sheets were made prior to editing. The editing of the film commenced on the 23rd Evening with the editor Mr. Vinod Kaul. It was continued on the 24th and completed by the evening with the help of the editor and the producer Mr. Balakrishnan.

Group B: ETV Programme on 'Set Theory'

Team Members: Kishor Desai

Pramod Chandra Sharma

Ravi Shankar Yadav

On the 20th of Febraury the script was finalised after consultations with the media experts. On the 21st, discussions were held with Dr. M.C. Sharma and it was decided to get 15 students from the D.A.V. School for the shooting of the film. Students were briefed.

On the 22nd, the film was shot with the children. The shooting took up most part of the day.

On the 23rd, the rushes were seen by the participants and

the cue sheets made. The film was edited on the 24th evening.

Group C : Tape Slide Programme on 'Geometrical shapes.

Team Members: Charan Pal Singh

Maharaj Kishen Kaul

Suman Yadav

On the 21st morning, after the script was finalised Prof. Bawa and Mr. Chainani were consulted at the I.P. Estate. On the 22nd morning, Mr. Chainani started framing the visuals according to the script. Paper cuttings were made throughout the day for the visuals.

On the 23rd, captions were made which were given for computer processing. The team members worked with Mr. Chainani for the art work & with Mr. O.P. Gupta for the 'COMPUTER' processing. The templates were readied by the evening and the photography completed.

The finishing touches to the commentary were given on the 24th after the language of the commentary was checked by Dr. M.C. Sharma. The audio recording for background music was done at Mother School.

Group D : ETV film on Water Pollution

Team Members: Anil Bharatiya

Kitty Nanaya

Lakshmi Rao

Nirupma Jaimini.

On the 17th of February, 1989, the script was discussed with Dr. Jagdish Singh, Dr. M.C. Sharma and Dr. Misra. Some suggested revisions were . . . then carried out. The team then previewed some films to get the required stock shots.

On the 20th of February, the script was finalised and the stock shots were selected.

On the 23rd, some shots required for the film were taken by Mr. Prem Lal the Cameramen. The same day, the audio recording was done with the help of Sh. Vinod Kaul. In the evening the film was edited with the help of Mr. Yeshwant Rawat and the producer Mr. Balakrishnan.

On the 24th of February, the titles of the film and the music were added with the help of Sh. Vinod Kaul.

MODULE VI

Project Work

The last ten days of the course were taken up for project work. The participants were devided into four groups. Each group finalised one topic in consultation with Resource Persons. Finally four topics i.e. one for tapeslide and three for ETV production were considered selected. The topic assigned for production to each group were :

Group A: ETV Programme on "The fuse wire and its use"

Group B: ETV Programme on "Set Theory"

Group C: Tapeslide Programme on "Geometrical Shapes"

Group D: ETV Programme on "Water Pollution".

The scripts along with objectives for the above programmes were finalised in consultation with experts from CIET. After that, production of the programmes was undertaken with the help of producer and technical staff of CIET. Different formats like demonstration drama and documentary, were used in the preparation of scripts for the programmes.

For the project on tape slide production, group—C was sent to GPE Division Indraprastha Wing of CIET where art work and slide were prepared. The audio recording was done at ER Division Mother School Wing of the Institute. Finally four programmes—one tapeslide and three ETV were prepared by the participants.

Evaluation and Summing up Session

Evaluation

On the concluding day, the success of the course was evaluated with the help of well designed strength weakness Action Programme. (SWAP) PROFORMA". Most of the participants registered satisfaction of the course. Since the course was organised during shifting of studios, hardship in conducting practical work were felt. However, the suggestions of participants were recorded. Some of them were of view that intensive course in ETV production needed to be organised. Their suggestions of time management for devoting 3/4th of time for process of production like editing, shorting and handling of equipments were also noted. Observations of participants for inadequate facilities of technical staff, non-availability of suitable cameras and editing table were also noticed from swap proforma. They also desired more time for handling and operation of hardware. They expressed their feeling of adequate orientation of theoretical and practical dimension of E.T. in the course.

Summing up Session

The valedictory function of the course started with welcome of Chief Guest Prof. A.K. Sharma, Head, Department of Teacher Education, NCERT by Prof. C.H.K. Misra, the Course Director, Prof. Misra, pointed out the main objective of the course and expressed that this type of course had been organised by CIET for the first time. The experiences of this course would be useful for organising further courses.

Dr. M.C. Sharma, the course coordinator presented summary report of the course (Appendix). He pointed out that intensive efforts were made to achieve the objectives of the course but due to limited resources for production, the programme produced by the participants are not of professional quality. Expressing his satisfaction for achieving the main objective of the course i.e. orientation towards theoretical and practical dimension of E.I., Dr. Sharma added that professional quality production need intensive training in production only which was not the objective of the course. He also expressed expectation from participants that they will utilise this training on the preparation of software needed for production. He desired that participants would not only involve themselves in training others but would also produce programme themselves and would be constantly interacting with CIET.

Preview of four programme was arranged and two participants also expressed their reaction about the course. According to them, the course had provided rich experiences. They also desired more time for production and handling of equipments.

Prof. A.K. Sharma, the Chief Guest, distributed the certificates to participants' and wished them to utilise the rich experiences of the course in their respective institutions. He desired for qualitative software from teacher educators. According to him, software must be linked, with curriculum. He expressed that effective use of media must be based upon qualitative software production. He further expressed the need of educational programmes (ETV/audio/tapeslide) for training specially for new coming up institutions like DIET. He congratulated CIET for organising this type of course.

Prof. M.M. Chaudhri, Joint Director, CIET, in his presidential address said that one should be actually involved in production rather than getting training and training others. He stressed that special care must be taken for the management aspect of production. Emphasising the importance of enrichment programmes, Prof. Chaudhri pointed out that our ETV programme must be designed in such a way so that these could broaden the spectuary education. For this, one could even drift from the curriculum. Summarising the experiences for setting up SIET's he suggested that the utilisation of equipments (hardware) is more important rather than only acquiring them. According to him, man power is insufficient in the field of ETV in our country. Dr. Chaudhari expected that teacher educators would try to handle and use the equipment. He further desired that participants of this course would try to involve themselves in actual production.

Dr. M.C. Sharma proposed a vote of thanks for the Chief Guest, the President, faculty, participants and their organisations. He expressed gratitude for the technical and secretarial staff for their active cooperation in organisation of the course.

APPENDICES

Course Content

This course deals with basics of Educational Technology. It consists of six modules. Each module deals with one major aspect of E.T.

MODULE I

Theoretical Frame Work of Educational Technology

The module familiarises the participants with the concept and theoretical basis of E.T.

Course content. E.T.—meaning, nature and scope; Communication—process, principle of communication and relevance to educational media a modern learning theories/ instructional models and their applications in designing of instructions:

Systems approach—concept and its application in E.T., approaches in E.T.,—need, methods/techniques and utility in improving systems, programmes and materials.

Practical work—designing of instructions/Application of

systems designing in E.T. programme, audience profile, need assessment and testing of scripts.

Duration. Six sessions each of one hour and practicum/ demonstration of 6 hours (total 12 hours).

Mode of Interaction. Lectures, Experimental Sessions, demonstrations, discussions.

MODULE II

Graphics

The module acquaints the participants with various aspects of graphic aids—their nature and potentialities.

Course content. Graphics aids in education—nature, types, characteristics : Non-projected aids—charts, maps, globes, models, boards (type and process of production and utilization), Projected aids—film strips, overhead transparencies, tapeslides.

Practical work. Operation and use of Hardware used in projected aids, Demonstration of Low Cost Teaching Aids and tapeslide programmes.

Duration. Time allotted to this module is 5 lectures each of 45-50 minutes duration and 5 hours for practical work.

Mode of Interaction. Lecture, demonstration, discussions, and practicum.

MODULE III

Audio/Radio Programmes

In this module, the participants would be acquainted with planning of content, development of script and production approaches/techniques in Radio/audio programmes.

Course Content. Audio/radio in education—planning of

content and production approaches for formal and non-formal education, process of development of audio/radio programmes—scripting, format and production techniques evaluation—creative observation, formative and summative.

Practical work. Operation and use of Hardware of audio programmes, stages of programme production and evaluation of programmes.

Duration. 5 lectures each of 45-50 minutes duration and 4 hours for practicum are alloted for this module.

Mode of Interaction. Lectures, demonstrations, auditive practicum.

MODULE IV

ETV Programme

This module familiarises the participants with nature, scope of ETV and acquaint with process of development and production of ETV programmes.

Course Content. Television in education—nature and scope; ETV curriculum—need and preparation; process of programme production—feed forward research, development of concept, production and evaluation; script writing for educational television—techniques and formats.

Practical wark. Operation and use of hardware for ETV, play back of ETV programmes.

Duration. Time for this module is spread over 6 lectures (each of 45-50 minutes) and 6 hours for practicum.

Model of Interaction. Lecture, demonstration, preview, practicum.

MODULE V

This module familiarise the participants with modes/

methods and importance of information and dissemination systems.

Course content. Information and dissemination—needs, methods and modes, media Resource Centre—Establishment and function, visit to Central Film Library.

Duration. 2 lectures of 45 minutes each.

Mode of Interaction. Lectures.

MODULE VI

Individual/Group Project

In this, the participants would be required to specialise in production of material using one of the media such as graphics, projected aids, audio or video using principles of educational technology. This also includes evaluation of course.

Duration. 10 working days.

Mode of Interaction. Attachment Project method.

LIST OF HANDOUTS

1. Educational Technology: A Modern Approach
2. System Approach
3. Modern Instructional Models and their application in designing instructions
4. Research in Educational Technology
5. Testing of ETV Programmes—Practicum
6. Graphics in Education
7. Visual Communication
8. Tape-Slide Material in Education
9. Black Board
10. Low Cost Teaching Aids
11. Planning of Content and Production Approaches for Formal & Non-Formal Education
12. Process of Production and Techniques of Audio Programmes
13. Scripting Audio Programmes & Formats
14. Educational Television in India
15. Script Writing for TV
16. Scripting for Educational TV—Principles & Formats
17. Educational Communication by Television
18. ETV Curriculum for Teachers
19. The process of Television Production
20. ETV Transmission
21. Information & Dissemination

ORIENTATION COURSE OF EDUCATIONAL TECHNOLOGY FOR TEACHERS EDUCATION

Day to-day Programme

Date	Morning Session			Afternoon Session		
	10.00—10.30 a.m.	10.30 — 11.30 a.m.	11.45—1.00 a.m. p.m.	2.00—3.00 p.m.	3.15—4.00 p.m.	4.00—5.30 p.m.
31.1.89	Registration	—Welcom/Introduction of participants —Objectives of Course (MCS) —Key note address (JSR)	—Modern Approaches to E.T. (CHK)	Systems approach and its application in E.T.	Communication principle & process (CB)	Revelance of Communication to educational media. (CB)
1.2.89	Summary Report Presentation	Instructional Models & their application in designing instructions (MCS)	Practicum Application of systems designing/in ET Programme/Designing of Instructions. (SPM/MCS)	Research in ET-Method, Techniques. (JS)	Practicum/Demonstration related to Audience profile, need assessment, Testing of Script. (HMK)	

Date	Morning Session 10.00—10.30	10.30—11.30	11.45—1.00	Afternoon Session 2.00—3.00	3.15—5.30
2.2.89	Summary Report	Graphics Aids in Education I (TRB)	Visual Comunication (Demonstration of Non-Projected Aids (KKC)	Non-projected Aids Boards-Types characteristics. (SPM)	Low cost Teaching Aids HC/MCS
3.2.89	Presentation	Graphics Aids Charts (Process Production eradication) (TRB)	Projected Aids Films Stripts/OHT/Tape-slides. (KKC)	Hardware used in Projected Aids. (MCS & TECHNICAL STAFF)	Screening of Tape-slide Programmes.
6.2.89 (Mon)	Summary	ETV in India (MMC)	ETV Curriculum need & preparation (CHK)	Educational Communication by TV (CB)	Practicum Demonstration
7.2.89	Report	Scriptwriting for ETV—1 (GDS)	Techniques & Formats (Demonstration) (SPR)	Scriptwriting —II (MP/GDS)	Short Exercises for Scriptwriting (MP/MM/GDS)

Date	Morning Session			Afternoon Session	
	10.00—10.30	10.30—11.30	11.45—1.00	2.00—3.00	3.15—5.30
8.2.89 (Wed)	Presentation	Process of ETV Production-II Concept to Programme (CB)	Operation and use of Hardware in ETV (AST)	Process of ETV Production-II (CB)	ETV Production Play back exercise
9.2.89		Evaluation of ETV Programmes (JS)	ETV Transmission/play back of ETV Programmes (HL)	Demonstration of ETV Studios facilities (AST)	
10.2.89 (Fri)		Information and Dissemination (SCV/SKC)	(...............Educational Tour to IIMC/CCRT/DD.......)		
13.2.89 (Mon)	Guidelines for Teachers ETV Programmes (JSR/SPB)	Preview of Teachers Programmes	Group work for Selection of Tonic/Indentification of Objectives etc.		

Date	Morning Session 10.30—11.30	11.45—1.00	Afternoon Session 2.00—3.00	3.15—5.30
14.2.89 (Tue)	Audio/Radio in Education (LGS)	Planning of Content and production approaches for formal and Non-Formal Education (LGS)	Scripting of Radio/ audio and formats (SP)	Process of production and techniques (SG)
15.2 89 (Wed) at CIET, MSW	Evaluation in Audio/Radio (LGS)	Playback of Radio/ Audio Programmes	Playback of Radio/ Audio Programmes	Demonstration of Audio Studio/ Recording etc.
16.2.89 (Thurs)	Selection of Project	Group formation	Analysis, reference work, briefs etc.	
17th & 20th to Feb. 89	Project work for	(A) Tape Slide programme Production (TRB GEP STAFF)	(B) Audio/Radio Programme (LGS & STAFF)	Production (C) ETV prog. production (CB & ETV STAFF)
27.2.89 (Mon.)	Evaluation of Course/Valedictory		TA/DA Disbursement	

SUMMARY REPORT OF THE COURSE

Dr. M.C. Sharma,
Course Coordinators

The course was intended to orient teacher educators towards theoretical and practical dimensions of Educational Technology so that they could in turn train teachers in their respective Institutions.

The specific objectives of the course were:

—to familiarise participants with theoretical basis of educational Technology.

—to orient them towards characteristics and potential of different types of Graphics aids and Media (small format and Mass).

—to acquaint them with process of development of different types of Graphics aids, Audis/Radio & ETV Programmes.

—to familiarise them with Hardware (equipment) used in the production of tape slide/Radio-audio, ETV programmes.

—to impart practical experiences in preparation of instructional materials/scripts used for different types of Graphic aids/media.

—to make them aware about the utilization, evaluation & dissemination of various types of broadcasting & non-broadcasting programmes.

On the basis of the objectives, the course was divided into six modules.

Modules   I—Theoretical framework of Educational Technology.

Modele   II—Graphics.

Module   III—Audio/Radio programmes.

Module   IV—ETV programmes.

Module   V—Information and dissemination.

Module   VI—Project work for production of Tape-slide, audio or video programmes using principles of E.T.

The first two days of the course devoted to discussing the theoretical basis of Educational Technology like concept, the application of systems approach, Instructional models and evaluation. Practicum exercises were also conducted in this model. In the next two days, the graphic aids in education—their process and production—were discussed in details.

In the second week of the course, the module and programmes was taken up. This included sessions on ETV in India, ETV animation, script writing for ETV, process of production and evaluation of programmes. The participants were also given practicum exercises on script writing in the same week the module on information and dissemination was also completed. The participants previewed many films during the sessions for evaluation. Educational tour to Central Production Centre, Doordarshan was also arranged where participants were shown the largest Computerised equipments and lighting systems used in studios.

In the third week, the module on Audio/Radio was taken up. Various formats for writing scripts for audio programmes were discussed and a number of Audio/Radio programmes were played back for the participants. In the two sessions on ETV and Audio/Radio, the participants were shown the various hardware used in ETV and Audio/Radio.

The last ten days of the course were taken up for project work. The participants were divided into four groups and the following projects were finalised:

Group A—ETV Programme on "The fuse wire".

Group B—ETV Programme on "Set theory".

Group C—ETV Programme on "Water Pollution."

Group D—Tape-Slide Programme on "Geometrical Shapes".

The scripts for the above programmes were finalised in consultation with the experts at CIET. This was followed by the production of the programmes with the help of the producer and the technical staff of CIET. It may be mentioned here that different formats like demonstration, drama and documentory were used in the scripts. The script of the tape-slide programme was finalised and the group was sent to I.P. Estate for art work and prepration of slides. The audio recording was done at the Mother School Wing of the CIET. On the last day, the course was evaluated by the participants and their suggestions received.

Although great efforts were taken to achieve the objectives of the course, due to limitations of the resources available for production, the programmes produced by the participants are not of professional quality. But the main objective of the course was to Orient the participants towards the process of production and not make them professional producers. And it was in this context that the productions were done.

It is hoped that the participants who are teacher educators have been benefited by the course as far as preparation of software is concerned and they would have been enlightened with the process of production of different aids and media needed for Educational Programmes. We also have expectations from participants of the course that they besides training teachers in their institutions will also involve themselves in preparation of softwares and production of educational programmes for small format and mass media. They will also remain in touch with us by informing us about their creative work in the field of Educational Technology.

Video Equipment required for Educational Technology

S. N.	Equipment	Qty.	Cost (approx.)	Source of supply
	VCR	(J. Yen)	100	Y=12 Rs.
1.	EV—A 300E	1	1,09,000	SONY Video System Sony Corporation Tokyo, Japan
2.	EV—S 700E	1	2,10,000	
	Camera with Recorder			
3.	CCD—V8 AF—EK	2 pcs	5,14,000	,,
	Remote Editing Control			
4.	Vido Editing Controller RM—E 100V	1 pcs	25,800	,,
	Monitors—Audio/Video			
5.	PVM—6030 ME Trinitron Color	2 pc	1,70,600	,,
	OR			
	PVM—1371 OM Trinitron Color	2 pcs	3,08,000	,,
	AC Power Adapter			
6.	AC—V&E	1 pc	28,900	,,
	Batteries			
7.	NP—22 Rechargable Batteries	20 pcs	80,000	,,
	Tripod			
8.	VCT—600	2 pcs	71,800	
	Video Cassette Winder/ Eraser			
9.	BE—V 8	1 pc	17,400	,,
10.	Battery Charger BC—1 WA	1 pc	62,100	,,

(*Contd.*)

S. N.	Equipment	Qty.	Cost (approx.)	Source of supply
11.	LC—V 605 Carrying case	2 pcs	43,000	SONY Video System Sony Corporation Tokyo, Japan
12.	LC—V&5 Video Camera Jacket	2 pcs	13,000	,,
13.	Cables			
	(i) EURO Connector Cable (for Audio/ Video)		1,00,000	
	(ii) Other reqd. cables- to make the system complete from Sony.			
14.	Non Recorded Video Cassettes (Tape)			
	(1) P 5—30	10	15,000	,,
	(2) P 5—60	10	17,000	,,
	(3) P 5—90	10	23,000	,,
15.	VHS VCR	1	15,000	Local Market
16.	Colour TV Set	2	20,000	,,
17.	Console for setting up of the system	2 nets	12,000	,,
18.	Power Cable, Video and Audio Cable	—	5,000	,,